In and Out of Hollywood

SELECTED WORKS BY CHARLES HIGHAM

In and Out of Hollywood

A Biographer's Memoir

Charles Higham

Terrace Books

A trade imprint of the University of Wisconsin Press

Terrace Books, a trade imprint of the University of Wisconsin Press,
takes its name from the Memorial Union Terrace, located at
the University of Wisconsin–Madison. Since its inception in 1907,
the Wisconsin Union has provided a venue for students, faculty, staff,
and alumni to debate art, music, politics, and the issues of the day.
It is a place where theater, music, drama, literature, dance, outdoor activities, and
major speakers are made available to the campus and the community.
To learn more about the Union, visit www.union.wisc.edu.

Terrace Books
A trade imprint of the University of Wisconsin Press
1930 Monroe Street, 3rd Floor
Madison, Wisconsin 53711-2059

uwpress.wisc.edu

3 Henrietta Street
London WC2E 8LU, England

1   3   5   4   2
Printed in the United States of America

Library of Congress Cataloging-in-Publication Data
Higham, Charles, 1931–
In and out of Hollywood : a biographer's memoir / Charles Higham.
p.   cm.
Includes index.
ISBN 978-0-299-23340-2 (cloth: alk. paper)
ISBN 978-0-299-23343-3 (e-book)
1. Higham, Charles, 1931–.
2. Biographers—California—Hollywood (Los Angeles)—Biography.
3. Gay authors—California—Hollywood (Los Angeles)—Biography.
4. Motion picture actors and actresses—California—Hollywood (Los Angeles)—
Biography—Anecdotes.
5. Celebrities—California—Hollywood (Los Angeles)—
Biography—Anecdotes.
I. Title.
PN1998.3.H52.A3   2009
791.4309794´94—dc22
[B]
2009008136

To

RICHARD V. PALAFOX

and

WHITNEY LEE

Every silver lining has a cloud.
Old Hungarian proverb

Acknowledgments

Special acknowledgments are due to Scott Coblio, master of word processing; Philip Parkinson, my fine British researcher and devoted associate; and Edward T. Lowe, British genealogist. David Thomson, Patrick McGilligan, and Todd McCarthy were warmly enthusiastic and supportive. Raphael Kadushin, Sheila Moermond, and the entire editorial team at the University of Wisconsin Press were most helpful at all stages; I was lucky in having Diana Cook as the most skillful of copyeditors. Marc Wanamaker, peerless archivist and Hollywood historian, supplied the superb photographs, and Ned Comstock at USC proved as always a great help in supplying documents I had filed with him over the years. Without the help of those listed above, this book would not have been possible.

Some of the Cast

Muriel Spark
Dr. Marie Stopes
T. S. Eliot
Stephen Spender
Colleen McCullough
Kenneth Tynan
Rupert Murdoch
Jack Benny
Henry Fonda
Jack L. Warner
Samuel Goldwyn
Vincente Minnelli
Walt Disney
Charlton Heston
James Wong Howe
Hedda Hopper
Mary Pickford
Harold Lloyd
Dorothy Parker
Barbara Stanwyck
Bette Davis
Mae West
Marlene Dietrich
Rouben Mamoulian

John Ford
Pauline Kael
Orson Welles
Joseph Cotten
Dwight Macdonald
Bernard Herrmann
Mary Miles Minter
Cary Grant
John Updike
Ring Lardner Jr.
William Burroughs
Lew Ayres
Ginger Rogers
Dame Judith Anderson
Fred Astaire
Adele Astaire
Jean Negulesco
Cecilia de Mille Harper
Fritz Lang
Maria Rasputin
Lucille Ball
Clint Eastwood
Don Siegel
Jimmy Stewart

John Wayne
Mercedes McCambridge
Roman Polanski
Gene Hackman
Broderick Crawford
Johnny Mercer
Marlon Brando
Christopher Isherwood
Marjorie Main
Groucho Marx
Katharine Hepburn
George Cukor
King Vidor
Colleen Moore
Jed Harris
Josef von Sternberg
Sam Jaffe & Bettye Ackerman Jaffe
Jules & Doris Stein
Lew & Edie Wasserman
Alana & Sue Ladd
Alan Ladd Jr.
Anna Lee
Robert Stevenson
Elsa Lanchester

Eddie & Margo Albert
Olivia de Havilland
Joan Fontaine
Hal B. Wallis
Elvis Presley
Martha Hyer
Cornel Wilde
Jean Wallace
Rex Harrison
Richard Basehart
Alfred Hitchcock
Greta Garbo
Michael Powell
Francis Ford Coppola
Robert Duvall
John Milius
Arthur Cantor
Helen Mirren
Joan Collins
Michael Mann
Tammy Grimes
Leonardo DiCaprio
and
many, many others

In and Out of Hollywood

*I*t was a rainy, chilly January afternoon in 1969, at the elegant campus of the University of California at Santa Cruz. My office as Regents Professor looked out on an uninspiring picture of dripping shrubbery and somber redwood trees. I was feeling despondent as I had given up hope of obtaining access to the most legendary of lost movies: Orson Welles's *It's All True,* a Latin American epic, left unfinished in Hollywood vaults from 1942.

Hazel Marshall, head of the editorial division and stock footage department at Paramount, which now held the surviving reels, had told me that many more had been dumped off Catalina Island as useless stock and that I could not, ever, see the extant material as she had no idea who owned the rights. I was within inches of scoring a major coup in movie history scholarship and had been thwarted at the very last minute.

The phone rang and without enthusiasm I picked it up. To my amazement, Hazel Marshall was on the line. She addressed me as "Mr. Hyams," which didn't surprise me as my name is often mispronounced in America. She told me to come to Hollywood at once; the movie would be ready for me to see at 9 a.m. the following day.

I called the airport; no planes were flying in a storm. But late that night a plane suddenly became available and I left on it, bucked about through lightning and thunder for hours as the plane made several stops. Soon after dawn, I was at last in Hollywood.

I was at Hazel Marshall's office at exactly 9 a.m. She showed me an old, creaky, pedal-operated Moviola beside which stood a stack of small metal reels stamped IT'S ALL TRUE. Armed with notebooks, I spent the next eight hours without a break, writing down details of the remarkable footage, pulse racing, aware that in movie terms this was the equivalent of finding the Dead Sea Scrolls, a fifth gospel, or the Rosetta Stone. The footage included a single reel, edited by the great Mexican editor Joe Noriega, of a completed segment, "Bonito the Bull," about a boy who saved his animal from slaughter in the corrida in Mexico City by making a direct appeal to the president.

Exhilarated, I flew back to Santa Cruz. The next day, Hazel Marshall was on the line. She said she had made a serious mistake: she had confused me with a stock footage buyer named Hyams in San Jose, near Santa Cruz, and that I must forget all I had seen. I told her she had signed a clearance with my name properly spelled and my identity as professor made clear. She threatened legal action, and I hung up on her. The discovery made me famous, and all because of her error.

Such luck, a million-to-one example, has marked my whole life, including my years in Hollywood for the *New York Times,* and that luck began at a very early age.

I was ten years old. It was a windy day, and I was out on a long run in light rain through fields near our family home, the Mount, in South Godstone, Surrey, England. I had my head down, looking for wet mud that might cause me to slip and fall, and my school cap had blown away in the tempest that blew the russet autumn leaves in scudding confusion, that swept away the last ghostly "clocks," or heads, of dead dandelions.

I had lost my way, but I saw in my mind the ground that lay ahead: a low, sloping hill and clumps of sodden gorse, with rabbits and hares about, and I could hear crows cawing in trees blackened by a recent fire. Suddenly, I heard a voice: the voice of my late father, who had died three years earlier, telling me to look up. I did. Just a foot from my face was a long, sharp spike, protruding from a stone wall, which could have killed me instantly. I gave thanks and, looking up now, changed direction, my heart drumming loudly, every sense alert.

I was aware of a world around me that the eye couldn't see, where those who have crossed over survive, and I have had much evidence since of its existence, which I will describe in these pages.

$\mathcal{M}$y first memory is of a room whose predominant color was dark blood red and of the fear I felt in it. It was the master bedroom of our family's suite at Savoy Court, off the Strand in London, and adjoining the somber splendor of the Savoy Hotel. Aged five, I had been taken in pain from the Savoy Grill at luncheon. I had been seized by an attack of tonsillitis and had to be operated on quickly. The normal procedure would of course have been to take me to a hospital, but Father would have none of this. The operation was to take place in a River Suite of the hotel, converted into an operating theater. This had never happened before in that London hotel, and never would again.

A crack team of doctors and nurses arrived, led by the best known ear, nose, and throat surgeon in England, Sir Lionel Colledge, father of Cecilia Colledge, the 1936 German Winter Olympics skating champion, and Sir Thomas (later Lord) Horder, our own physician and attendant to the royal family. The uniquely staged operation was reported in the press; I was a tiny part of London history; and Stanley Jackson recorded the incident in his official history of the Savoy.

I knew very little of the father who had brought off this astonishing event. He was stocky, of medium height, already turned sixty when I was six, dressed always in Savile Row gray suits and Sulka ties and handmade shirts and shoes, a red carnation in his buttonhole, his overcoat lapels made of black Russian astrakhan. His voice was deep and hypnotic; no trace of his Cockney origins survived in what was now British American upper-middle class. He still talked of "Noo York."

It would be many years before I would learn of Sir Charles Frederick Higham's early life. Born in shabby Walthamstow, London, the son of a penniless solicitor's clerk, he had gone steerage with his widowed mother to New York. Risen from poverty by way of numerous enterprises, he had arrived back in London at the age of thirty, after numerous firings. He spent his last few pounds on a fine wardrobe and the cost of a luncheon for the business leader John Murray Allison, thus giving the impression he had succeeded in America and was about to bestow his knowledge on the backward Britishers.

The gamble paid off, and he rapidly became a famous figure in England, running his own advertising agency. In World War I, he adapted Lord Kitchener's poster of the pointing finger and the challenging words

Your Country Needs You, which, with the encouragement of the young Winston Churchill, he had posted all over London. He became a member of Parliament for Islington and was knighted for his services to the Crown. He founded the well-known veterans hospital, the Star and Garter at Richmond.

It is said that this polished huckster could convince you that black was white, that the moon was made of green cheese, and that there were people and animals on Mars. What is certainly true is that he became a supersalesman, claiming, with what veracity I do not know, that he had created both the famous His Master's Voice advertisement in which the dog stared into the phonograph horn and the Bisto Kids, urchins seen everywhere on billboards glowing with recently drunk Bisto broth, and that he had talked Americans into drinking tea—the Boston Tea Party in reverse. The Great I Am had a twenty-foot placard running two stories up a building in the Strand on which he advised the public to buy Dunlop tires.

He had divorced my mother, fourth of his wives, before I was three, and at the time I remembered nothing of her. There was talk of an adopted half sister, who was in a mental institution in Buffalo, New York, and of a first wife's suicide from the Brighton pier, of which not a word appeared in any biographical entry.

It was not the custom in upper-class families in England in the 1930s for parents to spend more than token, very brief periods with their children; nannies were my life, and I shall tell more of them later. My stepmother would appear briefly on her way to a party, heavily scented, in fashionable evening gowns, just before I was tucked up in bed at 6:30 p.m.; a kiss, a quick good night, and she was gone. Less often, Father would appear at the same time, the customary red carnation in his buttonhole, handkerchief neatly folded in his coat's top pocket, the cigar scent overpowering. On weekends, he would let me watch while, in Wellington boots, he built bonfires on the garden or supervised the cleaning of the goldfish pond.

We had a staff of eight, four living in and four, including a gardener and his assistant, housed nearby. Those living in included a cook-housekeeper, a lady's maid, a butler-chauffeur, and my latest nanny. We traveled by Silver Phantom Rolls-Royce to and from our home at Savoy Court in London.

The staff liked to whisper to me the strange goings-on of my parents; and even at five and six years old I was able to grasp most of their stories. It was said that both my mother and my stepmother had very peculiar marital histories.

My mother, born Josephine Janet Webb, was an anomaly in a family of brickworks owners in the dull provincial town of Cheltenham. Beautiful, well-read, and bright, she was sexually compulsive, drank heavily from the beginning, and had a wayward, neurotic, self-pitying, and self-aggrandizing nature, along with great charm. She was almost always unhappy, subject to fits of crying; she had artistic ambitions, and was a flower painter and writer of unpublished books with titles like *Spring Sorrow*. Of French Huguenot origins on her mother's side, her ancestors had seen Joan of Arc burn at the stake. Married early, she was divorced at eighteen; she then met a handsome Dutch tea planter, on leave from Java in London, named Adriaan Kochenius. He swept her off her feet and asked her to share his life in the Indies where she would, he promised, be *memsahib* of a plantation with a flock of servants.

The idea had an exotic appeal, and she set sail with my grandmother Amy for the distant Dutch colony. But on arrival she found herself in the same predicament as Leslie Crosbie, the wife of the planter in Somerset Maugham's famous play (and later film) *The Letter*. Her husband had a Eurasian mistress and made no secret of it; within days, my mother was on a ship bound for England, and the divorce court.

My stepmother was born Ruth Agnes Dawes-Smith, the daughter of an army officer, and always called Jill. She also fell in love with a South East Asian planter, Lancelot Victor Neligan. He was an agronomist and rubber specialist, headquartered in what today is Sri Lanka, then the British colony Ceylon. They were married quickly, and for reasons that excited some suspicion, he made out a will (he was only twenty-eight) in favor of his bride the day before the wedding.

On May 7, 1931, the couple were aboard the steamer *Cheshire,* in the Bay of Biscay, bound for Ceylon on their honeymoon, when (or so the servants gossiped and Jill later confirmed) Neligan told his bride that because he had contracted an illness named sprue (there were no symptoms), he could not consummate the marriage. She told him that time would take care of the problem but he would have none of it. He ran from the cabin in shame and flung himself overboard. The captain ordered a search, but it was fruitless. Jill returned from Gibraltar, took a job in my father's office as secretary, and won him from my mother.

Exactly what I made of all this at the age of five I am uncertain; all I do know is that, preferring the kitchen to the drawing room, I spent much time with the gossiping staff and retained what they told me in memory. The revelations would cease abruptly when a parent unexpectedly walked in, to ask why some household duty had not been performed.

The household at the Mount was run with the precise, accepted discipline typical of the time. At exactly 7 a.m., the grandfather clock in the entrance hall below chiming the hour, Nanny would wake me and lead me, dressed in pajamas and dressing gown, to my tiled, art deco bathroom, where she had already filled the tub from enormous iron taps marked H for Hot and C for Cold, mixing the water to the exact temperature suitable for Sonny, my nickname.

Across the tub from side to side rested a wooden bridge on which lay a large brown ocean sponge; soaps, including the semitransparent, amber Pears; a loofah, for scrubbing the back; and mysterious small balls of wire wool, never used. In the water, sometimes brownish from the insecure rusty drains, there floated a toy miniature yacht in full sail, a plastic duck, and a swan. I hung my clothes on heated silver rails and climbed in, giggling happily, soaking and enjoying Nanny's vigorous scrubbing of my back. Red and robust, I would jump out, and Nanny would rub me vigorously in a fleecy towel. Back in my room I would dress in woolen underwear, white starched shirt and smart Sulka tie, Savile Row suit, long gray woolen socks, and, almost always, brown brogue shoes.

And now came breakfast, the meal absent my parents; they rose later, still tired from very nearly nightly parties, balls, pedigree dog shows, or attendances at theaters and cinemas. The sideboard for the first meal of the day was well stocked as I walked into the dining room, with its French windows opening onto a garden that stretched for eighteen-and-a-half acres to the well-trimmed hedges of the adjoining property.

Unlike other meals, breakfast was always self-served. On the African mahogany sideboard stood a row of sterling silver chafing dishes, each engraved with my father's initials, CFH, and a conceit: a fake heraldic shield.

Nanny and I would walk after breakfast; I can recall Father accompanying us once. As we passed a woodshed, piled with timber, some of it blackened from recent flames, he told me not to play with fire, a wise instruction I have disobeyed ever since.

I would throw seed into the goldfish pond, mourning and burying any dead occupant. I would aim at crows with my pea shooter. I enjoyed exploring our local forest, the crackle of leaves and twigs under my feet, a sudden surge of bluebells, or in winter walking through the powdery snow from which I would make a snowman, complete with briar pipe and rakish hat borrowed from the gardeners.

Lunch was shared only with Nanny, or sometimes with a piano teacher, who tried in vain to have me master the instrument. I hadn't the patience, though I did have the ear.

Afternoons were spent playing croquet with child-sized sticks, balls knocked through hoops, with the neighboring Aisher children, or on rainy days, which were frequent, playing Happy Families and Old Maid card games, or Hunt the Slipper, or Sardines (a form of hide-and-seek).

I also liked board games, such as Halma, Tiddlywinks, and Drafts, or the newly introduced Monopoly, and Totopoly, its horse-racing equivalent. In the drawing room I enjoyed playing Bagatelle, a pin table affair in which one shot silver balls through nests of pins in the hope of having them hit a jackpot. And on the radio there was *The Children's Hour* at 5 p.m., in which the BBC created a ghastly place called Toytown, with bleating human sheep and a pompous mayor commanding them.

Just before teatime was for books: I was able to read at the age of four. Rag books were designed so as not to be torn by eager or impatient children's fingers, and standup books were, when opened, vertical displays of castle towers, country scenes, or fairy-tale forests. I relished them, as well as the Babar books, great thin, colored, shiny volumes relating the adventures of an elephant; and the Mumfie books, which I preferred, also dealing with an antic pachyderm.

A succession of German nannies, servants of Hitler's dictatorship, urged me to read *Grimm's Fairy Tales* while teaching me to count in their language up to ten. The Brothers Grimm proved horrific: feet and hands cut off in acts of revenge, witches baked in ovens. To this day I shiver at a mention of their evil Mother Holle. The Danish Hans Christian Andersen was even worse: I was haunted by the tale of the dancer whose red shoes carried her to a bloody death.

I was allowed one special visit to the forbidden night world of Downstairs, on December 10, 1936, when I was five, to hear the King, in a halting, uncertain, but determined voice, announce his abdication in order to marry Mrs. Simpson, whose name aroused derision in the room. Next day, Cook told me that she had been stoned by nurses in Regents Park. It was all meaningless to me.

Early in the winter of 1937, a court order gave my birth mother, of whom I remembered nothing, access to me for limited custody periods each year. She had become engaged to a steel foundry manager, Claude Manning, whose real name was Charles but because it was Father's name she made him change it. I remember to this day how I dreaded being dislodged from the Mount and Savoy Court to be housed, no matter how briefly, with a virtual stranger and a mother who had abandoned me at the age of three.

The chauffeur took me in the Rolls to Ashtead in Surrey, where Manning owned a fake Tudor house named Oakwood. It was all fumed oak and heavy, ugly carpets and chintz-covered armchairs and occasional tables heaped with magazines and books. There was one servant, a cook-housekeeper, and also a part-time gardener.

It was winter, and the house was poorly heated, with none of the ticking radiators and roaring fires I was used to, just an electric heater with two red bands that gave off a peculiar smell. My birth mother was beautiful, with alabaster skin, black hair (later dyed an unfortunate henna red), and always slightly over-made-up; my future stepfather was plump and gray faced, with a somber, irritatingly monotonous voice and no charm. Both were alcoholics and fought savagely with much drunken abuse.

Outings in Manning's Humber car were unappealing, and indeed I took no pleasure in the couple's neurotic company. Manning would beat me often for my lack of enthusiasm, or alleged rudeness, and I grew thin and sullen. Evidently Father had had enough after a month because he quite simply kidnapped me.

Meanwhile, it's clear that Father couldn't risk a counterkidnap by my mother, and I had to be whisked out of England at once. One winter night I was as usual lying awake in the dark when the lights were turned on, and Father, my stepmother, and Nanny walked in, telling me to get dressed.

We were driven by our chauffeur for hours, in the Rolls-Royce, through snow flurries. At last we were in a place with lights, shouts, horns sounding, a bustle of humanity. Now I saw great wooden sheds, whale-shaped warehouses, men with bales of unknown substances, and cranes, and I heard a howl of wind over water. We were in the port of Southampton.

We parked and got out. Porters came to pick up our luggage, including my pigskin overnight case and my stepmother's vanity case; it seemed that our steamer trunks had been brought ahead of us. I looked up at the great black and gold hull with red funnels belching smoke, a crowd in streamers, flung from the decks, and through the snow the ship's name, USS MAN-HATTAN, painted on the port side. It was close to midnight as we hurried up the gangway, and blue-uniformed American officers and white-clad stewards showed us to our A deck suite in first (then called cabin) class. We were, Father said, bound for America!

2

The trip to New York and Miami was exciting. I had no sooner settled back into the Mount on our return to England in March 1937 than I was told that I must spend some weeks with my birth mother and stepfather at Oakwood. I continued to find no joy there. All was unpleasant: my mother's drunkenness, the constant quarrels, the depressing array of adults who would turn up for cocktails and dinner, the deadliness of "Claude" Manning, with his gray face and hair and his reports on his iron foundry, of which he seemed to be a product.

Fortunately, my sulking and ill temper forced them to farm me out to my maternal grandmother, the wonderful Amy Webb, both at her ugly but welcoming house, Melincourt, in Cheltenham, and, more enjoyably, on a seaside trip to Frinton. There we were joined by my hearty, strapping Uncle Rupert, mother's older brother; her younger, sharply intelligent brother John and his wife, Peggy; her younger, sandy-haired, and gentle brother Brian—tubercular, yet smoking constantly in defiance of doctors' orders—and his plump, jolly, vigorously extroverted wife, Mabel.

Home movies that survive of that trip to the shore sometimes supplement, sometimes contradict, the vagaries of memory. It was at Frinton, with its rows of semidetached houses and boardinghouses overlooking a typically uninviting English beach of pebbles and no sand, that I started to know Amy and love her deeply.

She was fat, no doubt of it, at a time when that term was considered perfectly correct, and she rejoiced in her size. There was less shame in being heavy in her Victorian generation.

Her complaints were centered on her rheumatism and the pain in her right foot, which she attributed to an ankle injury in childhood from falling off a bathing machine (a hut on wheels used for changing at the beach) onto hard pebbles. A believer in Christian Science, she announced frequently that the pain she felt was imaginary and refused to have her foot treated medically. She hobbled gamely about, always laughing between grumbles, busy at the piano in both her home and the Frinton hotel, singing music hall songs, or "A Bicycle Built for Two" or "Ta Rah Rah Boom De Ay," in a remarkably secure soprano voice, to my everlasting joy.

Despite the miseries of Oakwood and the sadness caused a child by split parental custody, I see from the surviving Frinton home movies that I retained my infant toughness and joie de vivre. An outrageous scene stealer, I am seen, in a floppy white hat and swimsuit, running in and out of the waves, a picture of health and happiness, with no trace of neurosis or childish despair. I belonged to a generation that believed unhappiness could be cured by picking blackberries or galloping on a brisk pony; the very thought of psychiatry didn't exist in my world.

I spent much time digging for winkles and limpets or picking up strands of seaweed with their plump brown pods; I enjoyed donkey rides, and above all as the treat of treats even in that chilly spring, with a sun that gave no heat and drizzle that recurred almost daily, I couldn't wait for the ice-cream man to come by, with his cart's rattling tunes and white uniform and cap, to sell me, for sixpence, my favorite Wall's choc-ice cream. To this day I have felt no gastronomic pleasure equal to biting through the crisp brown shell to the shocking chill of the secret contents, or the first taste of fairy floss-spun sugar on long wooden sticks—and the pink and white striped sticks of Frinton peppermint rock, hard candy with the town's name printed inside. Seedy, run-down Frinton: it was a children's paradise.

Back at the Mount that summer, I learned that we would be spending several weeks in the Savoy Hotel. I loved the revolving doors that led to the Grill, running round and round until my stepmother insisted I stop. We were shown to our table by Manetta, the Italian headwaiter with his impeccable black suit and slicked-down patent leather hair. Father always had the same table, and woe betide the staff if it was given to someone else. Waiters pulled out our chairs and set out the pink Irish linen table napkins on our laps; we always had monogrammed silver serviette rings.

Father's favorite waiter, Thomas, invariably chose the meal for us from soup to savory (a salty snack that followed pudding, or dessert). It was during that stay I had my famous attack of tonsillitis and Sir Lionel Colledge and Lord Horder arrived to take charge.

Recovered, and bounding with energy one day after feeling I was at death's door, I heard that it was time I went to school. The news was welcome; at last I would meet other children. My entire life was surrounded by adults, and by the unwelcome disciplines of my stepmother.

$\mathcal{T}$he worst problem of school was that we pupils were required to attend church on Sundays, a rule never carried out at home by either of my sets of parents, since all were at best agnostic. On the occasions when I did attend Sunday services, usually just with Nanny Batchelder and in answer to local criticism, I disliked the experience intensely. The local minister at South Godstone, the nearest parish to the Mount, was High Church, so that the order of worship was almost Catholic, with a degree of liturgy and sermons threatening hellfire for unrepentant sinners, which seemed to include all of us, and would have frightened me, if my infant skepticism hadn't found them absurd.

The church was uncomfortable: first there was the standing to sing hymns, when few if any voices could be tolerated; the cramped wooden pews with the congregation's body odors in summer (regular bathing or use of deodorants was as uncommon in England in those days as decent cooking); then kneeling on the purple cushions as hard as stones, trying to think of some divine presence to pray to when all I felt was discomfort and boredom.

I realize today I was (without knowing what the word meant) a Manichean, one who, in keeping with an ancient heretical sect, believed that the world was torn between conflicting forces of good and evil, as impersonal as thunderstorms. I believed, as I do now, that adherence to the force of goodness, as if obtaining a daily transfusion of blood, could enhance any life, that embracing evil could only destroy it, eating into the system as well as into others'. Even Darwinians, I would learn later, talked of evil, but how could they acknowledge its existence and still insist that evolution was mindlessly at work on the world, with no morality beyond only the development of the species? Such thoughts were of course far beyond the mind of a six-year-old, but I am certain that a vague awareness of the idea stirred in me even then.

Above all, I felt that the stony, claustrophobic church, with its apse and altar and aisle, was not the home of a bearded God in the sky. Still, I saw Him in the glitter of snowflakes, trillions of individual jeweled forms; in the flights of butterflies fluttering from their chrysalises, a brief translucent glory; in the flights of birds migrating across thousands of miles to find miraculously their own species; in the gleam of dew on grass seen from my bedroom window at the Mount before the household rose for the day.

My school, Robinswood, near Limpsfield in Surrey, turned out to be neither grim nor repressive. It was run by the cheerfully masculine, angular Miss Benham, a woman in her fifties with gray hair drawn back in a bun, hollow cheeks, and eyes sparkling with good cheer. Thin as a crane, her upper lip marked with the suggestion of a moustache, she was of a type seldom seen in England today; a spinster by choice—she wasn't plain, though not pretty—loving children as if they were her own, she was devoted to making us happy. She usually wore a white silk man's shirt with a tie, a brown, buttoned cardigan, and brown walking shoes.

Sensible shoes she called them, and so was she. I loved her from the start. The school with its handsome gardens surrounded by scrubby elms was democratic and ecumenical, receiving children of all classes—a rarity in 1937. My best friend there, later a chief fire warden in Tasmania, was Tony Mount. Sturdy, twinkling, black haired, he was my constant partner at tennis. He was the son of a truck driver, but we felt no mutual class resentment. Another friend was David Sutcliffe, today untraceable, who came from a middle-class family. So there we were, Three Musketeers, proof at a time of class hatred that three boys could enjoy each other's company without actual or inverted snobbery.

I remember nothing of our indoor schooling, only that we were off on countless adventures in fields and over streams, in the course of what was called Nature Study. We learned from locals how to cure the white sprinkling of spots caused by stinging nettles: dock leaves rubbed on hands. We picked up horse chestnuts in their green prickly skin fallen from trees, peeled them, made holes in them, fixed them with string, and then, calling them conkers, fought with them. We found surprising pleasure in looking at cows; they gazed back at us with ruminant disinterest, switching away bluebottle flies with their tails and munching on grass, dropping large turd pats on the ground, which mysteriously formed thick crusts, like home-baked apple pies.

We explored rubbish dumps, where we found all manner of discarded metal objects, especially rusted old paint cans, smelling of petroleum, and shoes, hats, and (hilariously) women's stays. When we found a can that had a residue of blue paint in it, we melted the contents over a fire made of twigs and smeared our hand-me-down overalls in that color as a cruder form of meadlike dye.

We fished for tadpoles that flickered like living commas in the brackish stream water below the garden and ran through seas of bluebells, or golden carpets of buttercups, and examined the strange, lumpy gray forms of lichen on tree boles. Above all, we were fascinated by dragonflies, wondering if it was true that they had ten thousand facets in each eye and saw the world divided into a complex mesh, and also whether they saw in color.

Tony spent weekends at the Mount, where my stepmother, with Father usually absent in London, went out of her way to make him welcome. She taught him, as she had taught me, to be ambidextrous, a skill I have lost with time. She joined us in reading aloud such popular works as Richmal Crompton's William books, about an obstreperous schoolboy up to endless mischief, and A. A. Milne's *When We Were Very Young,* as well as Hugh Lofting's *Doctor Doolittle* books and the Swallows and Amazons series. The one children's author I disliked was Beatrix Potter; to this day I abhor literary anthropomorphism, in which plants, trees, animals, and birds are made to speak in human voices. I didn't appreciate Squirrel Nutkin, Peter Rabbit, and all the other Potter creations, and when they turned up predictably in a recent film biography of the author, I had to take off the DVD. *Wind in the Willows* annoyed me, with its badger and mole and road-hogging monster Mr. Toad. I could accept Lewis Carroll because the contentious figures in the *Alice* chronicles were merely figments of her dreams.

We were one of the first English families to own a television set. The sturdy walnut console in the drawing room had a screen that opened slowly to the touch of a button, like a Japanese fan, to reveal an oblong, pale gray and flickering little screen. I remember the entertainment as being numbing: boisterous regional knockabout farces, talks on how to take care of household and garden, lectures on wildfowl in the watery charms of the Lincolnshire Wold. In between enduring clumsy piano recitals, strident brassy themes from the BBC military band, and relentless hymn singing by the Chapel Royal Choir, I was excited by news broadcasts: a ship going down in a storm off Land's End; an airship's silver flight over London; the crash of an autogyro, a huge insectlike plane that was a precursor of a helicopter; and the wind-whipped palm trees of a Florida hurricane. I found myself an early acolyte of this ersatz shrine; children in ancient Greece must have felt this way when they visited the Delphic Oracle for the first time.

My stepmother was nine months pregnant by December 1937, a condition explained to me as the result of a visit by a stork. I asked if, for example, horses and cows had separate storks, and was silenced. Ordered, according to the now long vanished custom of the day, to spend weeks in bed, she was also, I thanked God, told not to exert herself later, so I suffered no slaps for many blissful weeks.

My half sister, Annabella, was a Christmas baby in 1937, and we were all in London at the Savoy Chapel for the christening. There could be no question of my stepmother breastfeeding the child, who was left at the hotel with a wet-nurse and day and night nurses as we all took off to see pantomimes at matinees.

To a six-year-old, these peculiarly British forms of entertainment were hilariously improbable, and magically absurd; they perversely mixed up the sexes. The Principal Boy, or hero, was a young woman in tights, the heroine in pretty dresses; their frequent kissings and dancings cheek to cheek were outrageously off-color. Mothers and sisters, ugly or otherwise, were played by ungainly figures of men. It was a topsy-turvy world, far more appealing than the real one outside. I especially enjoyed *Aladdin*, a riot of fake chinoiserie, in which the pretty girl in the title role had to deal with the cross-dresser laundress Widow Twankey in scrappy pidgin English.

Much as I relished the helter-skelter of pantomimes, I also found a place in my heart for Sir James Barrie's immortal *Peter Pan,* which again mixed up the sexes. That Christmas, I remember seeing, of all improbable Peters, the buxom movie star Anna Neagle, utterly feminine with her big breasts and hips, playing Peter, whom I had imagined as small, athletic, nimble—a typical boy. When she flew overhead, across the audience, it seemed that the wires were taxed to the limit to carry an actress who had become famous in films as Nell Gwynn, the chubbiest and cheekiest of royal mistresses.

I had wanted to see a film from earliest awareness, but had been forbidden by my stepmother (father was an addict). Now with her out of the picture I could see a movie at last; father's choice was *Snow White and the Seven Dwarfs,* shown at the New Gallery Cinema in Regent Street. I was bored by the opening scenes in which the pretty heroine was serenaded by birds and animals, but as soon as she was chased through an evil wood, where the tree boles turned into threatening faces and branches clawed at her viciously, I was captivated. I loved the wicked queen, peering narcissistically into a mirror with arched eyebrows and a red gash of a mouth, her oddly medieval costume of high collar and belt, her familiar with his smoky gargoyle face peering back at her from the glass as she asked, like any movie star, "Who is the fairest of them all?" and received the groveling answer she expected. I liked the huntsman who, conscience stricken, could not bring back Snow White's bleeding heart. The Seven Dwarfs made me laugh most of all in the transformation scene, in which the queen turns into a humpbacked crone, chased by them to the edge of a crumbling cliff in a realistic storm, the rock cracking under her feet as she plunges to a well-deserved death.

Back at the Mount in January 1938, my stepmother farmed out my half sister Annabella to nannies and resumed both her social life and her severe discipline of me. Now that I was almost seven, I was no longer confined to the nursery for lunch and dinner but had to learn the rituals of eating with the adults.

Pocket money of a shilling a week was to be kept in a small leather pouch; if I had folding money, it was to be kept in my right trouser pocket. I must stand when a lady came to the table at meals and when she left it. I must learn to "test" the game, pheasant, partridge, or quail, when it came in uncooked on a trolley before the meal, with my forefinger to see if it was sufficiently plump and soft and "high." I was to be seen and not heard; when I spoke at meals, my stepmother frowned and seized the occasion to slap me.

I escaped her because she was again unwell after her child was born and Father was in London to attend his doctors, who told him he was very ill; his smoking and drinking had set up the beginnings of a cancerous growth in his throat. Of course I knew nothing of this but I must have been surprised that he now spent a great deal of time with me, not realizing the reason: he had limited time now to love and to know me.

And now, Nanny Bachelder sadly left us, as it was felt I no longer needed her care. With Father, my stepmother, and baby Annabella we set off on a Mediterranean cruise aboard the ship *Arandora Star,* its fully realized replica seen today in London's Victoria and Albert Museum. She was a light, airy vessel, quite unlike the oppressive, art deco *Manhattan.* I can still see us on deck: the tarry scent of deck quoits as I competed with other children, the blue beach umbrellas over red painted metal chairs and tables as drinks were served in the sun, the sound of dance bands relayed through loudspeakers.

The Bay of Biscay made me seasick for the first time, but I soon recovered at Gibraltar and relished even the stench of goats being herded through narrow cobbled streets of Valletta, Malta. Venice brought a gondola trip on brackish waters down the Grand Canal to the tune of mandolins. Most desirable of all were the beauty of the Yugoslavian Bay of Fundi and the mysterious walled city of Dubrovnik, with its labyrinthine side streets and array of shops selling everything from abacuses to zinnias.

Back at the Mount, Father's condition worsened and his affairs were run largely by his lawyer, Maxwell Best, and by his excellent and properly named secretary, Miss Cleverly. He told my friend Colin Robinson, son of a staff member at Africa House, Kingsway, that he had lost 50 percent of his blood in surgery, a financier's term if ever there was one. Colin would share with me, Tony Mount, and David Sutcliffe rides in my brand new, bright red kiddy car, the noise of our merry laughter irritating my stepmother, who, now that Father was mostly at the London Clinic, again took fearsome charge of me.

Her scoldings grew more frequent and I closed myself to her, so that she called me a "blind boy"; she thrashed me with an ivory-backed hairbrush; she expressed derision for my every spoken thought. I see her still: tall, blonde, very thin, with sharp features; her shoulders often draped in fox furs, their button eyes as dead as her own; and accompanied everywhere by our five dachshunds.

She walked with a long, loping masculine stride, needling me endlessly: I mustn't slump, or I would get a hunchback; I was too pale (a slap took care of that); I mustn't moon about or read so much. When I lost a boxing bout with a neighbor boy she boxed my ears in punishment. She snatched away my favorite Black Magic chocolates and barley sugar sticks whenever she caught me with them.

And then, mysteriously she became affectionate. I had no idea why, until something happened to explain it.

3

*I*t was, as I recall, a morning in summer. I had taken my early walk at the Mount and was ready for breakfast but for some reason I went up to my room. I was walking past my parents' suite when I heard my stepmother call out to me, not in her usual snappish and commanding tone, but with an odd tone of seductiveness.

She was, I saw as I walked in, calling me from the bathroom. Father was in London, recovering, I believe, from yet another operation. As I walked toward the bathroom door, her voice was louder, and then she half-opened the door and pulled me in.

She stood there, next to the bathtub, naked. I was shocked; horrified; I had never seen a nude human being before. Her blonde hair was tucked into a rubber cap; strands fell on either side of her face. Her body seemed strange and repulsive to me; in clothes, she was slim, elegant, expensively dressed and coiffured, an evil snow princess. Stripped, she seemed ungainly, her breasts threatening and full, her nipples like ripened figs, her hips too wide, stomach heaving, and, though I tried not to look at it, her pubic hair a forest of black; could it be that her head hair was dyed?

She pulled off my clothes, twisting my arm painfully when I fought against her. Then, when I was naked, she gave me a conducted tour of her body, explaining why a woman's shoulders were narrow, her hips big, her body capable of housing a baby, the issue of blood that came every month.

She forced me to put my hand in her vagina, which was moist and clinging, like a sea anemone I had once examined at a beach. She said that Father had planted his seed in its depths, through intercourse, which was the supreme male experience and would be mine in a few years; that stories of storks bringing babies were ridiculous. She forced my hand deeper and moaned with pleasure.

At last I managed to wrench free and she struck me, calling me a vicious, foolish little boy. The steam from the bath, the glitter of white tiles in the bright electric lights, her naked form, and her savage, shouted anger were overpowering, and I ran out. It was only that strange detachment that marked me as a child that prevented me from crying, or from running away from home.

I said nothing to anyone about the incident; I must have been afraid my stepmother would kill me if I did. Certainly, seeing her eyes in a stare of anger, I am certain to this day she would have. To me, she was more than ever the evil stepmother of fairy tales; the brothers Grimm could scarcely have created anyone more frightful. A photograph of the time survives; no longer the cheerful outgoing boy of a Dorothy Wilding picture, I see myself, out with Father, the Evil One, my stepmother, and our pack of dachshunds on a walk in a gray, sad place that looks like London. I had become a picture of misery and secretiveness.

Father, I suspect, was disturbed by my new apathy and unexpected sourness; in turn, I was worried by his look of illness, his face unnaturally flushed, his neck swollen. When I asked I was told, by our Wimpole Street dentist Dr. Fry and others, that he had dental problems.

Appearances had to be kept up and my stepmother one day took me to a movie matinee in Godstone. Instead of an appropriate children's picture, she made me sit with her through, of all things, a romantic comedy for adults: *There Goes My Heart,* a typical thirties concoction about a runaway heiress who, pursued by a society reporter, falls in love with him. As I watched, I felt severe pain in my left ear, and I screamed. My stepmother jabbed with her elbow, telling me to shut up.

I doubled up in agony and screamed louder. My stepmother apologized to the people around; she hissed at me that I was pretending, to attract attention to myself. A uniformed usherette appeared with her flashlight to a chorus of shushes, and the manager had the lights turned on and, to everyone's unsympathetic annoyance, the film stopped.

I was carried into the lobby with its smell of varnish and linoleum, and an ambulance arrived, to take me to the nearest hospital. Doctors told my stepmother, who regarded all illness as a sign of weakness, that I had mastoiditis, a severe infection of the bone behind my left ear, and that the bone must be removed at once.

The nurses were no more sympathetic than my stepmother; this was England, where young men of seven were not supposed to weep or scream, and now I was rushed into surgery. I can still see the lamps overhead in their thirties, glazed glass globes, and I can smell the sweet and sickening chloroform, soaked into a mass of cotton wool in a steel frame, pressed to my nostrils. I tried to push it away; I felt I was being smothered. Then as I went under, like a drowned child, I had a dream: first, my heart began beating in a rhythm I heard many years later, in voodoo drums in Haiti; then I saw myself on a hillside, very much like the one on which I live today; a plane flew overhead, very noisily, and shook the house I was in so violently I was sent plunging into a valley. I saw the time as I woke: 4:30 p.m.

I recovered slowly and, as September faded into the chilly, damp October of 1938, I realized that my father was dying. He was brought back from the London Clinic and stayed most of the time in his front upstairs room overlooking his beloved garden, the monkey-puzzle tree, the summerhouse, and the eighteen and one-half acres of landscaped lawns. It was customary in those days to hide the truth from children, to say that a dying person had a bad cold and, when he died, that he or she had gone on a long trip abroad.

My stepmother, realistic to the last, told me that Father had cancer of the throat and mouth, that the disease was caused by smoking, and that he was still, she said, making passes at the nurses. She wouldn't allow me to see him until just before Christmas, which she conducted as always with presents round the tree and children in for charades.

I remember walking into the beautiful front bedroom, Father's bed set against the left wall. He was swollen, his neck enormous and marked with the black tracings of radium needles. His breathing was heavy and labored; he couldn't speak but tears ran down his cheeks as he saw me, the slim, fair-haired boy he had known so little, whose mother had given him so much grief, running out on him when I was three, and whose second wife was a terror worthy of some unbridled melodrama.

At sixty-two, he had not lived out his full three score years and ten. From his expression of melancholy and fear I may have guessed that despite a life of great success, a spectacular rise from poverty and obscurity, he wasn't content at the end.

He handed me, hands trembling, a parting gift: a small, plastic, reddish-brown bear cub stuffed with cotton wool, which I still have in my bedroom to this day, and have carried around the world. For some reason I never gave it a name. I thanked him and left, feeling numb. I never saw him again.

And yet, dismiss it if you will, I feel he has guided me ever since, that he has been responsible for the luck that I have known throughout my life.

On Christmas Eve, with of course no Santa Claus, no stockings on my bedroom mantelpiece for the visitor down the chimney, I was told he had died. On Boxing Day, my stepmother, my baby half sister, and I took off to London in the Rolls to attend the memorial service at the Savoy Chapel. My birth mother was refused permission to attend, as were my father's other previous wives.

Friends were there and the professional colleagues: Lord Beaverbrook and Lord Hailsham, as well as Sir Lionel Colledge, Lord Horder, and the advertising genius Philip Hill. The list was long. The bishop of London presided.

The graveside service and the internment followed at South Godstone Cemetery; my stepmother had the words Sleep Well Darling inscribed on the gravestone.

My birth mother embarked on a campaign to obtain lasting custody of me; my stepmother joined her in battle. The conflict had nothing to do with either woman caring for me; rather, it was an assertion of powerful egos. As for me, had it not been for her sexual abuse of me, I would have preferred to stay in my stepmother's care because of the luxuries involved and the promise of Eton; as it was, I was bounced from one courtroom to another, finding solace only in comic books, to which, at eight, I became addicted.

It was in the summer of 1939, with the war about to break out, at the somber, gray brick Law Courts in the Strand in London, that my mother, locked in the custody battle with my stepmother, felt forced to play her trump card: some maid at the Mount had presumably slipped it to her that I had been sexually abused. The result was that I was removed permanently from my stepmother's care and had to make my way in Manning's Humber to Oakwood again, this time for good.

Soon after my arrival there, depressed and wishing, despite everything, that I was back at the Mount and Miss Benham's school, I wasn't taught at all. Instead I had to put up with long, drawn-out days at home, the monotony broken only once when Manning invited me to witness a ceremony of the Masonic brotherhood, to which he belonged. I found the ritual repulsive: the figures in hoods, the chanting, the oath taking and threats of frightful punishment should I reveal what I had seen.

My mother drank more than ever, hysterical, always crying about one thing or another, telling me constantly that my father had been forced to draw up an "iniquitous will," which left her only a small income to raise me on, and my stepmother the bulk of the estate. She mentioned that the estate had greatly been reduced by treacherous business partners and crooked counselors. She railed endlessly against my stepmother.

She indulged in outside love affairs, which to a child of eight were not so much shocking as boring and incomprehensible. When her various lovers wearied of her self-pity and ill temper, she attacked them to me; since only days before she had described them as devoted and passionate, I was left bewildered. Today, I wonder why she couldn't have poured her grievances into the ears of women friends. Perhaps she didn't trust them not to tell her husband of her wanderings.

One afternoon, I heard a scream from my parents' bedroom. I ran in and found Manning kicking my mother in the ribs. I tried to pull him loose, a futile effort in view of my size, and he struck me, telling me he would kill me if I didn't let go. I ran out.

Manning took my mother and me out for a Sunday drive. They were enjoying a brief period of peace and relaxation, and perhaps my absence for several weeks had made my stepfather more sympathetic toward me.

The day was unusually beautiful, with clear, pale blue skies, a hint of actual heat in the sun, and flowers blooming in the hedgerows. Then, on the car radio, a musical broadcast stopped and a voice announced that the prime minister, the elderly and sickly Neville Chamberlain, would address the nation.

In a tense and halting voice, which displayed disappointment though not a hint of guilt, he stated that we were in a state of war with Germany. I have no idea how I responded. Is it possible I thought of how much of my upbringing had been ruled by German assistant nannies, how my parents had been obsessed by dachshunds, how Father had endlessly stated that there would be no war with Hitler? I think not; I feel sure no such thought entered my mind. But I rather suspect I was excited. A new element had entered my life.

We arrived at Oakwood to find something that for the first time in my memory had the three of us laughing together. An air-raid siren had sounded. Our gardener was in a panic, lying under a heap of sandbags that we had bought on written orders to protect the house in the event of air raids. His cowardice brought out the best and worst in us; for the first time, I felt we were actually a family.

The rituals of wartime began. I remember being fitted for a gas mask, which made me look like a figure in a science fiction comic: all snout nosed and goggle eyed, smelling of rubber. We were issued ration books, the small square brown pages to be marked off as we bought food or clothing.

And now, very strangely, circumstances reduced the drinking and quarreling at home. I suspect that millions of households were similarly affected; almost everyone felt that personal differences and slights were insignificant, that we must All Pull Together against Jerry, our word for the Germans.

My stepfather, now notably pleasanter, was called up for service. Overage, he had nevertheless flying experience from World War I, and was transferred to the reserve as a pilot officer in charge of training recruits at a Spitfire base at Cranwell, near Sleaford in Lincolnshire.

Why do I remember our leaving London, that winter day of 1939? It remains with me always: the sky black and spitting sooty rain; the long streets heading up to the Great North Road, dirty with windblown litter, a few pedestrians fighting the wind in mackintoshes, umbrellas, and shoes in galoshes; huddled figures in doorways looking like symbols not of fighting Britain but of an abandonment of hope. It was my first glimpse of poverty. In retrospect I may have felt that hell was actually this: not some Dante-esque pit of fire but a chill, empty, earthly existence with no hope of succor or warmth.

Lincolnshire turned out to be flat, misty, plagued by long downpours of rain, the sky almost always black. Snow, which I loved and longed for, never came. Our home at the Cranwell Air Base near the old village of Sleaford was a prefabricated bungalow, of which the most flattering thing that could be said is that it was utilitarian: made of wood, its walls covered in a bilious brown wallpaper, its furnishings matching suites of chairs and tables evidently bought at a bargain sale. It proved to be poorly heated, its two-bar electric fire intermittently going out due to some problem with the connections that was never fixed.

My stepfather was preoccupied in long hours of training pilots and taking them on trial flights. His absences were a considerable relief; when he came home at night he was too exhausted to quarrel. At last my mother had had enough, and without warning she left with me for London, having arranged some kind of separation allowance with Manning. We moved into 703 Keyes House, in the enormous block of flats called Dolphin Square on the Thames Embankment, in Pimlico. Others living there included the writer Gerald Kersh, the movie and radio stars Ben Lyon and Bebe Daniels, and the notorious Nazi sympathizers Sir Oswald and Lady Diana Mosley, who were arrested for treason and trundled off in the prison van popularly known as a Black Maria.

I left for Weston-super-Mare and St. Peter's, which was to be my prep school for the duration of the war, in time for the autumn term of 1940, and just before the heavy bombing raids of London; in essence, I was an "evacuee." Equipped with gas mask, school cap, gray uniform, long socks with elastic garters to hold them up, and sensible shoes, I joined the other new boys at Paddington Station. My mother and other parents were there to see us off. There were few tears shed; this was England.

After the three-and-a-half-hour journey we arrived at Weston-super-Mare, a sprawling seaside town where long mud flats stretched out to a sickly gray-green sea.

A school bus took us to St. Peter's, a handsome red brick pile with eaves, ivy and Virginian creepers, and spacious grounds that included a swimming pool, a tennis court, and a football field.

At an initial briefing, we new boys were welcomed by the tall, fair-haired headmaster, Geoffrey Tolson, who had been in charge of the school for years and had had Roald Dahl as one of his pupils (later he would have John Cleese).

The staff was excellent. My favorite was Captain Lancaster, a retired army officer with sandy hair and moustache, a good line in tweeds, a permanent tan from India, and a pleasant aroma of expensive pipe tobacco. In his private study, once a week, a group of us would gather as he read, superbly, and with all the correct dramatic emphases, the works of H. Rider Haggard. He brought to life the romantic sweep of *She,* a Victorian sexual fantasy about an eternal woman who awaits the arrival of a Greek god in human form, only to lose everything when she tries to follow him into the real world, and ages horribly, an idea copied by James Hilton in *Lost Horizon,* one of my favorite books of the time.

There was much to enjoy at St. Peter's: long walks in the surrounding hills looking for stone implements from prehistoric times or iron relics of the Roman occupation; learning Boy Scout crafts such as reef knots and sheepshanks and how to apply a tourniquet or dress an open wound; military whist drives, games with each team named for a particular country (mine was Sweden) and playing against other teams. Air-raid drills involved learning how to use a fire extinguisher and climbing up to the roof, then sliding down to the playing field inside a fifty-foot stocking made of parachute silk and used as an escape from incendiary bombs. We would plunge, laughing happily, clinging to a rope that was covered in chicken feathers but still left our hands quite raw.

Acting in plays was a pleasure and I received good reviews in the school magazine as Demetrius, the dashing young lover in *A Midsummer Night's Dream,* and Antonio in *The Merchant of Venice* (when Shylock talked of a pound of flesh, the audience giggled; where would he find it on my skinny frame?).

It was Geoffrey Tolson who sparked my early interest in movies. He personally ran the 16 mm projector, showing us, in the main school hall, silent movies supplied by the Wallace Heaton library. We thrilled to the real-life adventures of Cherry Kearton and Frank (*Bring 'Em Back Alive*) Buck as they fought jungle and swamp, alligators, poisonous snakes, and spiders to bring us vivid pictures of prewar tropical adventure.

We even went to films in Weston-super-Mare. The whole school walked to one particular theater to see what we were told would simply be newsreels and documentaries until the curtains parted on the big silver screen and to our whooping delight we were watching Bette Davis and Errol Flynn in *The Private Lives of Elizabeth and Essex.*

My sexuality emerged ahead of its proper time when I carved a knife from a tree branch into a phallic weapon, painted it silver, and began plunging it into boys' groins until it was confiscated, and I was caned. Whether anyone except Geoffrey Tolson knew what my attacks signified I rather doubt. I was in his bad books until I began to excel at soccer and rugby football, which I enjoyed hugely: huddling in my striped jersey with the others of my Crawford Butterflies team in scrums, then breaking free to carry the ball triumphantly past the finishing line; returning mud soaked on rainy days to the dormitory to scrape the dirt off the cork knobs of my football boots, then showering naked among the pink, healthy bodies of the other boys.

Above all, I enjoyed cricket. The autumn term of 1940 offered long, warm, sunny afternoons with the scent of new-mown grass in my nostrils. In cricket cap, white shirt, white trousers and shoes, and thigh-length pads, I would stand at the wicket with my shiny new bat, resined and sweet smelling, in my gloved hand, striking the ball as far as I could, then running happily until I succeeded or someone caught me out.

I enjoyed visits to Madame Tussauds wax museum in London. On the main floor were figures of historical importance, or current politicians and stars of stage and screen. I remember noticing that the Duchess of Windsor was glaring at former prime minister Stanley Baldwin, her nemesis in the abdication crisis.

I spent very little time among the waxen great; instead, I would make my way, time and time again, to the subterranean Chamber of Horrors, down a winding staircase with painted gray bricks suggesting the entrance to a gothic dungeon. One area was curtained off and marked ADULTS ONLY. Needless to say, I always peeked into it, to see an almost naked man, every muscle showing, hanging by his stomach on a hook.

There were sinister glass cases where for a penny one could watch medieval tortures in clockwork, the rack, the thumbscrew, and the water treatment, all with tiny figures that became unpleasantly lifelike.

Many of the figures in niches were murderers, often shown with their victims. The muscled arms of Marat, killed in his hip bath by Charlotte Corday, excited me guiltily. "IN THE VERY CLOTHES IN WHICH HE WAS HANGED," announced a placard next to Hawley Harvey Crippen, the American homeopath who accidentally gave his wife an overdose of hyoscine, a sexual depressant, so that she fell into a catatonic trance; he cut her up while she was still alive. He was hanged wearing his reading glasses.

The highlight of that summer was seeing *The Thief of Bagdad,* to this day my favorite movie. Its evil Grand Vizier, played by the great Conrad Veidt, with his heavy German accent, refusal to allow free speech or thought, and murderous attitude to those who stood in his way, struck me, even at that age, as a thinly disguised image of Hitler. Sabu, dark, almost naked, muscular and handsome, was a boy hero who evoked uncomfortable but exciting feelings in me; his scenes worked on me more than the hetero-sexual fantasy of the sequence when the vizier's latest victim is embraced by a clockwork figure of a Silver Maid, which stabs him to death at the moment of arousal.

I courted expulsion from St. Peter's by refusing to accept the wine and wafer of the church Eucharist, saying the ritual was sheer cannibalism. The school chaplain tried to explain that the ceremony was purely symbolic, but I would have none of it. If it hadn't been for my proficiency at sports, acting in plays and writing one (about an RAF base penetrated by a spy), or winning reading and spelling bee competitions, I think I would have been expelled.

At home that summer, I found my mother's taste in men had grown more exotic. She was sleeping with the famous black pianist-singer Hutch, Leslie Hutchinson, a man of dazzling looks and physique. One night I went with her to watch him play at the Café Anglais nightclub, which, of course, was normally out of bounds to children. I created a stir, not least because my mother's romance was known to all society. The dark Adonis strode in wearing white tie and tails, placed a black-and-gold Turkish cigarette in a cut glass ashtray on the Steinway grand piano, removed his white kid gloves, and began to play and croon, in a rich baritone, "Red Sails in the Sunset," his signature tune. The affair continued until Hutch met the even more beautiful Duchess of Kent and my mother again went into one of her "nervous breakdowns."

4

I discovered new avenues of escape during school holidays. I was captivated by newsreel theaters, small cinemas where the program cost only a shilling. It included three newsreels; three cartoons, including the sadistic Tom and Jerry series, with cat pitted savagely against mouse; and various shorts, lavishly produced by the major studios as program fillers.

Just as at feature film showings, the audience, unlike today, could arrive in the middle of the screening; after seeing it round, they would announce loudly that was where they came in, and leave. Nobody bothered to clean the auditoriums until after hours, if then; British hygiene was an oxymoron.

London was still, despite bomb ruins and smoke and vile weather, an intensely civilized city, where buying a gramophone record, after all these years of war, meant being offered hot cocoa or tea and shown to a private booth where the music played until the customer was satisfied. In the bookshops, assistants, all well educated, would suggest a new work and wrap the customer's selection individually in elegant paper.

And still the bomb attacks went on. Now we had the V-1 bombs, or doodlebugs, followed by the silent V-2s, both of which were guided from German bases across the channel. These new rockets were aimed at a target, and struck. Dolphin Square, scarcely damaged in the Blitz, now suffered a direct hit, and some young women on their way to a party were killed in an elevator. When my grandmother and uncle Rupert came to town they stayed at the Regent Palace Hotel and it, too, was bombed, with our whole family in the basement shelter.

My mother found a lover she preferred to the others. Peter Punt was handsome, fair, beautifully put together: an example of prime English upper-middle-class beef. He was impressive in his officer's uniform and much more polished then the others; his most irritating habit was having me take Whiskey, our Scotch terrier, for excessively long walks, while he made vigorous love to my mother. Transferred to Egypt, stricken with jaundice, he returned on sick leave looking ghastly, to tell her he was marrying someone else. Her tears and recriminations went on for weeks, and then she met another man on the rebound. Acting like a skittish woman, the new acquisition said he wouldn't have sex with her until they were married. Then fate, which she had tempted for so long, played a devilish trick on her: John Mallinson was impotent.

He looked like a cut-rate Napoleon, with a black, Brilliantined cowlick of hair; an oval, olive face; cold, staring coal-black eyes; and a hint of a belly. He was poisonous, detestable. Trained in the Royal Navy at Bermuda, he was retired early on health grounds and was busy making industrial documentary films, mostly on location in southern England; he had begun before the war as an assistant on a movie version of *The Mill on the Floss* with Geraldine Fitzgerald.

Now that she was forty, my mother was starting to panic. Mallinson may have wanted to punish her for some reason by condemning her to a sexless union. They got off to a bad start when she lied I was her brother. Mallinson knew better and told her so. I was not invited to their wedding at Caxton Hall Registry Office in 1944.

Had I remained strong and athletic, I could have handled Mallinson easily. But nature had played a trick on me as well, so that due to some glandular irregularity I shot up too fast and was nervous, strung out, and delicate where before I had been vigorous, sturdy, and robust.

Mallinson took every opportunity to savage me for my pallor, my state of nervous exhaustion, and my too-soft voice. He called me a "creeping Jesus" because I walked quietly into rooms, saying little. I was writing more poetry (and had verses published), which he called "verbal diarrhea." I had a violent quarrel with him, telling him that the reason he liked Whiskey was that a dog couldn't answer back. He screamed at me loudly over that.

His arguments with my mother were even more lethal. It's clear that his inability to make love to her drove them both to extremes of rage; it's unclear why she didn't at once seek an annulment. Perhaps she feared that a court case might reveal that even she could not arouse a man whose sexual capacities had vanished. Or perhaps she dreaded life without his income as a film director.

One day I heard a scream from her bedroom. Mallinson and she had fought, and he was picking up his hat and overcoat to go out. My mother shouted that she was going to kill herself by throwing herself out of the seventh floor window. Some days before she had been shocked by the sight of a workman falling from a loose coping stone on the roof of the flats opposite; he had died horribly. She yelled she would die the same way.

Mallinson broke the door down as we heard the window open. We burst in only to find her sitting on the bed, smoking, and reading a magazine. It was hard to forgive her for that, and a new quarrel broke out.

I don't recall whether it was then or later that my mother told me she wished I had never been born, that she had fought for three days and nights to keep me in her womb, that I had ruined her social life for good; and look what I had become: not the soldier, sailor, airman, or athlete she had wanted but a weedy poet, a sad bookworm, a freak of nature.

From then on, I felt not even the faintest vestige of affection she had managed to awaken in me during the war years. It was not until she died in 2001 that I received from a retirement home, among a batch of photographs and letters, pictures taken of her with me shortly after I was born, a robust fat baby on whom she gazed with maternal affection. Her screamed words, in short, were cruel lies, and so far as I was concerned, she committed a form of suicide then and there.

It was obvious I must go to public school. The family trust left no money for Eton or Harrow, and anyway boys had to be "put down" for these schools at birth. Instead, I was to be sent to the second-rate Cranleigh, in Surrey. It was about this time that the war came to an end.

I took off for Cranleigh with other new boys by train, in a specially reserved carriage. The day was heavy with darkness and rain and I felt a sense of ominousness: the school, I was sure, was not going to be a haven like St. Peter's, and my teenage companions were hostile, bullying me for my frail appearance and saying I was "death warmed up."

On arrival at the gloomy, unattractive school, I was soon told of the grisly ritualistic existence I would have to face. I was to be a "fag," which in England didn't mean homosexual; it meant servant. I would become a slave of a prefect, or senior boy, whose every command I must obey or be caned in the process.

The cheerless establishment with its dismal chilly schoolrooms was haunted by smells of body odor, chalk, varnish, turpentine, overcooked cabbage, and brussels sprouts. I had to make my prefect's bed, empty his chamber pot, carry his clothes to the laundry in a wicker basket, sweep the floor when he dropped crumbs on it, polish his shoes, and even brush his hair. I had to dust every inch of his cramped "study," which smelled of damp and urine every day.

I recall an early trip to class when I was carrying, balanced on a thick cardboard-bound exercise book, an obligatory bottle of black Swan ink and a wooden pen with a brand new nib. Noticing the time by my watch, I realized I might be late, and I ran. At that moment, someone tripped me and sent me flying. I blocked the fall with my hands but the ink bottle shattered and my exercise book was soaked, as well as the floor. A master walked by and told me to mop up the mess. When I asked with what, he cuffed my ear. I had to clean up with my pocket handkerchief and arrived late in class with black stains on my hands and face, to general mocking laugher. Had I stated I had been tripped, I would have been mercilessly attacked: a sneak was worse than anyone, the lowest of the low.

Almost at once, I was assigned to another school. Mallinson and my mother settled on Clayesmore, a progressive establishment in Dorset where there was no sadomasochistic prefect system and where boys would learn handicrafts.

I could have stayed the distance at Clayesmore but I was sunk by my own ineptitude.

I was incapable of doing anything with my hands. Before my traumas and before I became an adolescent I could as a Boy Scout effortlessly tie a dozen different kinds of knot, set up a tent and bring it down, repair a broken toy car or a toy train engine. Now I could do nothing; I had no practical aptitude, and I knew I must go. I ran away, without even a suitcase, and took a train to London with the last of my pocket money, to face the predictable abuse at home.

5

*T*here was talk of sending me to a "crammers," a private tutor's establishment where perhaps I might pass a university entrance exam. The very idea made me yawn; I had no interest in going to a university. Glimpses of Oxford and Cambridge convinced me I would be out of place in an atmosphere of ragging, debagging, drinking, boating, chasing women, smoking cigars, studying with learned professors in stuffy rooms going over ancient texts, then sitting for exams while an invigilator prowled about looking for cheats—the notion was appalling.

When it was pointed out that without a university degree, no openings would exist for me in medicine, the law, or finance, I shrugged. I had no interest in these professions and my existence at Dolphin Square was such, and my health so uncertain, I expected to commit suicide in a romantic gesture before I was twenty-one.

My sexuality, so suppressed at the time, again began to show itself as I watched a play called *Dark of the Moon*. In it, an almost naked Witch Boy, acted by the exquisitely muscled and proportioned William Sylvester, writhed about, dipped in oil, and provided rich fodder for countless wet dreams.

My mother, seeing my excitement, became alarmed; her homophobia resulted in her talking contemptuously of "nancy boys." Mallinson detested "queers." I wondered if his impotence resulted not, as my mother said, from some mysterious disease, but from really wanting men.

They sent me to an evil-smelling old doctor who with suspicious enthusiasm plunged a needle in my buttocks containing testosterone; I felt no different after three weeks of those hormones. Early in 1947 I was packed off to a crammers, which turned out to be a house in Guildford, Surrey, with only one other pupil, a South African cynic named Tony Jackson. It was with him that I had my next brush with the supernatural—or did I?

Each night, even when it was raining, we would take off on a long walk after dark, through the poorly lighted streets, for several miles. We would talk about love, which Tony didn't believe in, saying that "the real thing," meaning true affection between a man and a woman, didn't exist. He said that unlike myself he believed death brought only oblivion, and that any other conviction was proof of cowardice in face of the inevitable. Such was his gloomy nature at a healthy fifteen.

We always took the same route. Most of the houses we saw were unremarkable, from medium-sized villas to mansions, set back from the streets at the end of gravel driveways, most with garages. It was a prosperous middle-class neighborhood, whose lights were usually out by ten o'clock. One particular house was an object of fascination to us. Gabled, situated behind bare elms, it had what I felt was a sinister look.

One night we noticed something strange. A light shone under the closed garage door. Nothing odd about that. But then we heard a car engine running, which could mean that the occupant was threatened by death from monoxide gas. We wondered if we should alert the household. Then the engine was turned off; we heard voices raised in anger; and we decided to move on.

Next night at the same time, we were back at the entrance to the driveway. A woman in black, her face white and twisted under a pulled-down black felt hat, passed us, walked swiftly up the drive, and, at the front door, perhaps due to a trick of the light, disappeared.

Tony brushed off my suggestion that she might be a ghost; there was, he said, no such thing. Next night at the same time, we heard children crying in pain and fear; exactly where the cries came from in the house we could not determine; and then all the lights in the windows blazed, and went out. A moment later the same woman in black brushed past us, this time with an unpleasant laugh, and repeated her disappearing act at the front door.

Next morning, Tony handed me the morning paper. On the front page was a photograph of the woman we had seen. The article said that the house had been occupied by a well-known physician; that his wife, the woman in the picture, had died a year earlier of an unnamed disease and he had been unable to save her; that in his guilt he had killed himself in the garage by turning on the engine with the door closed; and that his children had found the body and called the police.

When I asked Tony if this convinced him of the existence of the supernatural, he laughed. Perhaps, he suggested, the woman we saw was the dead invalid's twin sister. I realized then that skepticism in such matters was impossible to shake.

𝒯y grandmother Amy was always a welcome presence while I was back in London for the school holidays. During the German rocket bomb attacks she had dissuaded my mother and me from going to shelters, and when a doodlebug flew past our windows at Dolphin Square, she said she would grab it and send it back. She usually liked to stay at the Cumberland or Regent Palace Hotel with my uncle Rupert and his wife and son, but now she stayed at the Royal Court Hotel in Sloane Square, so as to be near my mother's workplace at Peter Jones's store.

A small, mousy, inoffensive man, not bad looking, with a toothbrush moustache, also stayed there and courted my grandmother relentlessly. He flattered her that her piano and song recitals for the guests showed fine musicianship, that she looked no more than forty (she was, and looked, sixty-five), and that he wanted to marry her. For once my mother and I were in accord; he must go. He was clearly a fortune hunter, whose beady eyes could be seen frequently fixed on the fine pearls Amy wore with her invariable navy blue dress and hat.

She was upset when we said that the man was clearly a smarmy kind of gigolo. When she told George what we had said he suddenly gave up and moved to another hotel; we had the measure of him. Three years later, one morning at Dolphin Square, my mother handed me a morning newspaper. George's photograph appeared under the headline "WIDOW MURDERED AT ONSLOW COURT HOTEL." The Onslow Court was just round the corner from the Royal Court, and the victim, a Mrs. Durand-Deacon, resembled my grandmother. John George Haigh had killed her for her money after she agreed to marry him and made out a will in her favor. He had dumped her body in a forty-gallon vat of sulfuric acid but her teeth had survived, allowing for identification. I don't think Amy ever overcame her narrow escape from death.

I didn't do well at the Guildford tutorial and was sent as a last-ditch measure to the expensive and unpleasant Old Downs, a crammers housed near the well-named Gravesend, in Kent. I failed the exams again and it was decided not to even try to get me into a university but instead send me out to work.

In 1949 I was ready for my first job, which was to be in a bookstore, when quite by chance at an Indian restaurant in Cambridge Circus I met a busy Bengali film merchant-operator named Bishu Sen. He told me he had been struggling for years to interest the great Sir Alexander Korda, doyen of British film moguls, in making a version of the story of the Taj Mahal, a romantic tale of a seventeenth-century mogul emperor, Shah Jehan, who imported a teenage princess from Persia and married her. She died, very young, and in an agony of grief he had an architect design the Taj Mahal in Agra as her last resting place and then (Bishu Sen insisted) blinded the architect so he could never match the beauty of the sepulchre.

Bishu told me that he wanted someone to research the story fully and prepare an outline of the story. With a modest retainer, he sent me to the British Museum reading room for weeks to uncover what I could. It was a pleasure sitting in the glass-ceilinged rotunda in Bloomsbury, the desks lighted by green-shaded lamps; librarians, often snooty but usually helpful, helped me to find volumes in the rare books section.

I managed to sneak out of the library for a week through a translation of *The Thousand and One Nights* and felt strong stirrings at the descriptions of jisms (orgasms) and powerful male members waved about by handsome naked men, but I didn't dare request the illustrated editions, popular to this day among pornography collectors.

I finally wound up with a substantial file of information on the Taj, which I turned into a workable outline. It was given to the brilliant Michael Powell and Emeric Pressburger, currently famous for *The Red Shoes*, and they turned it into a scented, overripe affair; later, David Lean tried to develop the material with John Masters, author of *Nightrunners of Bengal*, but this also failed to work. Bishu Sen told me in 1950 that the Indians would not accept his choice of casting Richard Burton and Jean Simmons as stars, and the Western world would not have unknowns such as Shah Jehan and Mumtaz. This was thirty years before the advent of Bollywood; only one Indian movie, the frantic, sung-through, garish musical *Ahn,* had been seen in London in 1949.

Still not in the threatened first job, and with talk now of my being offered money to open my own bookshop, or obtain a directorship on some board or other when I passed twenty-one, I filled my days with writing when my mother and stepfather were blessedly absent in Kent on a documentary film shoot. I wrote a series of poems, at the same time translating Mallarmé's masterpiece *L'après-midi d'un faune* and Paul Valéry's *Ebauche d'un serpent* into English. I wrote poems of romantic intensity, influenced by Rilke, Hölderlin, Baudelaire, and Rimbaud, little realizing that the literary establishment would soon doom that rich style, prevalent in London in the 1940s, to oblivion.

With great boldness, I began submitting verses not to obscure self-printed magazines but to the prominent literary journal *John O'London's Weekly,* whose literary editor, the poet Richard Church, not only accepted my work but invited me to lunch at Simpson's in the Strand and told me that I had a future as a writer. Later he wrote to me, saying that I had a unique vision and must follow my own star alone; he emphasized the word "alone."

I sent poems to Muriel Spark; not then famous as a novelist, she was editor of the conservative *Poetry Review,* whose criterion was that a poem could not be printed out with equal success as prose. She accepted several of my works and was among the judges who later awarded me the 1949 Poetry Society Junior Verse Prize, a biography of Rimbaud by Enid Starkie, for my sonnet "Nocturne." She asked me to come and see her. Her office at the society's headquarters, 33 Portman Square, was just around the corner from my favorite pastry shop, which even in continuing rationing supplied the best raisin brioches I have ever eaten. She sat at a desk in the right-hand corner, her hair red and windswept, as if she had been out shooting grouse; her figure was full and womanly, not fat; she wore a form-fitting brown dress that showed off her heroic breasts.

Her eyes were as sparkling as her name; she paced as she talked, rapidly and brilliantly, with the wide-hipped swinging gait of a Bette Davis, sweeping back her hair from her forehead. She was extremely kind to the shock-haired, pale, elongated poet who sat before her, stretching his spindly legs; her encouragement was, after Mallinson's vicious discouragements, a candle in my darkness.

I was now the youngest much-published poet in London, and was taken up as one of her young men by the celebrated Dr. Marie Stopes, pioneer of birth control, known jocularly as Doctor of French Letters (DFL). Then seventy-four, she lived in an ugly Victorian house; with her dyed red hair, fox furs, brass necklaces, and arms clanking with bracelets, she resembled a male fortune teller on Brighton pier in drag. She would announce to visitors like myself that she was double-jointed and suddenly sink to the Persian carpet, twist a leg under her behind, and suck her right big toe. Her live-in lover was the wonderfully named Baron Avro Manhattan, a fair-haired, green-eyed Adonis who was over thirty years her junior; one night she announced to his embarrassment that despite the fact she was well past childbearing age, she insisted he wear "an authorized sheath" when he made love to her, to avoid possible contagion. Whereupon he turned her over his knees and spanked her, to general applause.

She invited me to appear with her and the baron in a reading of a play she had written about Adam and Eve, at a rented hall in Chelsea. She offered me the part of the serpent, as I was almost certainly the thinnest man in London. Edward Hulton's *Picture Post* was supposed to cover the event, but the reporters never came. Nonetheless it was a grand evening, with Baron Avro Manhattan as Adam and Marie Stopes as a seventy-two-year-old Eve. I longed to see a full production so I could enjoy the sight of the baron's body clad only in a fig leaf. Alas, I was denied the privilege; the play was never staged.

At the end of the reading, Stopes said to general laughter and applause that had Adam used a sheath there would have been no human race; and a damned good thing too.

I appeared at another reading in the hall, arranged by the poet and critic Howard Sargent, of bad verse; I brought the house down with the Victorian poet laureate Alfred Austin's "Summer is come and spring is over; / The cuckoo flowers grow mauve and mauver" and (on the illness of the Prince of Wales) "Across the wires the electric message came: / He is no better, he is much the same."

$\mathcal{M}$y mother somehow talked Mallinson into sending me with her to the South of France. The ostensible reason was so I could put on some weight on unrationed food and perhaps acquire a tan; the real reason was that she was having an affair with the prominent Hollywood screenwriter Ben Barzman, who was married but promised to meet her there.

First, we went to Paris where she enjoyed a rendezvous with that clever, to me physically unimpressive, man. The French capital in 1949 had a unique smell, composed of Gauloises cigarettes, chimney smoke, coffee grounds, urine, car exhausts, and sweat. The Métro, or subway, was particularly malodorous; youths cheerfully urinated on the platforms and in the carriages. The streets were filled not as they are today with traffic but with bicycles, spinning daringly along sidewalks, scattering pedestrians or darting in and out of occasional cars, and the popular Citröen minicabs.

Sometimes I would see a motorbiker, his girlfriend riding in front of him, his arousal clearly visible through his cotton pants. Above us roared prewar biplanes spelling out slogans in smoke or advertisements for Michelin tires and Château Margaux wine.

The only explanation for our staying at the very expensive Plaza Athénée hotel on the Avenue Montaigne is that Barzman paid for us. Certainly our foreign government allowance of sixty pounds would have failed to keep us there even in those days. In the lobby I could find enticements; the French male teenagers were everywhere, all handsome, dark, fit looking, sexy, kissing their girls openly, even fondling their breasts in public. They wore a uniform of berets, duffel coats, serge trousers, and sandals with socks. If they felt like publicly humping a tart, they did; they were insolent, free, open, and sharply intelligent and informed, and I was glad I spoke French. They filled the cheap seats of concert halls and theaters and movie houses; they were always sweating and laughing; apathy was as foreign to them as celibacy.

I spent hours walking the length of the Champs-Elysées, which was dirty and raffish in those days. In London, a first-run theater would announce only the title of the film being shown, with some stills in the lobby; here, enormous glowing posters announced the entertainment inside, showing men and women half undressed, luring the public in. Epics set in ancient Rome showed gladiators hurling virgins over their shoulders; inside, in the Gauloises-choked darkness, I saw, dubbed into French, Humphrey Bogart in *Dark Passage* and Joan Fontaine in *Letter from an Unknown Woman,* both supremely pleasing.

I walked more miles all over the city, enjoying the sense of being lost, relishing every vista, peering into the windows of mysterious dark shops that sold a vast range of jumbled goods. A favorite haunt was the Musée Grévin, the children's waxworks museum, a place of magic that made Madame Tussauds seem merely humdrum.

A hall of mirrors, reflecting the eager fresh faces of French students, seemed to dissolve and become a snowscape complete with mountains and polar bears; then it turned into a jungle, haunted by multicolored dragonflies and prowling pumas. Soon after that, we were in the minarets and plazas of some unnamed Middle Eastern city.

My mother and I took off to the South of France by the Blue Train; the contrast with England was painful as the roadbeds were perfectly laid, the compartment spacious, the dinner delicious: veal and sauté potatoes, served with excellent red wine—instead of Spam and whale meat. I remember waking in the morning with the sour Cinzano taste in my mouth, then, after washing up, going to the dining car for croissants and cappuccinos. For once, my mother and I were quite compatible, so long as she could introduce me to our fellow passengers as her brother.

At Cannes, we stayed at the Pension Madrilène, today long since vanished, in the flowery hillside suburb known as Californie. The view of the beach, the scent of night-flowering jasmine, the warmth of the air—all were captivating.

In London again, I had to face Mallinson's fury that I had not lost my pallor and that therefore the whole point of the trip was wasted; he hadn't guessed my mother's real reason—Barzman—for undertaking it.

I returned to the world of literature. I often went to the Institute of Contemporary Arts on Dover Street, where T. S. Eliot, who showed enthusiasm for many of my poems, would arrive to give readings of his work, owlish in horn-rimmed spectacles, looking more like a bank manager than a poet. With great tenderness, he would wheel in his tragic close friend the aesthete John Hayward, in a bath chair, the man's face swollen and weeping, his mouth gaping like that of some gross landed fish, the heavy shapeless form shifting restlessly in heavy rugs even in hot weather.

Edith Sitwell also read there at the ICA, dressed in the style of the Byzantine empress Theodora, her patrician face pale with powder, with the subdued composer William Walton at the piano, reciting her poem "Façade."

After more than fifty years, I can see and hear my Soho bohemian friends of that time; joyously the two closest, the gifted poets Iris Orton and James Kirkup, are still alive and in touch with me today. Orton, with her bulging forehead and hyperthyroid Bette Davis eyes, striding about in a black velvet suit and green army blanket with clasp used as a kind of opera cloak in all weathers; Kirkup, blond, handsome, wavy haired, and witty, like a Swedish prince marooned in darkest London. These were inspirations, guides into a world of friendly cafés and warm pubs, far removed from the glacial miseries of Dolphin Square.

The highlights of those literary years took place at the Ethical Church Hall in Bayswater, a dank cellar where I went often for poetry readings with Kirkup, Orton, and my friend the critic Bernard Bergonzi, among others. One memorable night, Stephen Spender was on the stage, dressed in a raincoat against the cold and damp; he had been a keen supporter of the Loyalist government overthrown by Franco in the Spanish Civil War. He had recently and rashly recanted, along with the novelist Arthur Koestler.

Apparently, the rabid conservative fascist poet Roy Campbell, a savage South African rhymester of famous ill temper, hadn't heard of the drastic recantation and invaded the hall, drunk, accompanied by his wife and his acolyte Rob Lyle, poet heir of the Tate and Lyle syrup fortune. He called Spender a fucking lesbian, a communist fairy and coward, and began hitting him hard so that Spender staggered and almost fell but in a spirit of passive resistance did not respond in kind. This excited still more contempt from his assailant, who spat at him and withdrew, to general booing and hissing.

I found a much less tension-charged atmosphere in the circle surrounding the new film critics' team of Lindsay Anderson, Karel Reisz, Tony Richardson, and Penelope Houston, who together published the film magazine *Sequence* in response to the dreary *Sight and Sound,* which they later took over. Lindsay published my first film review, of *The Furies* and *Winchester 73,* of Anthony Mann.

Working for a living was unavoidable. My first job was at Better Books in Upper Grosvenor Street, in Mayfair, which included delivering packages of the latest best sellers to the apartments of such figures as Mary Martin and Sir Simon Marks, owner of the Marks and Spencer department store. I would stand at the half-open doors, as I waited for someone to sign, looking into a world of gilded, richly upholstered luxury that reminded me painfully of the world I had left behind ten years earlier.

I lost the job quickly because of my mother. Dressed in an expensive beaver lamb coat, diamond bracelets sparkling on her wrists, she would invade Better Books and announce in a loud voice through tears that she was penniless and must have my entire wage package on the spot. Embarrassed, I handed it to her, and without a word of thanks she would sweep out. The genial manager told me that customers were upset by her appearances and that I must go.

I found a job at the Times Book Club on Wigmore Street, where I met the young woman who was to be my wife. We worked together in a catalogue room, meaninglessly shifting cards from one drawer of a wooden cabinet to another, but with plenty of time to talk.

Norine Lillian Cecil was the Eurasian daughter of a railway family in Mussouri, India. Small, dark, with burning brown eyes, she was too plump and too round faced to be conventionally pretty, and she showed the scars of smallpox under her heavy makeup. But she loved me and I loved her; we had in common a love of movies and of literature; we would walk together in rain or shine, mostly to a favorite spot in Hyde Park, where after work or on Sundays we would sit for hours on a bench under a spreading chestnut tree, holding hands, too filled with joy to speak.

I told John Mallinson and my mother I had found a woman I loved and expected them to be pleased that I hadn't turned out to be what they never tired of telling me they feared most: a queer, a pansy, a nancy boy. Instead, they were appalled; Norine wasn't white and she didn't come from a good family.

It was as much as they could do to be polite to her, and I decided to move out and live with her away from Dolphin Square. We found a bed-sitting room in Nottingham Place, with a gas meter that had to be fed a shilling every hour or there would be no fire; we ate fish and chips wrapped in newspapers; made love, not always skillfully; and were as close to pure happiness as it's possible to be in this world.

We were married just after my twenty-first birthday, on March 8, 1952, at Caxton Hall Registry Office, with my mother, posing as a pleased parent, present with our best friend, Ronald Burn, a member of the staff of the British Museum. Somehow, we had managed to save enough money for a honeymoon in Europe; certainly my mother would never have come up with the cash from my trust fund she was stealing.

Back in London, Norine and I had to obtain work quickly. I doubt we had twenty-five pounds (a hundred dollars) left between us, and my mother still hung on to my allowance, illegally spending it all. My wife hit on the idea of starting a newsstand selling papers from all over the world, a novelty at the time, and the next few weeks were spent in raising money from her relatives in India; getting a license from the London authorities, a predictably slow and dreary process; and persuading distributors to let her put out their publications. In view of the capricious London climate and the frequency of rain and fog, this meant not only buying a barrow but also heavy rainproof sheets, and fending off "teddy boys," the local gangster gangs, who threatened to overturn her place of business. She triumphed over every obstacle, but only for a while.

I obtained work at Macmillan, many years later my publisher, as a clerk in the educational department run by the cold, lumpy, bespectacled David Kay, under the general direction of Daniel Macmillan, the brother of Harold, the future prime minister. Kay asked me to be a spy, using excuses to sneak out to him from other departments the opinions people had of him. I told him only what he wanted to hear, not what they actually said; he glowed with self-approval.

Norine and I were still living at the time in Nottingham Place, not far from my old haunts of the Classic Cinema in Baker Street and Madame Tussauds wax museum. The room's only decoration was a threadbare wall hanging, covered in stitched figures of skiers in white. Her magazine stall wasn't doing well, chiefly because of thefts and vandalism and heavy rain or snow; she gave up and took a job at a bookstore in Charing Cross Road. One of her customers was Kenneth Tynan, the most gifted young theater and film critic of his generation, and when we were lent a fancier flat, at 68 Vandon Court, Petty France, near the Houses of Parliament, we invited him there with his wife, the novelist Elaine Dundy.

Tynan was as dramatically self-created as his friend Marlene Dietrich. He had turned himself into a reincarnation of a late nineteenth-century fop, a figure reminiscent of the great illustrative artist Aubrey Beardsley, with just a dash of Oscar Wilde. His lank brown hair flopped forward despite his attentions over his high, domed white forehead; his eyes sparkled sharply in a face of yellow parchment; his shirt was ochre, his tie green silk and floppy, his suit lavender, his socks the same color, and his shoes pale gray suede. He chain-smoked, holding his cigarette in a theatrical mannerism between the third and fourth finger of his right hand.

Elaine Dundy was by contrast conventionally dressed, in a well-fitted black suit and a white blouse, her hair trimmed into a neat, cupcake style. She was working on her soon-to-be-famous novel *The Dud Avocado*. Tynan held the floor, telling outrageous stories about the stars; his stammer, surprising in so eloquent a man, invariably delayed the punch line, so that one waited breathlessly, no doubt to his secret pleasure, for some startling revelation, and then at last he would deliver the coup de grâce. I asked him why he hadn't written plays himself, and he replied that he could never think of a plot. I thought: That isn't the real reason. Managements whose stagings he had slaughtered would take great pleasure in rejecting his work.

His flat in Hyde Park Gardens was surprisingly drab. I had expected an exotic environment to go with his clothes: nineteenth-century vases and furniture, framed portraits of the theatrical great, rich Indian or Chinese carpets, exotic plants in brass Indian bowls. Instead, he offered only one couch, covered in a shabby, fake tiger skin throwover, badly upholstered armchairs, a threadbare carpet, and, in the middle of the sitting room, an ill-kept playpen where the Tynans' baby daughter, Tracy, crawled, screaming loudly, quite ignored by her parents and with no nanny in attendance.

To increase the din, Tynan turned on the phonograph and subjected us to the raucous strains of my least favorite American comedian, Phil Silvers, in his current Broadway show, *Top Banana*. The ordeal was alleviated by the arrival of the genial and attractive young composer Sandy Wilson, whose 1920s musical spoof, *The Boy Friend*, would soon become a sensation, starring the newly discovered Julie Andrews.

In the bedlam, conversation was almost impossible. Tynan and Dundy were in strong support of the U.S. Democratic candidate, Adlai Stevenson, and were busy using the "Madly for Adlai" slogan. Sometimes the couple would fight in front of us, seemingly enjoying our discomfiture.

It was at this time that Erica Marx, a rich woman who lived in Kent, embarked on a series of publications entitled *Poems in Pamphlet,* in which she would introduce new writers whose work had not found acceptance in major publishing houses like Faber and Faber.

T. S. Eliot at Faber had written to me praising my work; but he felt that the poetry list he edited was already too long: a major disappointment. But Erica Marx accepted me at once, and I met her. Genial and tweedy, she wore Robin Hood felt hats with feathers in them. She was my discoverer and mentor, and when *A Distant Star* appeared, I enjoyed almost uniformly favorable reviews.

These were good times, although my mother, my stepfather, and my boss David Kay gave me no word of congratulation. This was painful, and even when I was published by C. Day Lewis (father of Daniel, a fan of my work), in the prestigious PEN Anthology, and later in subsequent PEN volumes, I heard nothing from them. I even managed to obtain the much-envied assignment of compiling crossword puzzles in the *Listener* and later I won the Ximenes Crossword Prize in the *Sunday Times,* and was toasted at a banquet given by the newspaper at the Trocadero in Shaftesbury Avenue.

I also managed a minor literary hoax. I had become irritated by the (to me) pretentious tone of *Sight and Sound* in reviewing current films. The idol of the new school of critics headed by my friend Lindsay Anderson was John Ford. I invented a film called *So Alone,* directed in London by Ford, and dealing in misty poetic-realistic terms with the lives of two tramps dwelling by the Thames. The review appeared in *Sight and Sound* and the nonexistent movie turned up in encyclopedias of film under John Ford for many years. The film was discussed at length in Andrew Sinclair's well-received biography of the director.

With friends like the Tynans, and acclaim from critics for my verse, I seemed to be on top of the world, even in a state of near poverty (but we always managed to eat). But then something happened that would drive us out of England.

6

*Q*uite suddenly, our marriage had begun to turn sour. We had wanted a child and without having the common sense to have examinations by doctors—we both had a horror of hospitals and I had recently endured a hemorrhoidectomy—blamed each other for the failing. Norine suffered from depression after losing her job at the bookshop and, following a savage quarrel, she cut her wrists and took an overdose of pills.

I managed to apply tourniquets from a torn bedsheet and sent the bloodstained linen to the laundry. At St. George's Hospital, a stomach pump saved Norine's life; I don't think she was grateful.

No sooner was she back at our flat at Vandon Court than the police arrived. They said a murder had been committed in the building and that the laundry had reported blood on our sheets. They were about to arrest us when the manager ran in to announce that the culprit had been caught.

The couple who lent us the apartment got wind of the incident and flew back from Italy to ask us to leave at once. My mother turned up, full of recrimination against Norine, who was only now able, and shakily, to get out of bed and walk. They screamed at each other, and my mother seized Norine by the throat and began to strangle her. Norine kicked her in the groin and they fell to the carpet, locked in a wrestling grip.

I managed to separate them and threw my mother out of the flat. We never spoke, for the rest of her life, again. I am certain she would have killed Norine if she could.

We moved to a depressing small apartment in Wembley Park, near the famous stadium; there we found each other again. But our sexual relationship was sporadic; our hearts were no longer in it after two years, and we gradually became just friends, with occasional unsatisfactory erotic episodes. I had come to dislike my job at Macmillan and we decided finally to get out of austerity England and go as far away as we could: to Australia.

It was a serious decision, influenced in part by the literary atmosphere of London. For a time, I had been attending Wednesday evening readings of new verse at the home of the critic G. S. Fraser; there I would meet such prominent figures as W. S. Graham, David Gascoigne, John Heath-Stubbs, Dannie Abse, Michael Hamburger, and Kathleen Raine. These fine poets, despite some skepticism, continued to work largely in a newly unfashionable, romantic vein. Soon, the New Movement in verse took over everything; the emphasis was on Marxist principles of realism, in stark imagery; disillusioned, dry urban verses that offered no solace. Philip Larkin, John Wain, Kingsley Amis, like the Young Turks of film criticism, Anderson, Lambert, Houston, and Karel Reisz, rejected outright the colorful, the pastoral, the glowing rich excesses of their predecessors. Even Dylan Thomas, our master, was disdained.

My second volume of verse, *Spring and Death,* also published by Erica Marx at her Hand and Flower Press, was received as well as the first, but I saw the writing on the wall.

It was time to go, and Australia seemed farther away than anywhere else. I had no idea whether a London intellectual like myself would find a place there. The travel brochures and books showed lean, brown men, with wide brown hats that dangled corks to keep off flies, beaches crowded with gods and goddesses, and no indication of "culture." Our British friends Ronald Burn, Ian Pavitt, and the wonderful African British Ianthea Matthews urged us not to go out to what they felt must be a cultural wilderness. The expatriate Australian communist Jack Lindsay, a close friend, was equally discouraging. But our minds were made up.

For a time, it seemed that our plans were doomed. Since Norine was half Indian and there was a White Australia policy, to arrange immigration she had to pretend she was purely English and swore out a false document to that effect. Since I had a suspicious shadow on one lung that might have indicated sarcoidosis, I also was in jeopardy. Ruled out for a virtually free passage, offered to young immigrants, we had to agree to pay the full fare of sixty pounds (then about three hundred dollars) each, and we didn't have the money.

I went to see the family solicitor Max Best, who forced my mother to restore my income on pain of trial and imprisonment. But I still had to obtain the fare, and I went to see my stepmother Jill Deacon. I hadn't seen her except for one afternoon in 1944 when for some forgotten reason she was allowed to receive me and gave me a copy of the *Curdy Stories* of the Scottish fabulist George Macdonald.

She lived in a pleasant house in Sutton, Surrey, with her much younger and very handsome husband, Alan Deacon, and my half sister Annabella, blonde and curly haired at fifteen. It was obvious my stepmother was shocked at my unkempt appearance, surprised that I would want to see her after all those years, and secretly delighted she could show up my mother by offering me help. She liked Norine at once, calling her Nonie; she had mellowed with time. I had forced myself to forget her abuse of me as a child and I never told Norine about it.

It turned out that I was lucky; Jill had a brother, Peter, in Sydney, and her mother was there for a stay. When I gave her my assurance that I would never see my mother again and that in effect I had come back to her, she advanced me the passage money. On November 5, 1954, Norine and I left on the SS *Oronsay* from Tilbury dock.

Sydney ravished our senses. The *Oronsay* sailed in just before Christmas in stunning heat, the famous harbor blue and studded with yachts manned by handsome boys in shorts, the inlets and headlands glittering in the white Australian sun.

Unable to find lodgings with a double room we could afford, we stayed in separate locations, I at the YMCA, Norine at the YWCA. It was hard to sleep in the humid heat; I heard men in slippers trailing past my room to the bathroom at all hours and at dawn the shower room was full of men, big and heavily muscled, running to fat in their twenties, good natured and boisterous.

When I was unable to obtain work, Norine managed a transfer to her firm's Sydney branch, and I found a job at Graham's Bookstore in Martin Place. We were able with our joint salaries to afford a flat, at the very Australian address of Boomerang Street, Maroubra, near a beach.

Air-conditioning was rare in Australia in those days, and working at Graham's, or living at Boomerang Street, was, in the summer of 1955, like living in boiler rooms. At Graham's, frail as I was, the long hours of standing, with only half an hour in an airless stockroom for lunch, were exhausting. Drenched in sweat, I would help choose books for customers, wrap them individually, make out the sales slips, and ring up the sales. I would carry heavy parcels of newly arrived volumes from the delivery truck. Somehow I got through the days.

And I did make new friends at Graham's. Barry Humphries, then an obscure writer and serendipitist of oddities of science and literature, was a lank, yellow-skinned, streaming-haired figure who would one day become famous as Dame Edna Everage. When, during one of his Broadway seasons, I wrote suggesting a meeting he replied saying that he remembered me, not from my career as a best-selling and prize-winning author, but as a shop assistant at Graham's. It was his little joke; I didn't appreciate it.

Colleen McCullough was not yet the best-selling author of *The Thorn Birds*. Tall, hefty, broad-shouldered, always laughing, she was unmistakably Irish, with her red hair streaming in the Maroubra beach winds, her stride forthright and masculine, yet her interest in men was explicitly sensual. This Valkyrie had with her at all times a bulky, shapeless typescript of a novel in progress; I read it with dismay, seeing, I regret to say, no promise in it. I gave her what advice I could to improve it, which, no doubt to her betterment, she ignored.

Hence: *The Thorn Birds*.

I met Colleen again at the height of her success in the 1990s, in the green room of a talk show in Los Angeles. Instead of hugging me as an old friend, she coldly announced that our situations were now reversed: she mentioned the fact that I had become a much-published book critic and columnist in Australia when she was obscure and struggling; now she was a best-selling author and what was I? I showed her the *New York Times* best-seller list. My latest book matched hers—on the nonfiction list.

The novelist Patrick White didn't become a friend—he was too misanthropic, distant, and bleak for my taste—but I was grateful for the verbal support of this great Australian writer, who later won the Nobel Prize. I can still feel the shock of pleasure when at a book exhibition he recognized me as poet, critic, and littérateur. At the same time I discovered a lifelong friend in the sharply intelligent critic Joel Greenberg, who would one day collaborate with me on two well-received books, and would help me introduce the term *film noir* to the English-speaking world.

I joined the Sydney Poetry Society, run by an old expatriate English bohemian named Imogene Whyse, who wore flowing robes and spoke in a high, fluting voice. I didn't realize it then, but becoming a member started me on a new career as an Australian writer.

I read my poems aloud to the group, catching the eye, one memorable evening, of the distinguished Roman Catholic poet James McAuley. Gaunt and severe as a monk painted by Zurbaran or El Greco, he was at heart warm and kind. He mentioned my name to John Douglas Pringle, the shrewd, tubercular Scottish intellectual who edited the *Sydney Morning Herald*; I was working at the time at Penfolds, a stationery store where I spent most of the time in a gray cotton coat running up and down ladders fetching ledgers for sale. Pringle came to see me, was shocked at my situation, and offered me the chance to review books for him, which I eagerly accepted.

In my lunch hour, I would take a bus across town to the enormous, gray, and uninviting pile of the *Herald* building, riding a creaky elevator, saturated with the stench of newsprint, to Pringle's large but austere office, with grimy windows looking out onto a featureless townscape. Books for review were piled up on a side table, and instead of offering me any of them he asked me to choose two. One of these was Kenneth Tynan's *Bull Fever*, an account of traveling through Spain with Orson Welles and an encomium to the rituals of the corrida, which Norine and I had witnessed at Nîmes.

A phrase in my review, that bullfighting was no more than an unpleasant way of turning bulls into beef, pleased Pringle, and he told me I could review as many books as I liked, and for as long as I liked. It was the first book review I had written.

At the same time I began writing many of the so-called hysterical historicals, garish features of two thousand words each, published in the young Rupert Murdoch's Sydney *Daily Mirror*.

I had an inkling, even then, that Murdoch, my boss, would one day be an overwhelmingly important figure. He was still in his twenties, lean and dark and sparkling, and exuded enormous energy, charm, and chutzpah. Although he owned the *Mirror*, he would run up and down stairs with proofs under his arm, personally examine each page as it was pulled off the printing press, and know by heart the names of everyone who worked for him.

He also read every word of the newspaper articles, and that included mine, but I never heard criticism from him. When my editor William Joy retired and was replaced by the less cultivated Irish Australian Brian Marien, who would hurl article pages across a room at me if they displeased him, Murdoch took an equally keen interest in my work.

Royal mistresses, murderers and murderesses, despots, pirates, saboteurs were grist to my journalistic mill, and fires, earthquakes, tornadoes, shipwrecks—the test of my acceptance was sensation, the most horrendous aspects of the world's unsavory past. I began publishing anonymously, in the *Mirror,* about two pieces a week, which, with the *Herald* assignment, allowed me to live as a freelance, earning twice my wages at Penfolds, which I left quickly.

7

By 1956 Norine and I were no longer happy with each other. The quarrels over money and my constant mess of books and papers had worn her down. We moved into separate bedrooms at Boomerang Street.

She began work as a trainee nurse at a hospital. She had in her a frustrated maternal instinct, and in addition to taking care of her patients she brought others to our home. They were gay men, whom she had us feed and clothe. One of these ragged dropouts with a green face had developed gangrene and died only minutes after the ambulance arrived. I found the use of our flat as a home for waifs and strays hard to deal with; my lack of sympathy in the matter shocks me in retrospect. At all events, it was obvious our marriage was over.

She told me, one afternoon, that she had fallen in love with a fellow female nurse, who was friendly with her and with Colleen McCullough, who was also working at the hospital. They would share a home in the future.

For years, memory played a trick on me, convincing me that the day Norine moved out I walked the length of Maroubra Beach in the heavy rain, much too shattered to speak. But now I know that in fact I took her departure as I have taken others in my life, very coolly in my stride; we had had a good time while it lasted, and it was the right moment to move on.

Was I shocked to find that she was bisexual? Not really. Despite our wanting a child, I always felt, despite our love for each other, that neither of us was fully committed to a heterosexual relationship. I didn't blame

53

her and only felt sad for the loss of so much. Emotionally at a standstill, I embarked on a long period of celibacy.

Rooming at a flat in Double Bay, I decided to build myself up physically. Celebrating the publication of my first Australian collection, *The Earthbound and Other Poems,* I took the advice of my friend, the writer Chris Koch (later, he would write *The Year of Living Dangerously*), and enlisted with a personal trainer, the copper-skinned Apollo Bruce Langstaff.

He understood my fear of being seen at the beach in swim shorts, that my thinness and pallor and lack of muscle tone were to me causes of misery and despair. He found a little-used beach on the harbor, near Rose Bay, and began training me in shallow water; I slowly overcame my fear of drowning. The exquisite subtropical surroundings of sand and sea and flowering jacaranda were inspiring, and the diet Bruce put me on—oatmeal, fruit and whole wheat bread with peanut butter, fresh fish and vegetables, and light custards—gave me some badly needed pounds.

Within six months, I had obtained an acceptable physique and a decent tan; I could go to the beach and feel proud of my body and swim quarter miles at North Sydney's Olympic pool, in freestyle, with tumble-turns at the end of each lap. I soon learned to prefer saltwater pools; I even ventured into the surf and began shooting waves.

Those hours of pleasure are with me still: the hot sand or concrete on my bare feet; the run into the ocean, watched by lifesavers in their towers; the sting of salt on eyes and lips; the scent of ozone; the feeling of strength as my arms carved through bright green water.

I made new friends. Robert Hughes, later the famous art critic of *Time* magazine and the brilliant, best-selling historian of colonial early Australia in *The Fatal Shore,* was fair haired then, comely, slight, dazzling in his erudition and cynicism. He was going through a stormy affair with a pretty actress named Noeline Brown. I visited them often at the home of his brother, Tom, who later became attorney general of Australia. I became close to Jack Lee, the famous British director of *A Town like Alice* and *Robbery under Arms,* married to Isabel Kidman, a relative of Nicole. Long summer afternoons, at their beautifully restored colonial house, were delectably civilized and enlightening.

Life became much more agreeable. A plump, energetic journalist named Tom Fitzgerald started up a weekly, *Nation,* which ironically was the exact political opposite of the liberal American journal of that name. Robert Hughes became the magazine's art critic; I, at twenty-six, the film critic.

At a party at the home of the American consul in May 1961, I met Peter Hastings, the weekly *Bulletin*'s huff-and-puff editor. Lanky and awkward, he had grown a regimental moustache to hide a harelip; he added to that a personality that suggested the character he aped.

He asked me for suggestions. The *Bulletin* was an anachronism: it still had reports of sheep-shearing contests, recipes for salt beef and damper, politics in remote areas; it reviewed only Australian books, published only Australian rhymed poems. I told him it should start by including interviews with visiting movie stars. For years, the only Broadway, Hollywood, or West End figures who went Down Under were already on the skids. The successful, with rare exceptions (Katharine Hepburn in a Shakespeare season was one), wouldn't be seen dead there; playing Sydney was just one step above a cruise ship. But now the seductions of the city had begun to be understood abroad; promoters were paying enormous sums to lure major performers; and the possibilities of enjoying in bed so many fine local human specimens of both sexes were irresistible to many of the famous visitors.

Peter Hastings hired me not only as a consultant but as his first interviewer of the stars. In 1956, at a midnight screening at the Metro Cinema, Kings Cross, I had been electrified by the birth of rock and roll in the movie *Blackboard Jungle,* with the brilliant attack and energy of Bill Haley and the Comets on the sound track.

Now, at the giant, tin-roofed Sydney Stadium, Joel Greenberg and I sat enthralled as such great performers as Johnny Rebb ("Go Johnny, Go!"), Connie Francis, the Everly Brothers, and the locally famous Johnny O'Keefe and Col Joye almost burst through the ceiling with their joyous, highly sexual performances.

Whether the nights were hot and steaming in the un-air-conditioned arena, or cold, with rain thudding on the roof, these evening performances were to be treasured. And as well as the rock stars there were more traditional figures to interview.

Charlton Heston was as large, thunderous, Jovian voiced, and monumental as I had expected. He told a story I still treasure. When the movie *The Ten Commandments* was mooted, its producer-director Cecil B. De-Mille held a meeting with his actors and writers. Heston, cast as Moses, asked who would speak the voice of God, talking to him on the mount. DeMille, in ringing tones, shouted, "YOU DARE TO ASK?" And thus the matter was settled.

Heston asked me if I knew any Australian poems that he could include in an international tour for UNESCO, reading one verse from each country he visited. I at once pulled out of my pocket my effusive verse "Harborscape"; he read it, smiled at my cheek, and slipped it into his briefcase. He read it all over the world.

Judy Garland was the saddest of spectacles. Her early spunkiness, full-bodied attack, and charm had faded—understandably since, in poor health, she had flown for some twenty-six hours in those pre-jet days from America and was barely able to face the press. When, after a long delay, she at last entered the penthouse suite at the Chevron Hilton Hotel, she looked like a chicken newly emerged from its shell.

Thin and frail, her beautiful dark eyes filled with pain, she was accompanied by her equally exhausted gay husband, Mark Herron. Bland and nondescript, almost as thin as she was, he seemed barely able to speak, and was given little chance, as the bullying local press corps and their cameramen and TV crews kept pushing him away saying they didn't want him in the shots; who was he anyway?

Gallantly, Garland turned on the overweight and ham-armed reporters and told them that if he wasn't included in the shots, she was walking out. She told them that he was a fine actor and would soon be starring with her on Broadway (not true) in a play called *The Owl and the Pussycat*; he would be the Owl, and (with a laugh) she would be the Pussy. Herron took her hand as if he were drowning and was included in the photographs, though sadly they were cropped in darkrooms to remove him.

Garland gave two concerts at the Sydney Stadium, where she was greeted by the very large Sydney "camp" contingent (*gay* was not a term used at this time), who stood on their seats to cheer her. Just before she opened, one of her staff called me to say she must have a certain mind-enhancing drug or she would forget the lyrics—her supply had been confiscated by customs (the drug mentioned was prohibited in Australia). I said I wasn't a drug dealer and was about to hang up but the man begged me. If I didn't help there would be a disaster: Judy would disappoint thousands of fans who had bought tickets, and the local producer, Harry Miller, was broke and wouldn't be able to supply refunds. I gave the man the name of an abortionist; apparently that man (how did I know?) had access to forbidden substances. Had my help gotten out I could have been in trouble, but I was enthralled by Judy Garland's talent, even in decline, and wanted badly to help her.

At my own wish, I received no word or note of gratitude, which could have been evidence of my complicity. Instead, I was invited to accompany Garland and Herron on the train to Melbourne, where she would give her next two concerts.

It was a nocturnal journey; Garland slept all day. We were accompanied by her supporting star, Peter Allen, whose manager was a retired policeman, hired to act as his father and see to it that nobody found out the young man was homosexual. In the night, above the pounding of the train wheels, I heard Garland, in the next compartment, yelling to Mark Herron, "Fuck me, you faggot, fuck me." Apparently, he didn't, because her shouting went on until dawn, making sleep impossible.

Her concert next night was a disaster. A huge crowd of gays had assembled to see her and gave her a standing ovation when she walked onto the stage. But apparently she had used up the abortionist's remedy. She managed to stumble through "Over the Rainbow" and then she was done for. She was booed and catcalled by the same crowd that had cheered her minutes before, and she fled in terror.

Matters were worse in Hong Kong. Peter Allen had fallen in love with Mark Herron and in Melbourne, Mark commuted from Judy's bed to Peter's. The dual demands on Herron's underpowered sexuality continued in Hong Kong. The men decided they dared not continue the relationship openly, so it was decided that Mark would marry Judy and Peter would marry Liza Minnelli—later. No time was wasted in organizing the "beard."

Before her first concert, Judy was stricken with pneumonia and a nervous breakdown, and a typhoon broke out over her hotel. Screaming, she was carried out on a gurney, inadequately covered, and was soaked to the skin. She barely recovered in the hospital.

Needing a vacation, I took off by plane and ship and plane to New York; on the way, the SS *Himalaya* stopped at Port-au-Prince in Haiti. I had always wanted to be present at a voodoo ceremony; I knew from extensive study that voodoo was not black magic, or an experience of diabolical evil as presented in very bad old B-movies. It was instead a form of anthropomorphic religion in which there was a god for every animal, bird, or plant. The gifted film director Maya Deren had evoked the realities in her documentaries, which I had seen long ago in London.

For a white person to see voodoo was almost out of the question, but the local tourist authority had devised cabaret shows in exotic settings to deceive visitors into thinking they saw the real thing. I had written in advance to the Ethnographic Museum in the republic's capital, Port-au-Prince, enclosing my books of poetry along with my credentials. I had received a response stating that I should contact the museum's director on arrival.

The letter contained no promises. But when, with a fellow passenger I will call Jeff, I visited the museum, I was told that I had been approved and that if I were to appear at the Episcopalian cathedral at midnight, and meet there by the high altar a man in a red shirt, he would be our guide on a trip to the mountain hideout where the appropriate voodoo priest would await us.

At midnight, as arranged, Jeff and I walked up the apse and saw a giant mural, painted with primitive force, a copy of Leonardo daVinci's *Last Supper*. Christ and all the disciples were black, with one all too significant exception: Judas.

Our guide was prompt. Handsome, tall, and muscular, he indeed wore a red shirt. But first he proved a disappointment; despite his no doubt detailed instructions on where to take us, he kept trying to lure us to various tourist spots in Port-au-Prince where the nonsense version of voodoo was in full swing. Luckily, I spoke French and, while his knowledge of English was very limited, he spoke Creole. I was able to understand his patois and he was able to understand me. I handed him twenty dollars, enough to feed him and his family for a month, and insisted on being taken to "*le vrai voodoo.*" And at last he gave in.

He took us to a small house on the outskirts of the capital. The owner, clearly a voodoo priestess, was enormously fat and jolly, in a flowered muu-muu. From the ceiling of her airless central room, with its mud floor, hung fetishes: voodoo symbols such as miniature figures of men, women, animals, and birds in what appeared to be colored wax; bird claws; dried spiders; shoes that belonged to a zombie, a living dead man, we were told; and long, dangling black strings decorated with dead men's teeth.

She examined us closely, finally approving our appearance and non-threatening effect. Given her approval, our guide drove us up through the outermost areas of Port-au-Prince into the hills.

In the darkness, pulsating with dozens of drums, reverberating like thunder from miles away and carried on a burning wind, we saw wooden houses open to the street, whole families squatting or sitting in side circles formed by their furnishings, and by rings of candles, suggesting that they were seeking protection from the powers of darkness. Men danced past us, in leopard skins, making no sound. Then the drums increased, a hundred more perhaps, or two hundred. The sound they made matched my heartbeat, heard years ago as I went under chloroform in England.

Now we were free of Port-au-Prince, and the long ascent began through the city of Pétionville and beyond. Once we were in the hills, the darkness was intense; there was no moon, only the flares of torches. We bumped along at one mile an hour on a dirt track not devised for cars. The doors opened at the back and hands came in and felt our shoulders, our chests, our genitals, and finally our faces.

The exploration wasn't sexual but rather, I sensed, to gauge if we were enemies, or afraid. Finally, we reached a clearing, the hills dark and tree covered on either side. I saw what I knew to be the *hunfor*, or priest's house, with no doors or windows, a kind of horse stall, open to all weathers.

At its exact center was a pole, some twenty feet high, decorated in vivid colors. A painted serpent wound around it, head first, tongue hanging out; the ceremony was about to begin.

Our guide told us to hand some money to the priest who, also in a red shirt, greeted us in Creole and told us to sit against the wall facing the night; we were not to move, no matter what happened, until he gave us permission. This man was also a magnificence of animal grace and muscularity; I had to fight against my feelings as I looked him over.

He subjected us to a test of courage. He drew a machete knife from a scabbard and, to show its sharpness, sliced a melon in half. He danced, almost naked, erotically, beautifully, in front of us, the whirling knife missing our faces by inches. Had we bent forward, we would have been killed.

With a sigh of approval, the priest smiled at us; we had passed muster. He signaled an attendant to open a door that was almost exactly behind us.

I looked around; an inner room was crammed with teenage girls, all in white shifts with nothing on underneath. Once the door was ajar, an icy wind on this hottest and sultriest of nights swept out of there; I felt it pass through my body like a sword. No stage magician could have conjured up so arctic a breeze.

One by one the girls, visibly aroused, their nipples erect under their white cotton shifts, lay down at the foot of the pole. I thought the priest would make love to them but instead in some trick of the torchlight the painted serpent seemed to penetrate them one by one, bringing screams of pleasure and spilling virginal blood on the sawdust floor. They crawled out into the night hissing like snakes, as the priest began sacrificing chickens and cows until we had to leave; our ship was sailing in the morning.

We had been present at a ceremony rarely witnessed by white men: the ritual of Damballah-Uedo, the serpent god, one of the leading figures of the voodoo family of deities.

I found the experience exhilarating, but Jeff was affected by the strain of pretending fearlessness and the shock of seeing the erotic and barbaric ritual at firsthand. When I wrote to his parents a few weeks later, as I hadn't heard from him, they told me he had died, at twenty-three, of a heart attack.

My fourth collection of poems, *Noonday Country,* was scheduled for publication in Sydney. When it appeared, the reviews were glowing. Then, quite suddenly, Peter Hastings of the *Bulletin* offered me the job of entertainment and literary editor, a remarkable appointment for a man in his early thirties.

And yet, I hesitated. Freedom to find and make love to men carried with it the constant risk of discovery and imprisonment; as a freelance, I could make my own hours when the danger would be reduced. Now, I would have to be in an office for at least eight hours a day, and on Saturdays go to the printing press near Mascot airport and help supervise the finished pages. I would have only evenings, when I would be tired, and Sundays, always the time of the greatest police vigilance with agents provocateurs in the form of gorgeous men sent everywhere to entrap and destroy.

My mind was made up for me. It wasn't so much Hastings's threat that I wouldn't otherwise enjoy a guaranteed future, that I wasn't "going to set the world on fire, kid" (but I knew I would, and much later, did), but rather the decline into death of my generous landlady, Hilda Stanley-Lowe. Matters had become strained at the house on Marine Drive when, now at the peak of physical fitness, I was suspected of an unnatural interest in her grandnephew, age eighteen; actually, she imagined it, and so did the boy's mother. But when Hilda was dying, carried down the steps but barely making it to the ambulance, I knew I had to leave and earn my living in a job.

The *Bulletin* offices were housed in gray, ill-swept, and dusty quarters on George Street, not far from Circular Quay. My room was bare, furnished only with a plain deal desk, a chair for visitors, and a filing cabinet. Just beyond the grimy window, a wrecking team was drilling round the clock to destroy an old building that was marked for demolition; the noise was bad enough, but although the window was jammed shut by the damp swelling from recent rain, dust somehow seeped through the cracks and settled in a film on my typewriter and blotting pad.

Once again, as at the *Nation,* I was, as a closet liberal, ironically involved with a conservative journal. Stemming from my mentor and friend James McAuley, and from various contributors of great influence, the *Bulletin* was concerned with fears of a Communist invasion of Australia (a most unlikely scenario I didn't dare argue with) and gave full support to the corrupt government of South Vietnam, hoping it would stem the Communist tide. I was happy that I was never asked to editorial political meetings; so long as I filled my back pages with reviews of books, film, theater, and music and wrote a cover story every few weeks, I would not be troubled further.

With no demur from Hastings, who gave me a remarkably free hand and even entertained me at his home, I swept away what was left of the old *Bulletin* with its agrarian emphasis, traditional poetry, and parochial emphasis on local work, and changed it for the first time into an international journal, not impossibly to be compared with the *Spectator* in London or the *New Republic* in America. I brought in old friends, London intellectuals and poets, including Bernard Bergonzi and James Kirkup, as correspondents. I even published poems by Marianne Moore and Robert Lowell, and reviews by such unlikely figures as the great New Zealand writer Sylvia Ashton-Warner.

Jack Benny's reputation in movies was as a skinflint, the meanest man in the world, the title of one of his films. I was startled to find that he was equally stingy in private. It was customary in those days for press agents accompanying stars to take a local writer out for lunch on the expense account, as it was known that we all had very meager allowances. I had expected Benny to want to go to Sydney's finest restaurant, the Caprice, but instead he elected to be interviewed over lunch at Cahill's, its cheapest. Once he opened the menu he picked his way through price after price, settling finally on the least expensive item, a ham sandwich. He didn't order drinks but asked for tea, and asked me also whether Down Under one paid for milk and sugar. I assured him we did not; he smiled and gave a good interview.

Henry Fonda was a surprise. I had expected the genteel, charming, posturally superb, rather countrified figure of the Westerns, his thin Nebraska accent correcting his mask of urban sophistication. Instead he turned out to be afflicted by a mild form of scoliosis of the spine, and was round shouldered, spiky, grumbly, and far from appealing despite his well-maintained looks. He wasted most of the interview settling scores with people of whom most of my readers would never have heard, and who had allegedly caused him harm, decades before. Only one story he told seemed to me interesting. Making *You Only Live Once* for the sadistic Fritz Lang, he had been dragged from his honeymoon bed with instructions from Lang to run in actual icy rain through a Los Angeles railway siding, until he was soaked and acquired a chill. Lang informed him that he might as well not go home as he would be required at dawn and anyway would be no good for his bride.

The attitude of most Australians was irreverent to famous performers. As for evangelists, they got short shrift. Where Oral Roberts appeared they burned his tents and kicked him out. Such irreverence was healthy but it had a downside: so much talent was unfairly dismissed; so many great figures were badly treated Down Under, which, fortunately for them, meant little in their careers. When Frank Sinatra's bodyguards, dubbed the Goon Squad, beat up the local reporters and photographers, they caused a national incident, but it was the paparazzi who deserved punishment. Frustrated by Australia itself, local celebrities realized they were unknown elsewhere, and thus created an unhealthy climate of envy, desperation, and iconoclasm.

Among the pleasures of working in Australia in those days, before American-style pressures for performance built up, were the relaxed scheduling and the mandatory six weeks of annual vacation required by the Union of Journalists. Still more pleasing was that one's bosses didn't resent that arrangement or fight against it, since the national ethos called for leisure as well as toil. With reviews assigned in advance, and two new cover stories ready to be printed, I was able, for the five years I was on the *Bulletin* staff, to travel each year the length and breadth of the Pacific, and, incredibly, free of charge and paid.

This was because of an arrangement whereby the P and O Orient Lines, still the dominant merchant marine force in the region, would take on prominent journalists and give them free first class passages on the ocean run, from Sydney to Auckland, New Zealand, to Fiji, Honolulu, Los Angeles, Vancouver, Keelung in Taiwan, Hong Kong, Manila, and then back via Adelaide and Melbourne. In addition to a spacious cabin, I was given a generous salary and granted an office and a female member of the staff as my personal secretary.

When I returned to Sydney, I learned of my deficiencies as a swimmer. I hadn't ridden a board, but I had learned to shoot waves at a level just below the lifeguard class. One afternoon I was swept out to sea by a riptide that rendered me helpless.

I felt myself weakening, and knew that I might drown. Then, again, calling futilely for help, I crossed the borderline I have mentioned often in these pages. I became aware of myself as a separate self, seeing a brilliant light bursting in my brain, observing my struggling as if I were someone else. Then, a voice, perhaps my father's, told me to swim forward and catch a wave. I did, and was flung onto the beach, face down, biting the sand. I recovered within an hour.

Peter Hastings resigned as editor of the *Bulletin* in 1963, and the more congenial Peter Coleman took over. He persuaded our boss the farouche Sir Frank Packer that circulation would improve if I was sent to Hollywood to interview stars, directors, and producers for a series of *Bulletin* exclusives, to be announced on billboards as CHARLES HIGHAM'S HOLLYWOOD. I had reached the top in Australia.

8

I was surprised to find that Australia was regarded in Hollywood as second only to Great Britain as a foreign market for films. When I sent letters to the heads of the studios' overseas publicity departments and called the local representatives, the response was overwhelming.

I left for Los Angeles on April 17, 1965, feeling fit, chipper, and ready for anything. Housed at the tarnished but still comfortable Hollywood Roosevelt Hotel (where Bette Davis's first husband had once been a bandleader at the Blossom Room), I enjoyed laps in the swimming pool, the bar, and the eggs Benedict for breakfast. I soon heard from my local contacts: Robert W. Vogel, ace publicist at MGM, keeper of many secrets; Don Prince, handsome as any movie star, of 20th Century Fox; Ely Levy of Columbia, still overjoyed by his admission as a youthful immigrant thirty years before, classically New York Jewish; Louis Blaine, stalwart of MCA/ Universal; and Carl Schaefer, lean and cool, of Warner Bros. They all would have limousines at my disposal, or drive me themselves.

It was Schaefer who invited me to my first night's event: a party at his studio for two thousand members of the world's press, held on Sound Stage Six. At my table were the aristocratic Counts Unger of Sweden, twins known as "strictly from unger" (one wore a monocle in his left eye, the other in his right, so they could be told apart). Also joining me was the legendary Ivy Crane Wilson, allegedly a correspondent for Australian magazines that in fact were long since defunct. Everyone was so fond of her that in her eighties (she had arrived in the Valentino era) she was still invited to everything.

After we finished our meal of soup, squab, and ice cream, a voice announced that our host, Jack L. Warner, would make a speech of welcome. A spotlight swung over to his chair. He wasn't in it.

The sound stage exploded in laughter. A moment later, Warner shouted from somewhere deep in the bowels of the building, "I'm in the john, ladies and gentlemen of the world's press, and I'll be out in a moment!"

A few seconds later, there was a roar of water as loud as if we were sitting under Niagara Falls. It was the flushing toilet, relayed by a mischievous sound department, at many times its noise level, through the public address system.

Warner strode in, smiling like a shark, with slicked-down, patent leather dyed black hair, blue blazer with gold buttons, starched white shirt, blue tie, white yachting slacks, and two-toned shoes. I liked him at once. Here was a grand old pirate, cheerfully unscrupulous, ready to take on the world.

As he spoke warmly of his appreciation of the foreign press, I recalled a story once told me by the late British financial writer George Schwarz. Warner had entertained Winston Churchill when the great man returned to the British prime ministership in the 1950s. Famous for his ignorance, Warner knew very little about him. He had his research department prepare a dossier, which he then, to everyone's annoyance, including his guest of honor's, insisted on reading aloud, all thirty pages of it.

At last, an hour later, he reached the end. He said, "I now call upon Winston Churchill to give his address." "Number Ten Downing Street" was the reply, and the laughter was deafening.

Three interviews were promised me to start with. I had asked to see the three greatest surviving figures: David O. Selznick, Sam Goldwyn, and Walt Disney. I was too late for the first of these: Selznick had just died and I attended his funeral at Forest Lawn. My chief memory of the event is Katharine Hepburn's reading of Kipling's famous poem "If," which, in fact, was deeply ironical. The poem called for a man to be a picture of integrity; when others lost their heads, a real man would not. But Selznick, though a great filmmaker, was corrupt, devious, and ready to blame everyone in sight for his own failings, both as filmmaker and man.

Goldwyn was a surprise. I had expected him to be short; instead he was, or seemed to be, tall. He placed his guests below eye level in low-slung chairs, so that even when he was seated at his desk, he could dominate them. I almost lay, looking up at his high-domed, bald, and wrinkled skull. With his yellow parchment skin, he resembled a Jewish Pharaoh, mummified.

I expressed my admiration for his fine productions of *The Little Foxes, Dodsworth, Wuthering Heights,* and *The Best Years of Our Lives.* He took the praise coolly, as no less than his due; then, to be polite, he asked me about Australia. His interest was, not surprisingly, minimal and his eyes clouded over as I began to tell him what I could. But then something made him sit up.

I told him that a group of his classic works was in circulation in Australia and New Zealand, distributed by a small operator named Sidney Blake. "New Zealand is the same as Australia, right?" he asked me.

"Not at all," I replied. "It's a separate country, though also in the British Commonwealth."

He jumped up from his seat and angrily pressed a bell. A nervous male assistant ran in. He asked the youth how the hell his pictures could be shown in New Zealand when they were licensed only for Australia. "Get your ass out of here and find out!"

Flustered, the young man left. For a few awkward moments, Goldwyn said nothing, staring at me, his gnarled fingers drumming on his blotting pad. At last, the assistant returned. "Well?" the old monster demanded.

"We sold the Australasian rights, Mr. Goldwyn. New Zealand is part of Australasia. It's a geographical term. I'm sorry to say, sir, we've been had."

"Find out who was responsible. I'll have his ass if it's the last thing I do! He'll be out of here so fast he won't know what hit him! And he'd better look for a job *in* Australasia!"

Next day, Bob Vogel was my host at MGM, entertaining me in the private dining room: a rare privilege. As we walked to it through the chrome-and-beige art deco commissary, created by the great art director Cedric Gibbons, we stopped at a table occupied by a grizzled man. Bob introduced us: "Charles, this is Mr. Douglas Shearer, head of our sound department. He's the reason our studio has the best recording quality in the business."

"Eh? What's that?" the head of the sound department replied. "Can't hear you. Speak up!" The head of the sound department was deaf.

We walked to another table where a man of the same age was seated. Bob said, "This is Mr. Charles Schoenbaum, head of our Technicolor division."

Schoenbaum looked at my blazer. "Unusual color, green. Popular in Australia I imagine."

The blazer was navy blue. The head of the MGM Technicolor department was color blind.

Another shock was in store. I was allowed to sit in on a conference of studio contractees on the subject of a new musical that finally wasn't made, *Say It with Music,* a biography in song of Irving Berlin. Vincente Minnelli, attenuated and fastidious, was the director present. He had the large, liquid eyes of his former wife, Judy Garland. The polished, silken writer Leonard Gershe and the cold, collected Gene Kelly were also present. Only the producer Arthur Freed, famous for *Meet Me in St. Louis* and *On the Town,* was unimpressive; he might have been an expensive haberdasher. Then came the big surprise: everyone had to shout, until Freed adjusted his hearing aid. The greatest producer of Hollywood musicals was as deaf as the head of his sound department.

Walt Disney's suite of offices in his Burbank studio building was light, airy, sunny, and designed in the pastel colors of his best cartoons. I was greeted on arrival by a harem of pretty, blonde young women. I wasn't surprised, in view of Disney's early infatuation with Hitler, to see that none of them was African American, Native American, or, so far as I could see, Jewish. Later, at Disneyland, I saw that the same racist rule applied. When Hitler's beloved propagandist filmmaker Leni Riefenstahl visited Hollywood in 1938, Disney was the only studio chief to give her an official reception, and a party at his house.

Disney was dapper, trim, and sunburned, with a smart moustache, a nice oatmeal cotton sport jacket, brown slacks, and two-toned shoes. He looked a picture of health, despite the fact that, as I learned later, he had cancer and was given only a year to live. We were accompanied throughout the interview by his familiar, or acolyte, the publicist Joe Ruddy, who, as it turned out, was highly embarrassed by his employer's revelations.

To my astonishment (I didn't know he had been given a death sentence), the great man decided to tell this visitor from Down Under all the painful thoughts that he had bottled up for decades. He said that he was, and I could take it from him it was God's own truth, bitterly disappointed in his own career.

I looked at him aghast, saying nothing, as Joe Ruddy squirmed in his chair. How could the idol of millions, possessor of one of the most famous names in the world, creator of masterpieces like *Snow White and the Seven Dwarfs* and *Fantasia,* not to mention Disneyland, possibly feel that?

His weathered brown hands clasped tight, he told me that his life had been adversely affected by his brother Roy, who was in charge of the business end of the empire and had been chiefly responsible for its dazzling success. While Joe Ruddy sweated with embarrassment, frequently wiping his brow, the great filmmaker talked of his early aspirations to being a pure artist, untrammeled by financial considerations, happy to be poor. He spoke of his early days in Kansas City, and how he missed them. He said that film after film had been ruined by his sibling.

I asked him for examples. He began with *Alice in Wonderland.* He told me he had wanted to make the film version in black and white, copying the original Tenniel illustrations, and preserving the delicate but revealing portrait of Victorian attitudes the book contained. Instead, his brother had insisted the colors scream, the characters be bullying and grotesque, the songs contemporary and grating. He shuddered at the memory.

I asked him about *Ichabod and Mr. Toad,* a dual presentation of Washington Irving's story of the supernatural, and of *The Wind in the Willows,* Kenneth Grahame's masterpiece of anthropomorphism. He said that the version of Irving was far too garish and broad in its approach, and he had wanted the "Grahame classic" to be a feature on its own, not pointlessly doubled up with an inappropriate American companion piece, to which it had no thematic resemblance. He had wanted what he called the "Willows book" to be realized in a replica of Ernest Shephard's famous illustrations; he disliked this noisy, overactive, tiresome burlesque with Toad as road hog, burning up the English country lanes and making a thorough nuisance of himself.

He detested *Peter Pan,* saying that the tiny, floating light called Tinkerbell in the J. M. Barrie play should never have been turned into a nubile, sexy fairy, and that the movie quite failed to reflect the gray, subdued light of the London in which it was set. Most of all he was annoyed by *Cinderella,* wanting it to be a delicate fantasy in which such scenes as the pumpkin carriage, the white mice, the slipper left behind, and all the other elements were to be conveyed in simulated woodcuts. Instead, he said the picture resembled "a musical about a sorority reject making her way to a senior prom."

I asked if anything in his pictures reflected his personal vision. What had survived his artistic crucifixion? He smiled and said up to now nobody had addressed him on the subject. He began with the terrifying scene in *Pinocchio* in which the boys turn into donkeys, sprouting large ears and braying. He went on to mention the thorn forest in *Sleeping Beauty,* a terrifying creation of which Gustave Doré would not have been ashamed, and the forest that threatened Snow White, also created by a wicked royal, the queen's transfiguration into a hunchbacked crone, and her death when she falls from a cliff edge.

But in only one sequence had he found his fullest expression, and of which he was deeply proud: the astonishing "Night on Bald Mountain" in *Fantasia,* in which the dead rise on skeleton horses from cemetery graves to the summoning of the devil, a terrifying naked figure whose domain is a volcano into which he sends the ghosts spinning into hell. Disney told me he ran the scene personally for the movie censor Joseph L. Breen, who, expressing shock, asked for it to be run again. After the second showing, Breen said, "Walt, we can't possibly allow this."

"Why not?" Disney replied.

"Those women falling into the pit."

"What about them?"

"You can see their naked breasts. You know that's not permitted."

"There are no bras in hell, Joe," Disney said, and Breen had to laugh, and let the sequence through.

In 1965 Hedda Hopper was still the most powerful gossip columnist in America, syndicated in hundreds of newspapers. A visit to her was obligatory, and on a warm, sunny afternoon, Bob Vogel drove me to Beverly Hills to meet her. He told me en route that her former chief rival, Louella Parsons, was confined to a mental institution, given a useless wooden telephone on which she could place calls to long dead or retired studio figures, demanding news of marriages that had taken place decades before and furiously denouncing publicists who had failed to give her information when they too had passed away.

We arrived a few minutes ahead of time at Hopper's elegant clapboard and brick house at the end of Tropical Avenue, with a blue slate roof, pencil pines framing the front door, HH on the welcome mat, and oleander bushes with their poisonous leaves flanking the sides. Bob rang the doorbell. No response. Then at the exact moment Hopper had invited us, and not a second sooner, the door flew open and there she was. Strikingly beautiful even in her old age, she wore a wide black-and-white straw hat, a brown silk suit, and diamond and pearl rings on her long, delicate white hands. Her face was fair skinned, and her eyes had the sharp stare of a lynx.

Raucous voiced, unabashedly vulgar, she showed us into her living room, which had the plush, claustrophobic coziness of a jewel box. Over the fireplace, framed as if it were a Rembrandt and flanked by votive candles in antique silver sticks, was Boris Chaliapin's 1940s *Time* magazine cover picture of her in a typewriter hat, blown up to a colossal size.

Visiting the bathroom, I found it decorated with rose wallpaper and a large single paper red rose in a red Chinese vase, as well as a three-foot pile of long-playing records. Had she, I wondered, nowhere else to store them?

She served us cocktails from a small, mirrored bar off the living room, and then she showed us her "memory corner," an area where she kept the tributes of the famous, who had wished to secure her approval: this woman whose words, barbed or supportive, could affect whole lives, whole careers. She told us that each Christmas she received hand-painted greeting cards from the great, each by her fixed requirement, actually painted by the stars themselves. She was especially fond of a pretty winter landscape done by "your fellow countryman," the famous gay Australian dress designer Orry-Kelly, and works by the writer Dorothy Kingsley, and by Mary Martin. She even had a card from Winston Churchill, sent from Morocco, and next to it a large, ivory-colored autograph book containing a galaxy of names, from Bud Abbott to Vera Zorina, each page marked with the appropriate letter.

I found out many years later that Katharine Hepburn, who told me the story herself, had under extreme pressure been required to send Hopper, for the first time, one of these votary Christmas cards, cosigned by Spencer Tracy. It was a painting of a nose, with a cautionary note inside, advising her to keep it out of other people's business.

As night fell, Hopper drove us in her green, hand-tooled Rolls-Royce, a gift from her British newspapers, to the Lytton Center, built on Sunset Boulevard on the site of the demolished Garden of Allah Hotel, for the first public screening anywhere of Vincente Minnelli's *The Sandpiper,* starring Richard Burton and Elizabeth Taylor. When we arrived and were seated in the back row, I saw that the Burtons were just in front of us. They turned round, nodded to Bob Vogel, and pointedly ignored Hopper.

The credit titles began to appear. As soon as she saw the panel devoted to the screenwriter Dalton Trumbo, who had once been blacklisted as a Communist, and had only recently been restored to eminence as one of Hollywood's leading figures, Hopper, who had been instrumental in his former ruin, began to shout. To a chorus of shushes this latter-day fascist screamed that Trumbo was supposed to have been run out of town, that she would make sure he would be run out of town again, that he was a goddamned Commie and what in God's name was MGM thinking of in hiring him?

Richard Burton turned round and shouted, "Shut your fucking mouth, you stupid old biddy! Go back to your backyard and stay there, you moldy old gossip!" "Yes," Taylor added. "Go the fuck home, *now!*" Hopper stood up to leave but Bob Vogel pushed her back in her seat. She had changed into a hat in the dangerous shape of a predatory bird. As she shook her head, its beak pecked me so hard it actually hurt.

In the circumstances, it was hard to concentrate on the movie, sentimental mush staged at Big Sur, and Hopper's angry mutterings didn't help. Back at her house, she was still seething. "You know," she said, as she fixed us a late-night supper, "they paid the Unfriendly Ten compensation money for losing their jobs. Why not just give it to the Moscow slush fund?"

Not content with lashing into Communists, she started in on gays. "The faggots are taking over Hollywood. Why, one of your stars, Bob" — he cautioned her to be careful — "a bobby-soxer's dream, was so busy being a fairy that another of your boys had to divorce his wife so your faggot could marry her and have a beard." She said she had to pay $100,000 to Michael Wilding to settle a libel suit after she had accused him of being a homosexual.

She seemed to think that Australia was a Man's Country; she obviously had no idea it was a paradise for gays. She said that her fellow conservative Bob Hope was going to take her to the Melbourne Cup Race and looked forward to meeting "clean-cut young men like yourself, Charles. I'm sure you've got several mistresses."

My next stop was at "Buckingham Palace": i.e., Pickfair, the legendary home of the late Douglas Fairbanks Sr. and America's sweetheart, Mary Pickford, named for both of them. Pickford had lived there with her former bandleader husband, Buddy Rogers, for many years in almost complete isolation, very seldom receiving visitors, and never the press.

But she couldn't refuse a visit to the house by Australia's Walter Winchell, and an MGM chauffeur-driven car took me to Pickfair on a warm, late April afternoon.

A housekeeper let me in. She took me through the somber living room, which still had a flavor of the 1920s. Over the fireplace hung Pickford's portrait in oils, heavily framed in gold. Now I was in the writing room, very French, with marble-topped tables, Louis Quinze chairs and couches, a fine commode, and a French white ivory period telephone resting on a gilded cradle.

I waited for the star to appear but nothing happened, and I sat for half an hour wishing I had brought a magazine. Then the phone rang loudly, many times; naturally I didn't pick it up and I wondered why nobody else had responded. The housekeeper put her head around the door. "Aren't you going to answer it?" she asked me.

"It can't be for me," I replied.

"Oh, but it is, Mr. Higham. Miss Pickford is calling you. *In person*. From the Chinese Room!"

Astonished, I picked up the phone. A voice said, "Welcome to Pickfair." It sounded like a recording. Not knowing what to say, I responded with, "I'm delighted to be here, Miss Pickford. I look forward to the pleasure of meeting you."

"Look to your left," she commanded, in a tone of royal authority. I obeyed. "You will see a marble-topped table at the end of the room. Upon it is a guest book. Pray bring it to the phone."

I wasn't surprised she had adopted the antique language of old silent movie titles. I told my absentee hostess that I now had the book in my hands. "Turn to page 122." It wasn't easy; the pages weren't numbered. As I went through the book, I heard a faint tut-tut of impatience on the line. At last I reached the appropriate page. On it was inscribed: "We had a wonderful stay at your home." It was signed by Lord Louis and Lady Edwina Mountbatten. I read it aloud. "Being British," Mary Pickford said, "I thought you'd appreciate that. Good-bye." And with that she hung up, and I was being shown politely to the front door.

Soon after that I visited the equally famous Harold Lloyd. His magnificent house, Green Acres, almost as grand as Pickfair, had in the living room a year-round Christmas tree, heaped with unopened gifts. My host, twinkling as a gag in the prop horn-rimmed glasses that made him so distinctive as a youth, suggested I look around the garden before the interview as he had to attend to some business.

I walked out onto a perfectly manicured lawn, carrying with me a recent biography of the star. Suddenly, I heard a hissing sound and was surrounded on every side by a circle of sprinklers; if I moved too far I would be drenched. I wasn't surprised to see my impish old host laughing uproariously from a window at his silent screen joke. I completed the act: I sat on a tiny spot of still dry grass, opened the book, and began to read it. Delighted, Lloyd turned off the sprinklers, welcomed me in, and announced that I would from now on be an honorary member of the Comedy Club.

My next target was Dorothy Parker, the doyenne of the Algonquin Round Table and one of my favorite humorists. When someone died, a reporter asked her at the funeral if there was anything she needed. "Yes," she replied. "Go to the deli on Sixth and Main, pick up a corned beef on rye sandwich, and tell them to *hold the mayo*."

She had become reunited with her former husband Alan Campbell, who had written screenplays with her in the 1940s (*A Star Is Born*; *Sweethearts*). They lived in a shabby West Hollywood backwater named Norma Place, renamed by those who knew them as Abnorma Place, and were busy working on a version of the French farce *La Bonne Soupe*.

Campbell was still handsome in late middle age, trim, tan, visibly gay, dressed nattily in casual shirt and pants. Parker by contrast looked her age in black silk, all the bitterness of her vision of life concentrated in her hurt, watering Pekingese eyes.

Two o'clock in the afternoon was too early for cocktails but clearly Parker was already into her fourth or fifth old-fashioned, and to be polite I had to accept one. She took me to the window and showed me the house opposite. "John Dall lives there," she said, "the queer star of *Rope* and *The Corn Is Green*. At night if there's nothing on TV, Alan and I start Dall-watching. We see him kneeling, his head on his mother's knee, as she reads to him." Surely, I thought, the doyenne of the Algonquin Round Table and one of the wittiest women in American literature would have something better to do?

She asked me, without a hint of interest, my hobbies. I didn't dare say old movies, swimming, and working out. Instead, I said, "Studying old murder cases."

"Mention one," she replied, trying vainly to show that she cared when she didn't.

I thought back to my days at the Chamber of Horrors in London. "Hawley Harvey Crippen. He was an American pharmacist and physician living in London. His wife, a music hall singer, was demanding in bed so he gave her a sexual depressant named hyoscine and overdid the dose. She went into a catatonic trance indistinguishable from death and he began to cut her up while she was still alive."

Parker looked Campbell in the eyes and said, "What are you doing to my arm?"

She asked me the color scheme of the Crippen sitting room. "Shocking pink," I pretended, with no idea how to answer her. Decades later I heard that the room was actually done out in that color. "It must," Parker said, "have been like living inside a lung."

She asked me desultorily about Australia. I mentioned we had one great writer, the novelist Patrick White, who later would win the Nobel Prize. "You don't mean . . ." she almost yawned, and left the room. Minutes later I heard a car draw up outside. "Your taxi is here," she said as she walked in. I hadn't ordered one.

Of all the great stars the one I admired most was Barbara Stanwyck. Joan Crawford and Bette Davis, her chief rivals, superb though they were, seemed to me dated, but Stanwyck never did. Her performances were not extravagant or overly marked by tantrums and tears; even in *Sorry, Wrong Number,* in which she played a neurasthenic, bedridden heiress threatened with death, her acting was controlled, disciplined, filled with emotional understanding, and conceived in clean, sharp, classically simple lines.

I was surprised to find that she wouldn't see me at her house in Beverly Hills, but rather in an apartment owned by her friend and long-term publicity assistant Helen Ferguson, once an actress whose name Stanwyck in an inside joke would use for her own character in *No Man of Her Own.* The modest flat was housed in a prisonlike complex structure called the Park La Brea Towers, all biscuit stone and beige carpeted corridors, in which I rapidly got lost.

For the first time in my life, I arrived a few minutes late. Miss Ferguson was waiting for me with the statement that her boss expected visitors to be on time. I said that I was delayed by lunching with George Cukor, and that helped a little with Stanwyck when Ferguson ushered me into the drab Early Pullman apartment living room with its matching beige furnishings and fake fireplace with illuminated logs that flickered on and off as if they were not plastic with bulbs but real.

As I sat down facing the star, both of us in wing chairs, Ferguson handed me a sheet of paper with a list of Stanwyck's films marked by one, two, or three stars. While Stanwyck sat silent and stony faced, the secretary told me that three stars allowed for long discussion, two somewhat less, and one for brief mention only. No stars meant no talk.

I was relieved to find that my favorites of her movies, *Sorry, Wrong Number, Double Indemnity,* and *Stella Dallas,* all had three stars and asked her about each. She began to melt, realizing I knew what I was talking about, but I still found her a poor interview: uninformative, taciturn, with no anecdotes to tell.

Bette Davis was a contrast: the very picture of melodramatic emphasis every bit as much as she was on the screen. The 20th Century Fox publicist Don Prince drove me to her house on Stone Canyon Road in Bel Air, past a witch's cottage, a Gothic mausoleum flanked with fake classical pillars, and a small French château that Prince told me housed a parchment Gregorian chant used as a lampshade. Asked to sum up the occupants of this wealthy city within a city, Don said crisply, "They eat their young."

Davis's brick-and-clapboard house was set back from the road. On the front lawn stood a black boy hitching post she had probably stolen from *In This Our Life*. We entered the house through the kitchen, as if we were delivery men. A man and woman stood there, crookedly, all in black, like the figures in a Charles Addams cartoon. Don whispered to me later that they were Davis's sister and brother-in-law, engaged as slaves, and that the sister was mentally disturbed and had just been released from an institution.

The star, small, full hipped, chain-smoking, greeted us in slacks and a casual jacket, taking us into the living room, which she had set up as a New England hideaway. A table was set with a lazy Susan, cruets in a circle to be spun around, and at the center a blue china bowl, brimming incongruously with white magnolias. Sporting prints on the walls, including *The Horse Fair,* and groaning bookshelves gave an air of agreeably bookish comfort. This was the home of a woman who, though afflicted by madness in her family, herself manic and driven and notoriously difficult to work with, was clearly well educated and well read: a rara avis among the stars.

I was surprised to find that, known as a liberal in her younger years, she had turned into a conservative. She condemned American youth as victims of an "ice-cream culture" that allowed everything immoral. She talked of people becoming too lazy, too fat, too lethargic, too much in bondage to TV commercials, too prone to buy anything on the hypnotic suggestions of manufacturers, thus creating a debtor culture.

She deplored the loss of romantic elements and the increase in realism in pictures. She was painfully aware that movies like her *Now, Voyager,* in which an ugly spinster is transformed into near beauty by Paul Henreid and an ocean cruise, would not be possible in 1965. Like Hedda Hopper, she was homophobic, ironical in view of the fact that she had reached an age, and a degree of patented mannerisms—arms flapping and circling to emphasize a point, so many outbursts of tears that she might have suffered from conjunctivitis—that made her appealing no longer to most straight men but to a devoted army of gays.

As for movie criticism, she risked future ill treatment by saying that critics were all "neuters." Perhaps she spoke in the certainty that Bosley Crowther of the *New York Times* and Phil Scheuer of the Los Angeles equivalent would not read articles published in Australia.

By late afternoon she was drunk, talking inaccurately of an affair she was supposed to be having with the director Allan Miner. At some stage, deep in her cups, she dropped her mask for a moment and said, "Don't write that I killed my first husband. I killed my second."

I didn't find the answer to this curious throwaway until almost forty years later, from her director Vincent Sherman (*Old Acquaintance, Mr. Skeffington*). He was having an affair with her. For discretion's sake, since she was married and the women's clubs and Legion of Decency were on the prowl, they decided to spend a week at the Hotel Reforma in Mexico City, on the excuse that she would be making local publicity appearances.

Sherman left by plane; she, again for discretionary purposes, left by train. Her second husband, an aeronautics engineer named Arthur Farnsworth, found out and boarded the train at Union Station in Los Angeles. He ordered her out of her drawing room and told her to leave with him. She refused. The train began to move. She pushed him and he fell on his head on the platform. Later that day, he died on Hollywood Boulevard, from a blood clot formed in the fall. The studio paid heavily and the autopsy proved helpful. Bette Davis escaped the gas chamber.

Next on my list was Mae West. Years later, she would become a friend.

I was uncertain how to find her; I had written from Sydney to Diane Arbus, who had photographed her memorably for *Show* magazine. Arbus responded from New York on cheap, legal-sized yellow-ruled stationery in purple ink, saying that the star was very well protected but that she was, of all things, listed in the Los Angeles telephone directory. It was true.

I called West and she agreed to see me, although she used the disguise of Beverly West, her sister's name, until I revealed who I was. She lived in the Ravenswood, a crumbling Gothic pile in the leafy Rossmore district of Hollywood. Several people told me that she bought the building in 1932 when the biddies in residence there got together and asked for her eviction on the absurd ground that she was a prostitute. She threw them out.

She had insisted that Adolph Zukor, who had signed her at Paramount, furnish her apartment in Louis Quinze. She had only a vague idea of what that was. The studio art department, headed by Hans Dreier, fixed her up with plywood imitations stored for use and featured originally in Rudolph Valentino's *Monsieur Beaucaire*.

Miss West didn't know the difference. Every now and again, a plywood leg would snap off a gilded table and have to be sent out for repairs. The studio kept her waiting for six months, pretending that the table had to be sent to a specialist in Paris, who, of course, didn't exist. Instead, it was placed in a carpentry shop on Melrose Avenue, then stored.

I rang her doorbell at four thirty one afternoon. The stars always preferred that hour; the light was kind, and with any luck the interviewer would be done by six when friends might drop in for cocktails and dinner. The door was opened by Paul Novak, her long-term bodyguard, who had appeared in a loincloth in her stage show *Mae West and Her Adonises*. Massive and monumental, he made me feel like a wimp.

He showed me a coat of arms in the hallway, with lion rampant and dog *couchant,* saying that Miss West was "of Norman origin." The living room was surprisingly small, all in white, with gilded tables and chairs, no doubt still of plywood, and a baby grand piano with a white silk shawl on it.

Mae West walked in, very slowly, with the cautious look at her feet of the old. Her blonde wig was piled high in the style of the late nineteenth century; her face was plump and with only a few lines running upward from her upper lip; her brow was remarkably unwrinkled. She wore strange glasses: navy blue lenses punctured with tiny holes that must have refracted her vision like a dragonfly's. She was surprisingly décolleté, her flesh unwisely betrayed in the plunging-necked pink silk gown, when most woman of her age would have been hidden from toe to tippet. She coughed, and I realized she wasn't well; I was touched that she would see me in that condition. I began by asking her what was the greatest moment of her life. She replied without hesitation: "When I was a lion tamer."

In the film *I'm No Angel,* she reminded me, she actually had to control these beasts. "They wanted me to go in the ring in an ermine wrap and cap, but something made me refuse. Just as well, dear. The lions would have mistaken me for a bear and torn me to pieces." As it was, they liked her when in spangles she cracked a ringmaster's whip over them and made them jump through hoops ("I felt such a wave of power that I can't describe it").

At last I had found a star who loved gays. She reminded me she had created a play called *The Drag,* which in the 1920s caused a sensation as it showed, and favorably, two men locked in a passionate love affair. She said she liked men who loved each other and that they were more intelligent, more sensitive than so-called normal men.

She mentioned her spell in jail at Welfare Island in New York for obscenity on the stage. "I had a very handsome jailer," she told me, "and he brought me caviar and pâté de fois gras. Champagne too, but I don't drink, dear."

I left her in the certainty that I would one day get to know her better.

I had been back in Sydney only for a few days when my editor Peter Coleman told me I would be covering Marlene Dietrich's appearances in Melbourne and Sydney, sure proof that Australia was no longer considered a show business backwater. She had always fascinated me: I had enjoyed her obvious intelligence and sense of humor on screen, subtly humorous and self-mocking in her kitsch vehicles for Josef von Sternberg: *Morocco, Shanghai Express,* and the others, a mixture of champagne and soda water, and, as she herself called them, ineffably camp and foolish, though the objects of a lasting cult. Absurd though her most famous film moments were, they stuck in the mind: dancing in a gorilla suit in *Blonde Venus,* or riding up the palace steps on horseback as Catherine the Great in *The Scarlet Empress.*

By 1965 she had re-created herself as a nightclub star, performing with great success in London, Paris, Berlin, and Las Vegas. She was fitted with a rubber body sheath to give an illusion of youthful contours, but it was far too tight and caused her painful discomfort and falls. She wore opaque white stockings to conceal bruises and veins.

Her face had been worked on so much that it was hard for her to smile. Yet she was said to be down to earth, a good hausfrau, ready with chicken soup for sick friends, and very well read, with a grasp of literature in several languages.

The press conference for her was held at Melbourne's Southern Cross Hotel, on the afternoon of October 4, 1965. I knew I had to make an impression; fit and glowing from my recent sojourn in Hollywood, tanned to the hairline, I dressed with all the deliberation of a male whore out for a wealthy target: white cotton jacket, smart red silk tie, black trousers, expensive shoes.

Before anyone arrived I planted myself dead center in the front row of chairs arranged in a semicircle in the ballroom, and notice me she did.

Her answers to questioners were bright, smart, and very much to the point. I felt I had enough for a piece and returned to my hotel room to change for her black-tie opening night performance. The phone rang.

"It's Dietrich here," the voice said. "I want you to have midnight supper with me, after the show."

I accepted, of course, trying not to seem uncool by showing a fanlike excitement. But my heart was beating very fast. Would the night end there? If not, I would, I was sure, be equal to her demands, but as it turned out, they weren't made.

Her show that night was excellent, a feast of great songs, superbly delivered, in the famous clinging gown Jean Louis had designed for her: songs of pain, of tenderness, of war and peace, of love gained and lost, and with a sprinkling of contemporary works, including Pete Seeger's haunting "Where Have All the Flowers Gone?" I had never thought Australians could become hysterical, but the crowd outside the stage door was overwrought, women fighting each other for her autograph, others grabbing the photographs I handed out and spilling them on the ground. When we got into her specially imported Pontiac (she would ride in no other make of car) a seven-year-old boy's arm was caught in the door and as she released him, he screamed. She was terrified we would run over other children, and indeed they seemed to almost fall under the wheels while their parents pawed at the windows and tilted the vehicle till I feared it would turn over.

With two lighting men from the theater, we dined at Antonio's, the city's best restaurant, in the fashionable Toorak district.

I soon discovered that, despite her inevitable narcissism, Marlene was also interested in others. I asked her about the German and Austrian expatriates she had known in Hollywood during World War II: Jewish refugees from Hitler like Max Reinhardt, Bruno Walter, Thomas and Heinrich Mann, Lion Feuchtwanger, and the directors Fritz Lang and von Sternberg. She said that many of them found living in California painful; they missed their native foods and comforts, and yet they knew if they went home they would suffer certain death in the concentration camps. She added that most were tragically wasted by the American film industry.

After Marlene opened in Sydney, she called me often and we formed a friendship, yet only in a limited sense, because the give and take necessary, the confidences, the criticism, the frankness were impossible; everything had to be centered on her. I didn't resent this; a troubled narcissism as a necessary element of stardom was well known, and the fierce concentration of energy called for in a woman in her sixties to appear at her best night after night was very demanding on her.

But she had time to discuss others she admired. She adored Edith Piaf, the Little Sparrow, Charles Aznavour, Noël Coward, Alfred Hitchcock. She had fallen in love with Harper Lee's novel *To Kill a Mockingbird* and was delighted when I brought her a similarly spare and classic work, my Australian friend Elizabeth Kata's novel *Be Ready with Bells and Drums,* later filmed as *A Patch of Blue.* She would often discuss with me the works of Hölderlin, Heine, and Rilke, and shared my passion for Marc Chagall.

She could even take a joke against herself. She asked me one day why she always had a headache in Australia. I told her it was because she was walking upside down on the bottom of the world. She threw back her head and laughed. Her daily regimen was insane: she rose at noon and had no lunch, at three she had a single glass of champagne, at six another glass, no food in fact until midnight when she ate enough for a marine—heavy, rich soups; steaks or baked fish; a creamy dessert; and black coffee. And then she wondered why she couldn't sleep without an anal suppository, which she called Fernando Lamas, after the handsome but soporific Latino movie star of that time.

I arranged a dinner party for her in conjunction with Elizabeth Kata. Her rules were clear: No woman must be present younger than she, but all the men must be younger, and attractive. No woman must wear a dress that might threaten to upstage her Chanel. There must be an equal number of men and women, and the chairs in which she would sit must be lighted by a lamp with a pink bulb and heavy shade, and not face sunlight or moonlight. Dinner was to be served at eight, no earlier.

She arrived by Pontiac at seven, her hair girlish in a pale blue ribbon, her Chanel costume pink and gray, her stockings opaque as usual. I shall not forget her as she walked to the duplex apartment building, splayfooted, like a girl on her first date. Later, when darkness fell at the cocktail stage, she sat on a window seat and looked out at the ferries twinkling magically by, against a black and silver harbor, sirens sounding from the sea. "I feel I am seeing Australia for the first time," she said, with an approving sigh.

Digging into a baron of beef, of which she approved, she also referred to a German expatriate journalist who had written disparagingly of her in the Sydney *Daily Mirror*. His name was Uli Schmetzer. She raised her champagne glass in an ironical toast: "To Uli Schmaltzer." "To Uli Shle-mieltzer!" We all laughed.

That Sunday, Joel Greenberg and I took her out to dinner. Knowing she would hate the fashionable restaurants like the Caprice, with women in hats and blue rinses staring at her throughout the meal, I found an obscure Norman fish café in Watson's Bay, on Sydney Harbor. Despite the spectacular drive past the ocean, she complained that we seemed to be going to "the other side of the moon," so long was the journey, but when we arrived at the modest shack, she was overjoyed. She talked to the French couple from Normandy who ran it, clucked over their baby, and read the blackboarded dishes without glasses.

She murmured approval of the moules marinieres and sent the bouillabaisse back to remove the garlic. She let her hair down and began to gossip. Cary Grant, she said, was "queer" and had to refuse to make love to her on *Blonde Venus*; his lover was Randolph Scott. I was surprised to find her homophobic. Didn't she realize that the largest audience she had internationally was gay?

It was clear by now that Marlene and I would not be lovers. Even though I had invited Joel Greenberg along as a less than subtle hint, she must have guessed, even while attacking gays, that I might be one myself. On the other hand, I could have satisfied her if she had wanted me, even though she was thirty years my senior.

I wasn't her type. I was a slender swimmer and she wanted a bull-like boxer, a Hemingwayan square, heavily muscled, vigorously heterosexual.

One morning I received a call from a colleague, the twenty-six-year-old Hugh Curnow, who was built like a prizefighter, with massive shoulders and arms the size of my legs.

He told me that our boss, Sir Frank Packer, had threatened to fire him unless he obtained an interview with Dietrich. So far, I was the only writer in Australia she would see. Married with children, Hugh was afraid of poverty.

With great cunning, he wrote to Marlene asking her to cooperate and said that if she didn't, his children would starve. It was a sure way to her heart. She called me and asked if she should talk to him. I knew at once he was her type but didn't want her to be instrumental in breaking up his marriage. I told her I couldn't advise her not to see him but that if she did, she might not like what he wrote. "So it's six of one and half a dozen of the other," she said.

Hugh stayed on after the first interview she gave him, satisfied her in bed, and became her lover; his wife and children didn't know. Although he was scarcely comparable as a stud to her favorite flame, Yul Brynner, he almost certainly surpassed, if his own account was accurate, her previous inamorata, Jean Gabin. He told me she preferred cunnilingus to penetration, and she joked to Hugh that one of her lovers had thought it was an Irish airline.

She was determined to continue the relationship at her home in Paris, and on tour in Europe. She and Hugh cooked up a plan. He would ghost her memoirs, *Tell Me, Oh Tell Me Now,* a no doubt fictitious reworking of the facts to give the impression that she was a model of rectitude. She had never divorced her husband, Rudolph Stieber, whom she kept on a California chicken farm with his mistress, Tamara Mapul. When Mapul died some years later, Marlene went to the house and destroyed the dead woman's menagerie of glass animals, which she despised. Leaving the house, she bent over to clean out a dirty chicken coop. A chicken clawed off her wig. It fluttered with the hairpiece into a tree. Dietrich was unable to coax it to come down and when it proved stubborn she climbed a stepladder and grabbed the screeching bird. That night, she cooked it for dinner.

Hugh's gleaming face at work showed that the deal with Marlene had been made; he had sold his body to her, and now he bragged to me he would become rich and famous. Packer agreed to grant him a leave of absence provided that the newspaper had the world rights to the memoirs' serialization. It was decided that he would follow Marlene to Paris, not accompany her on the plane as that might create a public scandal and precipitate a divorce.

The loving couple began their trip in Hollywood, where they attended the first night of Charles Aznavour at the Huntington Hartford Theater. Hugh's articles of the trip were well written and published in the *Daily Telegraph*. Then there was a long silence as he worked with Marlene in Paris.

I was amazed to see him on a Sydney street one afternoon six months later, and asked him what had happened. He said that he finally could no longer endure his life with her there. Sex had to take place at midnight by the clock; evenings were spent going over her scrapbooks. Bad reviews were marked in black or crossed out altogether; good ones were marked in red ("Kenneth Tynan, he's a dream").

A paid prisoner, Curnow had begged for an evening off, to enjoy a Pernod, not, he insisted to me, to make love to another woman, but she refused. One night at last they went out to the Duke and Duchess of Windsor's house. Judy Garland was there. Marlene took out a long-playing record and placed it on the turntable. She sang *Falling in Love Again*. There were recorded cries of "Bravo" from an English audience, followed by "Ole" and "Brava" from a Spanish crowd, "Magnifique" from the French, and so forth, in a dozen languages. For one hour the guests had to listen to the applause, and then Marlene left.

The couple went out only one more time. Marlene said this would be a treat for Hugh's birthday. Her chauffeur drove them to the elegant suburb of Neuilly where they arrived at a tall, shuttered house and entered from the back, climbing a steep flight of stairs to a long, narrow, dark room. They sat, and a beam of light penetrated the murk. Suddenly they were watching *The Blue Angel* on the screen.

Hugh told me that such an existence was humiliating, defeating. He had lost his marriage and his children; he had lost the rights to the co-authorship of *Tell Me, Oh Tell Me Now*; he might now lose his job. He gave up and came home.

Sir Frank Packer knew how to punish unsuccessful writers. On the worst possible assignment, a grim contrast to the glamourous imprisonment in

Paris, he dispatched him to cover an oil discovery, of all things, off the coast of the state of Victoria, in vile, stormy conditions.

In a foul mood, Hugh had to accept or be fired on the spot. He was aboard the rig in heavy waves when a television team flew in to take some overhead shots. Their helicopter went in too close and, in the high wind, tilted over, and the blades swept through every man on board. Hugh, age twenty-six, was beheaded; his body was cut to pieces. He can't have known what happened.

By an unpleasant coincidence, Marlene opened in Melbourne that same night. When her impresario Kenn Brodziak brought her the news, she went very pale, leaned against the dressing room door, and said she would go on. She made one small change in the program. She began with *Where Have All the Flowers Gone?*—Hugh's and her own favorite song. She had the discretion not to attend the funeral, which would have caused a riot. Instead, she sent twelve white roses, the symbols of innocence.

In the wake of her departure, I began to feel the tide running out at the *Bulletin*. My Hollywood pieces, and profile of Marlene, had won approval at the top of the new organization, but a move to new quarters and a new editor, Donald Horne, not my fan, spelled an uncertain future. Horne, with his steely eyes, cold voice and manner, and lack of interest in show business, was critical of my cosmopolitan approach, and, Peter Coleman tells me, he was jealous because I had succeeded as a poet when he could only manage doggerel.

A journalist's strike held us up in 1967. To avoid paying more, Packer downgraded us all; salaries were based on grades and suddenly I became a C grade, about on the level, with Horne's approval, of a cub reporter.

When he tried to drag me into editorial meetings I resisted, as Australian politics, his chief subject, baffled and bored me. Further trips to Hollywood or even major pieces on stars were out of the question. I began staying home.

The assistant editor Patricia Rolfe called to warn me I might be fired if my absenteeism continued, and I resigned. Free of work for a time, I embarked on all the pleasures of Sydney, capital of attractive men and unlimited gay sex in those pre-AIDS days. The fact that discovery could result in arrest and imprisonment never bothered me; my self-confidence was so complete I was certain nothing would happen. And besides, many men on the police force were said to be part of the fun.

Even straight Australians were natural exhibitionists. In a country with fewer women than men, they endlessly stripped down in locker rooms and beach changing sheds, showing each other their muscles. Even the strictly heterosexual pub atmosphere, with huge men drinking beer by the king-size glass (schooners), offered little conversation about women (sheilas) and how they were in bed. The emphasis was usually on sporting victories, with much discussion of "great body on him, mate." Of course most were married and had children.

The gay bars were crammed almost every night. The most popular were located in the raffish, cockroach-ridden Kings Cross, Sydney's Greenwich Village. The most glamourous was the basement bar of the Chevron Hilton. There, the magnificent Australian boys, jacketless, sleeves rolled up to display powerful brown biceps, shirts unbuttoned invitingly down to the navel, pants tight and revealing, provided a spectacle of which Michelangelo would have approved. The conversation was less inspiring: cocks, screwing, whether this one was butch or bitch, Arthur or Martha in bed, and whether "lunch"—i.e., head—was offered by so and so. Few voices were falsetto; these racy comments were delivered in Australian deep tones, as if racing form was being discussed.

It was there that I knew I would find a lover; and after three weeks of workouts and lying in the sun to deepen my tan I walked in, wearing the approved clothing. But I soon realized that even in my shape at thirty-six I was already, so far as the gilded barflies were concerned, over the hill. I was about to leave when a man caught my eye.

He was seated at a table under an open window, lighted by a brilliant red sunset. He was in his early twenties, with black curly hair, a dark handsome, gypsyish face, and a sturdy body like that of Leonardo's Bacchus, in the required blue jeans. He smiled at me and our eyes locked. Within minutes, we were in a cab and headed for my home.

Hand in hand, we walked into my apartment, and without need for conversation we stripped each other, slowly, button by button. I thanked God for the work I'd done on my chest. He lay down not in the bedroom but on the sitting room couch under a tall, metal-framed window through which the moonlight streamed.

His body gleamed with health, not a weight lifter's but rather the natural product of good food and light exercise: the shoulders square, the arms ticking with defined muscle, the chest broad and carved, the stomach flat,

85

with the sudden bristle of hair above the genitals. I stood for a moment, drinking in the beauty of his youth, growing steadily more erect. Then I lay on him, and our bodies blended into one.

Gay life in Sydney was more exciting than ever. The rituals of existence were unvarying. Weekends began with Saturdays at Balmoral Beach or Camp Cove, where almost every man was handsome and desirable and no women were seen. At sundown each sunbather was handed a card inviting him to this or that party. In various stuffy, overfurnished sitting rooms with their "lounge suites," heavy curtains, and framed visions of Bondi Beach done in purple velvet, we were required to strip on arrival, give our host our clothes, and receive in return a rubber wristlet, with a numbered metal token on it. Everyone was up for grabs; nobody could be refused.

Saturday nights were especially appealing. It was typically Australian that in the humdrum suburb of Roseville, a Rotarian hall, devoted for the rest of the week to dreary evenings of religious lectures, discussions, and debates on local politics, now became the scene of a bacchanalian frenzy of the physically fit.

On arrival at 8 p.m., I handed my shirt and jacket to a seductive custodian who gave me the necessary wrist tags. Walking into the great hall, I saw strobe lights revolving in the ceiling, bathing over two hundred half-naked youths. Flashes of light turned us all into whirling dervishes as we spun in the currently popular twist, the watusi, and the froog. We changed partners frequently along with addresses and phone numbers or, when the music slowed, danced cheek to cheek, as our parents had once done.

At midnight, a ring-a-rosy was formed with one circle of men on the outside, another in the inside, dancing faster and faster as the band struck up a rock tune, inner circle clockwise, the outer counterclockwise. Then the music stopped and you found yourself with a partner. He was guaranteed for the night, and I had many Saturdays to Sundays filled in as a result. I lost count of the men who would walk with me eagerly to the cloakroom, exchange wristlets for clothes, then pile with me into a cab.

There were other rendezvous: Chez Ivy, where we danced close to records; Chameleons, where there was a DJ and room for six hundred men; and Jools, with a bar and restaurant on the ground floor, a drag show upstairs, and a brothel at the top.

Everyone in gay society was required to have at least one orgy of his own and I was no exception. Living now at MacMahon's Point, on Sydney

Harbor, with a friend I staged an event to which we invited the best-looking men we knew. The rule was followed exactly, clothes piled up in my friend's bedroom, each perfect specimen available to the others, towels on the floor spread out to catch the falling sperm, and no music to attract attention from the neighbors. At midnight there was a circle jerk, with each guest, if he had anything left over, spilling onto the chest of a prone, naked athlete. It was the night of nights of my life.

In spite of all this activity, I had a series of love affairs: with Kevin Garty, who later died of AIDS in California, with a beautiful, sweet-natured New Zealander; with a man I will call Louis Roche, a dark, moody, heavy-drinking Tasmanian painter; and "Marcus," a part-Aborigine dancer. Best of all I liked "Ivor," who would turn up at all hours of the night, guessing by some uncanny instinct I was alone, and strip, ready to serve and be served, then leave as silently as he had arrived.

I was running out of money again and needed a new job. With no desire to return to Rupert Murdoch's *Mirror* and churn out more Hysterical Historicals, I again had a stroke of luck. The same day I decided I must obtain work I read that Craig McGregor, the *Sydney Morning Herald* film critic, was going to America to live. I at once called my former editor and mentor John Douglas Pringle, who by another coincidence had just been restored to office after an absence in London as assistant editor of the *Times Literary Supplement*, at his harbor home and took a bus and ferry to his house.

He agreed on the spot that I should take over from Craig and asked me to write a regular book column and contribute articles both on local film-making and on trips to Hollywood along the lines of my *Bulletin* excursions. Was anyone so reckless so fortunate?

9

Today, Helen Mirren is deservedly famous, the recipient of an Oscar, brilliant as Elizabeth in *The Queen.* But when I first met her, in Queensland at the time, she was unknown.

Michael Powell, creator of my favorite film, *The Thief of Bagdad,* arrived in Australia to film *Age of Consent,* with Mirren and James Mason, and I met him off the plane and took care of his settling in. A young and talented actress, Clarissa Kaye, called me and anxiously asked my advice as *Herald* film critic: should she accept a part in the film? I asked her what it was. She said it was as James Mason's mistress and involved a sex scene in a Brisbane hotel. I told her to go ahead; it might lead to something. It did; they repeated the sequence in real life and soon after that they were married.

I spent a week on location with the movie in the Great Barrier Reef. Helen Mirren was in one sequence diving after fish, her magnificent bare breasts causing the male movie crew difficulty in concentrating on their work. Voluptuous and sensual in the picture, Mirren seemed cold and distant in person.

Decades later, I ran into her at a screening at the Directors Guild in Los Angeles and reminded her of that meeting when she was just starting out in her first film. Instead of smiling at a happy memory and sharing my affectionate thoughts of our mutual friend Micky Powell, she was as cold as before, snapping dismissively, "I am with Taylor Hackford," her director husband. As if I had tried to pick her up.

Joel Greenberg and I brought out *Hollywood in the Forties,* which introduced the term *film noir* to the English-speaking world. In Hollywood, while I wrote articles for the *Sydney Morning Herald,* we spent weeks interviewing directors, including Alfred Hitchcock, George Cukor, Fritz Lang, and Rouben Mamoulian, for a book entitled *The Celluloid Muse.* Asked when it was published what *The Celluloid Mouse* [*sic*] was about, I told a locally famous TV interviewer's large audience that it was an account of a struggling artist in Kansas City in the early twenties who on seeing a mouse run across the floor of his garret decided to draw it in a series of sketches which he then transferred to celluloid and thus Mickey Mouse was born; hence, *The Celluloid Mouse.* I went on to discuss Mickey's future career and that of his creator, and neither the host nor my fellow guests seemed to know I was talking about a book that didn't exist.

John Ford was the director who got away. I went to see him alone and found him in bed, ill, his last picture finished. As I walked into his bedroom, he raised his unshaven face, glowering and harsh, and fixed me with rheumy eyes behind heavy horn-rimmed spectacles. "Are you an Aussie bastard or a Limey?" he demanded. "Both," I replied. "Then you're a fucking two-time loser!" He spat a tobacco chaw to within an inch of my nose; it splattered on his expensive paper. I left at once in disgust.

I discovered that he was a chief supporter of the Irish Republican Army, along with that other Irish Australian Errol Flynn. A great director, he was so detestable a human being that I wondered how, as implied in his favorite actress Maureen O'Hara's memoirs, he could have had an affair with the very decent Tyrone Power, or with my friend, the delicate and fastidious English patriot Anna Lee, later the star of *General Hospital.*

Back in Australia, living now in the fashionable area of Double Bay, I was eager to return to California, my unspiritual home. Then, out of the blue, the opportunity came, in the autumn of 1969. An old friend, Bill Lillyman, whom I had encouraged against his doubts to go to Europe to advance his skills as a scholar of German literature, was teaching at the University of California at Santa Cruz and recommended me for the post of Regents Professor and Writer in Residence. This very high honor was accorded once a year to a representative author or poet from one country at a time. He suggested I be the first Australian poet to be chosen and that I combine teaching with seminars on film. I had established an international reputation as a motion-picture critic in articles in *Sight and Sound, Film Quarterly,* and the *Kenyon Review.*

The letter of invitation was signed by Governor Ronald Reagan. I accepted at once by telegram but suddenly realized I had no money to make the trip. Once again, the P and O Orient shipping line came to my rescue and offered me a free passage to Los Angeles in return for the usual presswork on interesting passengers aboard.

I attended the first anniversary of *Hair* at the Aquarius Theater on Sunset Boulevard. The nude men and women on the stage were testimony to the physical beauty of young Americans, and the open sexuality (though highly commercialized) was refreshing indeed. I had arranged to meet a friend in the lobby afterward, but he didn't turn up; after everyone had left I found myself alone . . . except for a tall Texas cowboy with Stetson hat, fringed jacket and chaps, and not, as I soon would find out, a hustler. He asked me whether I had been stood up and I nodded; he said he had been too and suggested we go to my hotel, the Hollywood Plaza, to make up for it.

We made passionate love. After it was over he said that the night was still young, and he suggested we go to a party given by a wealthy and famous producer at a house in the Hollywood Hills. Once there, I found myself in a crowd from which the middle aged, the unfit, and the unattractive had been excluded.

I spent Thanksgiving at the home of my American literary and film agent, Marcia Nasatir, later head of Columbia. She started me off on a friendship with Pauline Kael, then at her peak as a contentious and brilliant film critic, the doyenne of the *New Yorker.* Marcia telephoned her from the party, and I spoke to her; she was warmly welcoming. Soon afterward, she came to Los Angeles and we had lunch at the Polo Lounge of the Beverly Hills Hotel, surrounded by a Carmen Miranda decor of banana leaves and yellow Technicolor walls. I could see she was attracted to me, but I didn't find her physically appealing, though successive directors, including Robert Altman and Irvin Kershner, did, and had affairs with her.

With her uncanny instinct she clearly saw that I was gay, so she made no suggestion of spending the night, which was her wont when she desired a man. This was a relief and we parted friends, with a promise we would meet again when I came to New York.

It was time, after Christmas, to fly to Santa Cruz and take up my appointment. From the first, I had a strong dislike of the place that seems to me, in retrospect, disturbingly irrational.

I was awarded a house to live in, elegant and bare in the Swedish manner, and situated on the edge of a redwood forest. After the heat of Australia, mild even in winter, and of Southern California, basking in winter sunshine, I knew serious damp and cold for the first time since I had left England. The house was beautiful, but in an inhospitable and austere style I didn't find appealing, and it was infested by beetles that crawled out of the underbrush and invaded the rooms, with a particular fondness for the bathtub. Although a swat team appeared and eliminated most of them, they came back later—the stench of the insect repellent made me dizzy.

Bill Lillyman was away. I found no group of teachers to receive me warmly, but was left to my own devices to set up the curriculum for my classes. I felt more alone and isolated than I had ever felt. Over a weekend, with still no party or delegation of welcome, I flew in a state of annoyance to Los Angeles, picked up a handsome but unhappily alcoholic lover I will call Steven Day, and set up house at a motel in the town of Santa Cruz itself.

I decided to teach verse and film, the first to a limited group of no more than a dozen young men and women, the other to a much larger and more enthusiastic group of film students. There were no grades at UC–Santa Cruz.

My literature class was friendly enough but bored when I started to make comparisons between Australian poets, supported by a Literary Fund, remarkably lacking in neuroses; American poets (I singled out John Berryman and Sylvia Plath) alienated from a commercial society, reduced to teaching, sometimes driven to suicide; and British poets of an older, romantic generation snuffed out by the New Movement of Larkin and Amis, with its emphasis on urban realism. This left the class half-asleep and when I would arrive in the mornings, they were busy playing Bob Dylan, the Beatles, Pete Seeger, and the Rolling Stones. I decided that at thirty-seven I would be considered on old fogey if I disapproved of this and instead I began discussing the lyrics of rock and folk songs, monotonous as prayer wheels: the papers the students gave me based on the class discussions were seldom written but rather done in garish-colored illustrations or long, spun-out snakes of handwritten doggerel.

For the film course, I embarked on an ambitious plan, and here my students were very much in approval (this was the age of polarization, liberal youth, tribal in assuming Native American styles, with long hair, fringed jackets, and moccasins, carrying babies on their backs). I embarked, for Ernest Callenbach, the brilliant and bohemian editor in chief of the University of California Press, on a book, *The Films of Orson Welles,* which would, without the subject's customary interference, stem from my seminars and teachings of the contents of every movie he directed.

I had as my seminar guest the notable Welles colleague Richard Wilson, who delighted the students with his lively answers to questions. It was incumbent on me to invite my fellow (and senior in age and importance) Regents Professor Dwight Macdonald, then Pauline Kael's chief rival as the most celebrated film critic in America, author of the admired *Against the American Grain,* to join me on the platform and introduce an Orson Welles film.

I walked over to his house, larger and more comfortable than mine, to find a bearded, choleric man in late middle age, dressed in a sloppy button-down cardigan, checked Greenwich Village shirt, baggy corduroy pants, and incongruous suede shoes. He was wheezing slightly, evidently suffering from asthma, eyes watering; cheeks red.

He offered me no refreshment on this chilly, rainy afternoon, but instead, without inviting me to sit down, asked me gruffly what I wanted. I reminded him that I was his fellow Regents Professor and he snapped at me, asking how I, a mere whippersnapper, had conned anyone into giving me the appointment.

I told him, not without misgivings, that I had been picked from the ranks of Australian poets and critics for the honor; he snarled that there was no Australian literature and I must be an imposter. I told him that he would have to talk to Governor Reagan, who had signed the letter of approval, and he responded that the man was an idiot to take me.

I went on to mention some of our greatest poets, A. D. Hope, Judith Wright, and James McAuley, and our superb novelist Patrick White. Seeing an understandably blank face, reddening further by the minute, I switched the subject rapidly to film.

I soon discovered that this leader of movie criticism attacked almost everyone except the academic idols, Eisenstein, Pudovkin, D. W. Griffith. I told him I wanted him to address my class on Orson Welles. He said Welles made only one film. I replied that he had made several, and assumed he was referring to *Citizen Kane* and meant that Welles had made only one *good* film.

He glared at me and didn't answer. I asked him if he intended introducing *Citizen Kane* or *The Magnificent Ambersons,* Welles's second film, an elegy to a lost America of Stanley Steamers and gaslit balls. He replied that *Kane* was "an old German picture lit by a match," and that although it amounted to very little, *Ambersons* at least improved on Booth Tarkington's novel (of the decline of a midwestern family, with which it had nothing to do). He would, he said reluctantly, talk about it.

I couldn't let this pass. I told him to his face that he was wrong; that *Ambersons* followed the novel so completely that the entire opening narration, spoken by Welles, was drawn from Tarkington's text without a word changed; and that the only alteration from the novel itself was an enhancement of the character of Aunt Fanny, the flustered spinster who symbolized the sexual frustrations of the era, and was dazzlingly played by Agnes Moorehead on the screen.

"Rubbish, bumblepuppy, fiddlesticks," he exclaimed. "You are wrong, whatever-your-name-is from Down Under. You may have conned yourself into this job but you can't tell *me* about American literature."

"I *am* telling you," I replied. "And I may as well warn you, my film students have been reading the novel, seeing the film, and studying the screenplay. If you say anything that's incorrect, you'll be laughed at in class."

He wheezed; he muttered; he waved his hands at me in contempt; and I left. The seminar took place the following night. I was on my way to the lecture hall in driving rain when I saw him carrying an umbrella, in a snap-brim fedora hat and trench coat with collar turned up, sneaking like some elderly villain in a 1940s film noir, out of the library, looking furtively to right and left. He didn't see me in the darkness, and to make sure I hid behind a tree. From the glow of a lamp I could see a copy of *The Magnificent Ambersons* tucked under his right arm.

I introduced *Citizen Kane.* He dozed through most of it. Now it was his turn to introduce *Ambersons.* Without so much as a glance in my direction, he began by saying it was based "word for word on Booth Tarkington."

He got away with it that time but not the next. At a seminar a few nights later I asked him, with some misgivings, to introduce *The Lady from Shanghai*, Welles's confusing but electrifying melodrama about a corrupt lawyer who takes his wife and her sailor-lover on a sadistic yachting cruise from San Francisco to Mexico. He attacked the movie as rubbish, thus annoying the students, who were in love with its abandonment of an understandable plotline and its vividly exotic and surrealist imagery.

After he finished his diatribe I asked him if he didn't at least admire the cinematography of Charles Lawton, who, if he had been attending, he would have seen listed in the credits. "Charles Lawton!" he exclaimed angrily. "You idiot! He's not a cameraman, he's an actor!" I painstakingly spelled out the name as the audience burst into laughter. Red faced, he stumbled from the stage.

A few nights later, the chancellor gave a dinner party for him and Gloria, his wife. Like him, she affected the dress of a Greenwich Village bohemian with worry beads, a Mother Hubbard that went down to her ankles, and rope sandals.

The conversation turned to the polarization of America, the need for added police security for Governor Reagan's imminent visit to the campus, and the advent of such drug gurus as Timothy Leary. Nobody talked to Macdonald about the New York literary scene, and he became restive. Suddenly, he began to wheeze, and his face dropped into his soup. The academics present didn't so much as raise an eyebrow; presumably they thought he was drunk.

"He does this all the time," said Gloria Macdonald, "if he finds he's not the center of attention. It's all an act; he's faking."

"I'm not," came a wheezing voice from the soup plate. "I'm dying."

"Silly old fool! Sit up!" she commanded. The guests continued to eat as if nothing was happening.

It was therefore up to me, the outsider, to take the matter into my own hands. I urged the chancellor to call the campus paramedics. He looked at his wife, saying nothing; I pleaded with her to do something. Gloria Macdonald glared at me as if she could have killed me. America's most belligerent critic was still wheezing, asking for help, saying he was about to die.

I abandoned all etiquette and ran to the phone. The guests stared at me in astonishment at my sheer impertinence. The paramedics arrived with screaming sirens. As they carried Macdonald out on a stretcher, Gloria kept shouting, "You're wasting your time. He's just pretending. He's as fit as a fiddle!"

But he wasn't. He was narrowly snatched from death on arrival at the campus hospital. I had saved the life of a mortal enemy, and I was proud of it.

Soon after, following a disastrous lecture on film, to everyone's relief he and Gloria returned to New York, where his comments on Californian ignorance and the stupidity of the UC–Santa Cruz students and staff no doubt caused much merriment in intellectual circles.

Those were turbulent weeks. In the grip of the affair with my sad alcoholic lover, I moved from Los Angeles to San Francisco to Santa Cruz in ever increasing circles, but still managed, despite my disordered psyche, to give a well-received talk at a college banquet in my honor, the students laughing loudly at my Hollywood stories. Then at last I ended my romantic interlude without too much bitter recrimination.

I continued to prepare the book on the films of Orson Welles for the University of California Press and, in the process, embarked on what was to be the greatest adventure of my life. In 1942, shortly after Pearl Harbor, the unreliable genius had made a multifaceted movie in Brazil, *It's All True*. Never finished, it had vanished; I had to have this lost treasure; to achieve the find would put me on the map forever.

The story of its making was found easily. Abandoning *The Magnificent Ambersons*, enjoying the sexual opportunities offered during Rio Carnival time, shooting much documentary footage, Welles embarked also on the story of the *Jangadeiros*, the raft fishermen who, without a hull or compass, sailed their fragile balsa craft from the hump of Brazil to Rio to carry word to President Getúlio Vargas of their poverty-stricken condition.

During the re-creation of the Jangadeiros' arrival in Rio harbor, an incident occurred that caused the raft to overturn, and Jacare, the leader and a national hero, drowned in front of thousands of his fans. Welles, disguised as a washerwoman, fled, or he would most certainly have been lynched.

After much effort I found out that hundreds of cans of partly edited or unedited footage of the lost picture had lain for decades at RKO Studios, which was finally sold to Lucille Ball and Desi Arnaz's Desilu company. I made an appointment to see Miss Ball, who shuddered at the mention of

Welles's name. She said that his "Mardi Gras" footage was useless and that he still owed her fifty thousand dollars. She had hired him to make a pilot for a *Twilight Zone*–like series, which he had written and appeared in, entitled *The Fountain of Youth,* and he had squandered most of his budget on a lavish party to which she and her husband hadn't even been invited.

But she did tell me that the footage was housed at Paramount, and I soon found out that it lay stacked high in cans in the editing division, in the charge of an old studio cutter named Hazel Marshall. (The rest of this part of the story is told in chapter 1.)

In 1994, one Myron Myzel, with a group of others, had the effrontery to issue a laser disc of *It's All True's* surviving footage with the absurd claim that he had found the film for the first time.

After talking to several survivors of *Kane* and *Ambersons,* including my friend Joseph Cotten, Agnes Moorehead, and the director Richard Wilson, I knew I had to talk to Bernard Herrmann, the brilliant and erratic composer of the scores for both films, who was said to be inaccessible and a devilish old curmudgeon whom nobody liked. Everyone told me I wouldn't stand a chance with him, and then something happened—my luck again. A friend, Milton Lubowiski, owner of Larry Edmund's movie bookstore on Hollywood Boulevard, called to say that he had found the original score of *Salammbô,* the fake opera in *Kane,* in his stockroom; it had been thought to have vanished and was not in the music file on the film, kept at the still extant RKO offices.

Herrmann was said to have been looking for it for years; he hadn't known that the studio had auctioned the only copy in World War II to raise money for the troops. Somehow, it had wound up in Milton's shop, and he gave it to me as my trump card to force Herrmann's hand.

I called the *monstre damné* at his home and he growled that he never gave interviews. Then I told him that he would talk to me. He screamed at me, "Why?" I said I had something he wanted very badly. "What the fuck could you have that I would possibly want?" he asked, and with great pleasure I told him.

He declared me a fucking liar and said that anyway he had several copies of the work himself. I replied that *he* was lying, not I; that Milton Lubowiski had given me the only copy of *Salammbô* in existence.

"Who the fuck is Milton Lubowiski?" he screamed.

I told him. "How the hell would he have the money to pay for it?"

"It went for peanuts."

"Peanuts schmeanuts. I want that fucker. It belongs to me."

"It doesn't. It *did* belong to RKO but they chose to auction it. It belongs to me, and me alone."

"Whaddya mean it belongs to you? Who the fuck are you anyway?"

"I'm Professor Charles Higham of UC–Santa Cruz."

"Shit. How much dya want for it?"

"It isn't for sale."

"You'll give it to me then."

"No, I won't. Unless . . ."

"Unless what?"

"Unless you give me the source for the libretto, in French. The first words are 'Ah, cruelle.'"

"Oh, that. We'll see."

"No source, no deal."

Herrmann agreed to meet me next day at the Hollywood Roosevelt Hotel, in those days a seedy, tarnished shadow of its once almost glamourous self. We met in the lobby. I carried a copy of the score—not the original—in a cardboard cylinder under my arm.

Thickset, pot bellied, with a mop of gray hair and heavy horn-rimmed spectacles, the great composer-conductor bristled with the expected degree of hostility. His flabby pectoral muscles jiggled under an unflatteringly tight T-shirt worn under the jacket of a sagging double-breasted gray suit, and his voice, even more than on the telephone, had the shrill, whining emphasis of a vacuum cleaner.

I took out the opera score and he tried to snatch it from me; an unseemly struggle ensued as I refused to give it to him and I warned him not to continue as the pages might be torn.

People began to stare, including the uniformed doorman. Insisting once again on having him reveal the source of the libretto, I extracted from him the words "an obscure work by Racine." Then he snatched the copy, thinking it was the original, and left.

I had little time to spare as I was due to give a lecture at Santa Cruz that night. I took a cab to the downtown public library, an ancient firetrap filled with deadbeats and the stench of urine. There I found a concordance to the works of Racine and turned to "Ah, cruelle." Of course the libretto wasn't drawn from an "obscure work by Racine" but from *Phaedra,* his most famous play.

My next target was George Fanto, the cameraman of *It's All True.* I had an instinct he would have kept all the still photographs, which could make up a montage showing what the film would have been if it had been completed; there would be no chance, after my contretemps with Hazel Marshall, of Paramount yielding any pictures that had survived.

George Fanto was now, of all things, president of Daks Slacks in New York, and in no time I was on a plane there to see him. I walked into his palatial office high up in a skyscraper tower, and he pointed proudly to a desk covered in pictures stacked high, unforgettably re-creating the entire lost masterwork.

My semester at Santa Cruz over, I had no alternative but to return to Sydney and write the book there for months. I was in correspondence with Ernest Callenbach, drafting and redrafting the manuscript according to his inspired suggestions, wishing I could be doing the job in California, with promised access to the RKO files maintained by Richard Wilson. Instead, I had to continue at a disadvantage but, thanks to some local string-pulling, was able to see the Welles films again and again, describing every image. I was afraid that my big scoop on *It's All True* would be revealed too early. It wasn't, and at the end of the work, I got an assignment from Penguin publishers to write a book, *When the Pictures Talked and Sang,* about the birth of sound movies. I moved permanently to America to correct the proofs and wait for the publication of *The Films of Orson Welles.*

At right, top: Charles Higham with his birth mother, Lady Josephine Higham, 1931

At right, bottom: Charles Higham as a child, walking in London with his father and stepmother, Lady Jill Higham, 1937

Charles Higham as a teenager in London, ca. 1948

Mary Miles Minter, 1938 (Bison Archives)

Marlene Dietrich and Elia Kazan, 1954 (Bison Archives)

Alfred Hitchcock, 1955 (Bison Archives)

Howard Hughes, ca. 1958 (Bison Archives)

Errol Flynn, 1958 (Bison Archives)

Joan Fontaine, ca. 1958 (Bison Archives)

Olivia de Havilland, 1963 (Bison Archives)

Mae West, ca. 1959 (Bison Archives)

Elvis Presley, 1960s (Bison Archives)

Mary Pickford, 1960s (Bison Archives)

10

I spent several weeks in New York, which I still loved and where I felt more at home than in Los Angeles. There I developed my first serious American contact: with Pauline Kael, then the doyenne of film criticism, who as we know had been introduced to me by my agent and her close friend Marcia Nasatir, later head of Columbia Pictures, over the long distance phone call to New York, at the Thanksgiving party at Marcia's Hollywood house. Pauline had given me her good wishes and said she knew my articles in *Sight and Sound* and *Film Quarterly* and liked my writing. Aware that my book on Welles was imminent, she was at work on one of her own, focusing specifically on *Citizen Kane,* its screenplay, production, and political content.

She had received a brush-off from Welles and Bogdanovich and was out for their blood. I spent evenings at her large, surprisingly gloomy and austere apartment on West End Avenue, a contrast to the cheerful, brightly lit flat on Park Avenue South where I was living with a group of crazy gay Argentineans.

She was having an edgy affair with the director Irvin Kershner; oddly for a critic, she became romantically involved with directors, later, with Robert Altman. This seemed to me a mistake, since how could she judge their work objectively during or after a sexual relationship?

I told her that once the Welles book was published I planned to return to Australia as the pace and tension of American life were difficult for me to deal with. Whereupon she told me I was mad, that I had everything going for me, and that she would arrange a job for me as film critic of some newspaper or other in the provinces, with a chance of promotion to a major critic in a big city if I made good. I was baffled. How could she possibly organize such an appointment?

I asked my new acquaintances, the critics Stanley Kauffmann, of the *New Republic,* and Andrew Sarris, of the *Village Voice,* and they explained that she had so much influence and fame that what they called the Pauline Doctrine was law; but the conditions of fiefdom were menacing. If I took such a job I must be a "Paulette" and convey her opinions only; I must check with her before reaching a judgment on any film. This was of course unacceptable.

Stefan Kanfer of *Time* magazine confirmed these statements. When I sat with Pauline watching awards shows on television, she would condemn or praise the nominees with an opinionated if humorous certainty that allowed me no room to say anything; she simply assumed I'd agree with her. Such egomania was astonishing; I would have expected it in a Hollywood executive or star but not in a former Berkeley, California, intellectual and art house movie theater manager turned *New Yorker* sophisticate.

One night I dared to mention that I had made a friend of the distinguished actress Maureen Stapleton in a game of charades, on an Amtrak train since Stapleton was afraid of flying, and Pauline glared at me, saying that the star had ignored her in the street and was definitely no good. I mentioned an early crush on Geraldine Fitzgerald and she dismissed her with a sneer, saying she was far too fierce on the screen, when fierceness wasn't called for.

I realized sadly that a lasting friendship with this remarkable woman was impossible, that there could be no give and take in the relationship. I was told that the reason she lost her director lovers was because she had dared to lay down the law on their work and they too were egomaniacs. She felt she had the right to correct their artistic vision, which no creative person could tolerate. Later, she would lose Robert Altman because of this fault.

My book *The Films of Orson Welles* appeared, and it was followed by a full-scale attack on me by the then-hot young director Peter Bogdanovich on the front page of the *New York Times* Sunday Arts and Leisure section. This was more than I could have asked for; it made a book that might have existed only as an obscure scholarly work nationally known. Bogdanovich attacked me on every level, and I figured ways in which to respond. I began by thanking him for making me famous, by telegram.

In the meantime, Raymond Sokolov, film critic of *Newsweek,* was, I was told, preparing a review but might be unable to write it as he was taking off to Europe. I called the magazine and lied that I was his British cousin and had to reach him at once, before he flew to London. Reluctantly, they gave me his telephone number in Brooklyn.

I called him and said I must see him at once to discuss my major revelations. He said he was busy packing. I kept talking until he said to come visit him. I did, he was cordial and full of praise for my work, and he wrote a splashy piece, not just a review but an encomium for me as the "film detective" and discoverer of *It's All True.* Overnight I was on the American map, but I needed to do something more. I wrote a humorous interview with myself, with the *Times* in mind, asking me why Peter Bogdanovich called my book destructive and a pack of lies. I answered that the reason was that Bogdanovich was writing a book on Orson Welles that would be all the things my book was not. Dirty pool? Quite so, but why let the public into the secrets of competitive authors?

I delivered the piece to the *Times* by hand, and it appeared uncut and unaltered on the front page of Arts and Leisure and created so complete a stir that I was booked on the *Today* show, and all local New York shows, to talk about it.

One radio interviewer rushed me onto his program without reading the book. He told me he had no idea what to ask me and would I write the questions for him? He handed me a yellow legal pad, and I wrote out the first question: Why do people say this is the best book of its kind published since World War II? He read the question without batting an eyelash.

On another show, the guest of most importance was Sir Michael Redgrave. The dizzy hostess asked him how, with so heavy a schedule as actor and director, he found time to father such lovely daughters as Vanessa and Lynn. "It didn't take very long you know," was his laconic reply, and his interlocutor didn't laugh.

I returned to Los Angeles to prepare for my flight back to Sydney. I was packing my suitcases when the phone rang in my apartment. Seymour Peck, the all-powerful editor of the *New York Times* Sunday Theater section, was on the line: Would I please return to New York at once?

I was on the next plane. When I arrived at the *Times* offices, I found Peck sitting in the corner of an enormous *Front Page* office, where dozens of men and women in that pre–word processor age were tapping away at big office Royal and Remington typewriters, oilskin covers lying beside them on their desks under glaring ceiling lights; the noise was like that of a thousand woodpeckers; the heat was stifling.

Peck and his charming assistant Guy Flatley greeted me warmly and told me that my interview with myself was unique and unprecedented in *Times* history. They also said that Rex Reed, their chief Hollywood feature writer, was leaving them to join the *Chicago Tribune* newspaper chain as syndicated columnist and there was a sudden vacancy on the West Coast. It wasn't a paid job, just that of a stringer, but they anticipated there could be a flow of freelance assignments and would I stay on in America and not go home?

I was hardly able to speak. I had suddenly reached the top of my profession: no other newspaper counted for as much; my mere presence in its pages put me on a pinnacle. I enjoyed a warm lunch with the newspaper's film critic Vincent Canby and met with the Book Review's editors. Pauline Kael called with her warmest congratulations. I cabled the *Sydney Morning Herald*'s editor Colin Bingham to tell him I would not be coming home and asked my Sydney flatmate Colin Baskerville to ship over a few items of furniture. It never occurred to me that despite the fact I didn't drive, had no car, had almost no money, and would be paid only two hundred dollars an article, I would be unable to succeed at the job of a lifetime.

I had to find other sources of income to sustain me in my modest digs on Hollywood Boulevard. The Australian *TV Times* gave me assignments and secured for me a visa that allowed me to work as its Hollywood correspondent. I of course had the contract from Penguin Books in London to write *When the Pictures Talked and Sang,* the account of the first years of talking pictures between 1928 and 1932. I managed to persuade the American Film Institute, then housed in a marble palace once owned by the murdered oil millionaire Edward Doheny (the killing had taken place on the premises), to advance me the money to conduct taped oral histories, under the aegis of the Louis B. Mayer Foundation, of two good and true friends, the great cinematographers James Wong Howe and Lee Garmes. Both are included in my pioneer work *Hollywood Cameramen,* a critically acclaimed collection of interviews with men whose creative contribution to movies had been largely ignored.

One of film historians' most wished for targets was Mary Miles Minter, the silent movie star whose involvement in the 1922 murder of her beloved director William Desmond Taylor had helped bring her career to an end.

She had refused to see any writer, until Milton Lubowiski of Larry Edmunds Bookshop recommended me for the assignment of writing her life story and she agreed. This was exciting; apart from the Black Dahlia, the Taylor murder was the greatest unsolved crime in Hollywood history.

Minter answered the doorbell of her Santa Monica house herself. No more than five feet tall, and at least three hundred pounds, she was Baby Jane with her ringleted blonde wig and huge blue eyes, cheeks lighted up by round applications of rouge, cupid bow painted lips, triple chins, and a baby blue puff-sleeved 1938 dress decorated with enormous marigolds.

She ushered me into a living room that might have been that of an Oxford don. Books were piled up everywhere, many with stained page tops and silk markers, or bound in red leather; paintings were of horse fairs or British country scenes. A clubfooted German maid named Emmy limped in and out. Soon, Emmy brought in Earl Grey tea and British cake and cookies on a silver tray.

Minter was anxious to establish, to a former Regents Professor at UC–Santa Cruz, her literary credentials. She began by showing me passages of favorite verse by Whittier, Longfellow, and Ella Wheeler Wilcox; I would have preferred Whitman, Lowell, and W. S. Merwin. She recited a doggerel she had written, about the cliffs above Malibu "crumbling, the ocean was mumbling."

She began to talk into the tape recorder, which she looked at as if it were a bomb about to explode. Finally, she got around to the murder, and I put in a new cassette. She lied that it had been committed by a runaway teenager who had escaped from arrest after robbing a gas station down the street. Piling fantasy on fantasy, she described going to the mortuary after Taylor died, seeing him lying on a marble slab, and hearing him speak her name. I became convinced as she rambled on that she had killed him, though the general view in Hollywood was that her mother, the formidable Charlotte Shelby, had done the deed.

There was enough here for the basis of a book, but I didn't get around to it for thirty years. Next morning I heard the loud honking of a car horn outside my apartment building, followed by a nervous rapping at my door.

I opened it and saw Emmy, Minter's maid, shaking and pale. She said that Miss Minter, whom I could see crammed into a gray Volkswagen outside, wanted the cassette back at once: she had decided not to go ahead with the project. Luckily, the night before I had taken the tape to a specialist laboratory that copied it; I handed over the copy. It was, of course, under-handed of me, but why deny posterity the interview of a lifetime? I had to wait for Minter to die before I used it; a year after the interview the origi-nal tape was stolen in the course of my being held up at knifepoint at an-other Hollywood Boulevard apartment; but more of this later.

When the Pictures Talked and Sang was canceled when my editor at Penguin died at a very young age of cancer and his bosses lost interest in the project. Instead, I embarked on two books at the same time, a life of Flo-renz Ziegfeld, for the Chicago publisher Regnery, and *Hollywood at Sunset,* an account of the decline of the film industry at that time.

Hollywood at Sunset was commissioned by Peter Kemeny, the inspired young Hungarian-born editor at Saturday Review Press who was widely admired in New York. I decided on the bold move to interview the surviv-ing eight members of the Hollywood Ten, the blacklisted writers of the early 1950s who had refused to testify against their fellows during J. Parnell Thomas's witch hunt. Many years later, John Updike used much of my material, with my enthusiastic approval, in his novel *In the Beauty of the Lilies,* and I received a very warm postcard from him, something to trea-sure always.

Of the unfriendly eight, Ring Lardner Jr., son of the famous *New Yorker* humorist, was the most impressive. He told me that when he was sent to a Danbury, Connecticut, prison farm for failing to testify against his fellows, he ran into J. Parnell Thomas, jailed for padding the commit-tee accounts, on his knees scraping the excrement from the poultry cages. "Still clearing out the chicken shit I see," Lardner told him.

John Howard Lawson was grievously handicapped, hobbling on a cane, a shadow of his former brilliant self. Albert Maltz was very well organized, his filing system on the case meticulously maintained; I had only to ask a question to see him open a metal drawer and pull out documents support-ing the facts. I asked him and the others why, since being a Communist was not a crime, and America had been a World War II ally of Russia and on the side of the Stalin-backed Loyalist government of Spain during the Civil War, they hadn't, when questioned by the committee, admitted membership of the party. They told me they hadn't been members, where-upon I was compelled to say that I had their party cards. At imminent risk of a punch on the nose, I produced them. It made no difference; they maintained their position, citing the First, not the Fourth, Amendment.

The hearings records were at the University of Southern California, and they proved to be a surprise, chiefly because so many major namers of names were not revealed as such in the press, even by the liberal critics.

Jose Ferrer, so sly in films like *Whirlpool* and *The Caine Mutiny,* turned out to be the ultimate fink; he named almost more names than anyone. Shockingly, Lee J. Cobb named such intimate friends as Sam Jaffe, to whom years later I had to tell sadly of this.

I was living at the time at Peyton Hall, pretentiously named after Grace Metalious's steamy best seller, *Peyton Place,* on Hollywood Boulevard, a few blocks east of the scene of my encounter with Mary Miles Minter's maid. My neighbor was the sad, broken daughter of Walter Winchell. I received letters addressed to the famous songwriter Sammy Fain, who apparently had fallen on hard times and had lived recently at this improbable, humble location. Opening one of the envelopes by accident, I saw that it contained a gangland threat over gambling debts. I sent the letters on, marked Not at This Address, and began humming Fain's tunes, "Secret Love" and "Love Is a Many Splendored Thing," hoping he had found better quarters.

After a brief affair with a man I will call Gregory, a very attractive blond who provoked a pleasing degree of envy in my gay friends, I was alone. One night I came home to find a young man in my kitchen, going through my cutlery and looking in vain for something worth stealing. He had next to him a box containing many of my taped interviews, of which I had luckily kept copies, including the indispensable Mary Miles Minter conversation.

The burglar wasn't someone I had picked up; he was a stranger, straight, and not to me good looking. He held a carving knife at my throat and asked me for my wallet. It contained only five dollars and he groaned when he looked into it.

I talked to him humbly, quietly saying I was a visitor from Australia, a technique used by a friend of mine on a similar psychopath, and it worked.

He crawled out and over the garage by the way he must have come in. My landlord's son, a college quarterback, caught him in a tackle in the street and sent him flying.

He was arrested and taken to the county jail; my belongings were held as exhibits for five years, despite every effort to retrieve them. A police officer picked me up and drove me to the courthouse, slyly suggesting I had picked the man up and that it was an inside job. My showing him the wedding ring I still wore for Norine didn't change his tune. As I gave evidence at the trial, a look from the defendant, who went to prison for six months, told me I had better watch out.

The police called soon afterward to say that he had escaped; they could offer no protection and outrageously suggested I buy a gun. I was about to move when late one night the doorbell rang and I regret to say I panicked, certain the man had come back to kill me.

Instead, as I opened the door, armed theatrically with a carving knife, I saw a former lover from Sydney, an Austrian boxer I will call Franz. We moved at once to a new address and took off to New York, where my editor of *Hollywood at Sunset,* Peter Kemeny, lent us his apartment while he went to Budapest to visit his mother.

Ignorant of Manhattan life, I had expected a modest place but not the filthy, roach-ridden dump we moved into. Indeed, in a Kafkaesque moment, I found a cockroach on my toothbrush the first day we woke up.

Next morning, I heard a loud banging on the front door. In those days, perhaps still, tenants kept a metal bar resting inside so that anyone who broke in would send it hurling to the floor, thus attracting attention. Franz and I, sleeping in separate rooms, and both naked after making love the night before, failed to get up and the bar crashed down. The landlord burst in with two policemen, one of whom, addressing me with "wake up sleeping beauty," pressed a gun to my forehead.

He accused us of squatting; it seemed that Kemeny had failed to report to the landlord that he had lent us the place. Only by waking up his secretary—luckily he had left me her phone number—were we able to escape arrest.

We got on the next plane to Las Vegas. While we were watching Paul Anka's dinner show, a man at our table managed to steal Franz's favorite ring off his finger. The two events broke our relationship, but its ending was memorable. Franz, who was only reluctantly gay, spent a last night with me at our new apartment. At dawn he asked me to stand naked inside the door of our bedroom, for a very long time in the half-light. Then crying bitterly, he picked up the suitcases he had packed while I was sleeping— and left me forever.

The episodes had a tragic aftermath. For reasons unknown, Peter

Kemeny, after his return from Budapest, threw himself in front of a subway train at the Forty-second Street station and died instantly.

Somehow I managed to fit in my *New York Times* assignments, of which the most memorable was a trip to San Francisco to interview Clint Eastwood and the director Don Siegel on location for *Dirty Harry,* a precursor of the primitive and bloody films of today. I liked both of them. Eastwood was everything a man should be: confident, strong, nobody's fool, he knew the names of all the crew members' wives and children and remembered their birthdays. He was the ultimate team player, with the rangy build of a quarterback. And yet I sensed a ruthlessness in his character and wondered if he had that degree of tenderness and vulnerability that could ensure him lasting success with women.

Siegel was marvelously grizzled, as rough and tough as his pictures, a no-nonsense prizefighter in the ring of life. Watching the two men work on stunts—at one stage, Eastwood actually jumped from a ramp onto a passing bus—was to see American machismo at its best.

Ziegfeld was a challenge. Of all the people who had known or worked with him, only a handful were still alive. His daughter, Patricia Ziegfeld Stephenson, was as protective as one would expect; his Girl Friday, the legendary secretary Goldie, had disappeared. Luckily, Laura Wilk, an old-time agent I ran into at a party, knew that she had left New York and was living in Santa Monica. I went to see her.

It was love at first sight on both sides. She was small, perky, full of life; the discomforts and pains of old age had not quelled her spirits. She had kept diaries and appointment books going back to the 1920s, including a vivid entry of the first night of *Show Boat* on Broadway on December 27, 1927. Without these records I would never have had a book. She told me all she knew except for the details of one event: Ziegfeld's act of murder. Later I found out that he had killed a rival for his mistress Lillian Lorraine's affections with a knobkerrie, a carved walking stick. Influence with the New York police had saved him from imprisonment and the electric chair.

Goldie and I went to the old Ziegfeld theater, the New Amsterdam, today the long-term home of *The Lion King,* but in 1971 a dirty and run-down grind movie house. She hadn't set foot there since 1927, yet the moment we reached the producer's long since abandoned offices on the seventh floor, she remembered everything. She led me to the cubbyhole where the telephone girl sat, to the coproducer Charles Dillingham's pokey office, and at last to Ziegfeld's far from spacious room, still with the original, ugly bottle-green paint on the walls and the view of the New Amsterdam electric sign through windows that probably hadn't been washed since.

"That," Goldie said, "is where Victor Herbert chased me down the stairs, and there's the spot where Jerome Kern pinched my fanny." They didn't succeed with her, nor did Ziegfeld, and she became known as "the last virgin on Broadway." We went down to the manager's office on the fifth floor where he showed us a spittoon and said it was Ziegfeld's and that this, not the seventh floor, was the impresario's. Goldie corrected him; the spittoon belonged, she said, to the vaingloriously named theater tycoon Abraham Lincoln Erlanger and his partner, Marc Klaw.

Suddenly, Goldie remembered that we hadn't visited the legendary Ziegfeld Roof, where spectacular shows were put on after the Follies, at midnight. It was pitch dark up on the eleventh floor, but without a flashlight Goldie walked straight to the bank of light switches for the first time in forty-three years and turned them on, flooding the rooms with startlingly sharp illumination. The Roof was still used as a rehearsal theater for Broadway shows.

We walked through the old dressing rooms, used now as prop storerooms by the theater's owners. A carpenter came over and told us that one of his men had seen a beautiful girl standing in a doorway while he was working, with enormous violet eyes, dressed in the style of the twenties, with the word OLIVE on a gold sash across her chest. She had appeared several times, holding a blue bottle with white crystals in it. Later he came across a book of photographs buried in an old cupboard and recognized the famous showgirl and actress Olive Thomas, who had committed suicide decades before, by poison from a blue bottle.

Feeling a need to relate to the living, I decided to visit a brothel for the first time. The film critic Carlos Clarens had told me of such a place on Seventeenth Street and Fifth Avenue, and I walked there from my hotel, the Waldorf, one dark and drizzly afternoon.

The building was a beaux arts structure circa 1909, its front of crumbling stucco, its doorway pretentiously reached up a flight of steps. On the ground floor I was greeted by a man at a desk who explained to me that women were available on his level, men upstairs, and which did I want? I wanted both but decided on a man. I paid fifty dollars in advance and walked upstairs. The narrow staircase was carpeted with worn red felt and flanked by pictures of naked gay and straight couples making love.

I was astonished by what I found at the top. I had expected a custodian with a book of photographs to choose from but instead I saw a long dark corridor with black curtains blotting out the daylight and only the palest glimmer of ceiling bulbs to relieve the gloom. Along the walls were standing at least thirty half-naked men, all young and attractive, ranging from the very lean to bodybuilders. They had a look of sullen but sexy resignation, on sale to men who probably were mostly middle-aged and unappealing. More than one, seeing me, perked up, and I was at once drawn to a dark youth of perhaps twenty-five, with the look of a young Warren Beatty, bare like the others to the waist.

He led me by the hand into a room with a large double bed and a single candle flickering in a silver stick. I expected passivity and perhaps a refusal to kiss, but instead, relieved no doubt that I was in good shape, he attacked me like a lover. He unbuttoned my shirt and kicked off his boots, then pulled me down on the bed, stroking my body with surprising tenderness. He groaned when a bell went off an hour later, announcing that my time was up. We kissed in warm farewell and I said I would return but soon after I met an antic Cuban and began a brief romantic affair. I didn't go back.

A profile I wrote of Robert Young, who discussed his alcoholism with me when his press agent said he would not, appeared in the Sunday *New York Times* Theater section without a word altered, and with the enthusiastic approval of Seymour Peck. I was assured of a future there, though the assignments were few and far between.

Back in Hollywood, I cemented a friendship with the director Curtis Harrington, though his addiction to astrology and his racism were alien to me, and I found a new lover, Perry Paulding, while dining with an Alka-Seltzer heir, Butler Miles, at the Gallery Room in West Hollywood.

Perry was lean, slight, dark—exactly my type. He had aspirations to be an actor, and he certainly had the looks, the physique, and the temperament. He needed a home; he wasn't a hustler but he was worried about being unsupported. In turn, I needed a companion and sex on a regular basis.

He had just broken off an affair with a famous musical star who lived in Hawaii and spoke of him warmly, always a good sign. We talked of his moving in with me to my apartment building in Sunset Boulevard, today the Mondrian Hotel. But first I needed time to think this one through, and I took off to Hawaii for a week's vacation.

I had a double motive: a youth I had been involved with briefly in Palm Springs and with whom I used to sunbathe on the roof of the Hollywood YMCA asked a number of eligible gays to meet him in Honolulu when he would select one of us as his lover for seven days there. Several of us answered the call and to my annoyance he chose another man.

In a bad temper, I walked the length of the beach from my Outrigger Hotel, in moonlight, past the dark ocean and the white curling lines of the surf. Music floated from the various restaurants and nightclubs and my spirit began to feel at ease. At last I reached the Tiki Hut, a gay bar at the very end, within close sight of Diamond Head, situated up a flight of wooden steps and built like a native house of bamboo, with a thatched roof. There I saw a very attractive man in his twenties, nursing a Harvey Wallbanger. In minutes he suggested we leave together, and in thirty more we were in bed at my hotel. We scarcely left there for a week, so completely impassioned that a maid's daily appearance to clean up was a maddening interruption. I had never felt so alive, or conscious of my body, until at last he left for his home in Seattle and I never saw him again.

Back in Los Angeles, I had a memorable meeting with the cinematographer Robert Surtees, for yet another book project, on Ava Gardner. I now had three in the works. He told me that Gardner and Grace Kelly, her costar in *Mogambo,* which he shot in Africa, had arrived in Rome and he had been asked to take care of them.

To his amazement both wanted to be installed in a brothel, Kelly as a pianist, Gardner as a prostitute. The arrangement was made and the future Princess Grace began tinkling away at the ivories as clients went into rooms with beautiful women.

Each dubbed herself a movie star, and when a sailor went into the room where Gardner lay naked waiting for him, he was horrified and ran down the stairs screaming at Surtees, "Shit, that *was* Ava Gardner." He couldn't make love to so famous a woman. Ava spent the night in a state of frustration.

On February 7, 1971, eleven days before my fortieth birthday, I received a phone call from the *New Yorker.* A checker on Pauline Kael's forthcoming book on *Citizen Kane* said that Kael had given her my number and could I tell her the exact dimensions of the living room of Xanadu, the Florida residence of Charles Foster Kane? At that moment the apartment building began to tremble and there was a great roaring; the earth was groaning. It was as if a huge angry dog were shaking my flat.

Looking out the window, I saw the water from the swimming pool splashing into the courtyard and the sky filled with colored streaks from the transformers. It was a great earthquake, the most violent to strike Los Angeles since 1933.

The *New Yorker* checker asked me if I had heard her question. I told her I was in the middle of an earthquake, and she said she was sorry but she was on a very tight deadline. I was about to curse her when the line went dead.

I kept a breakfast date at Denny's on Sunset, treading past broken glass with my friend Jac McAnelly, and I went to a brunch party at the home of the Australian architect Norman Parker.

Perry, who had moved in with me by now, called from his home in Oklahoma City to express his concern. It wasn't the concern of a man afraid he might have lost a meal ticket; it was the concern of a lover.

This great beauty and magnificent sex companion was deeply vulnerable, afraid of the future, and tenderly anxious to please me, though capable of turning on me at times with outbursts of violent temper.

These increased after he moved in, but on the whole we had a happy relationship, based on mutual respect and humor, and sexual compatibility. But then Perry began to bring in company for threesomes, and I was a little stuffy and jealous about that, even though I went through vigorously enough with these random erotic encounters.

Suddenly, he announced that we had been offered the use for one month of an East Side townhouse in New York; the owner was a famous sports star, the idol of millions of American schoolboys. Perry had, he said, been the man's lover a year before; they had broken up but remained friends, and the man would be away in Europe.

Just before leaving Los Angeles, on the cold but sunny day of March 15, 1971, I was amazingly lucky again. I never read *Variety* on a daily basis, but a few days before, for some reason, I did pick up a copy and read, in an obscure paragraph at the foot of a page, that Nicholas Benton, head of Time-Life Books, was embarking on a history of the American film on phonograph records, each disc to be narrated by a star. A Los Angeles interviewer had yet to be appointed.

I instantly called Benton in New York and told him I was the only man for the job. Amused, he flew to Los Angeles to see who this pushy Anglo-Australian might be, and I joined him at the swimming pool of the Century Plaza Hotel.

I rattled off a long list of stars and directors and studio heads who would undoubtedly talk to me. Benton, an amusing, witty, and intensely sophisticated man who had an endless string of jokes about the activities of hard hats and referred to the afterlife as "that big studio in the sky," became an instant friend and hired me on the spot.

Perry and I were reasonably comfortable at the sporting idol's house. I was out much of the time, traveling to Rochester, where at George Eastman House in conditions of great luxury the genial curator James Card showed me long-lost movies on superb 35 mm prints for my Doubleday book *The Art of the American Film*. I also began interviews with New York figures for Time-Life: the haughty Elia Kazan, who called the interview an audience as if he were the pope; Mrs. Ben Hecht; the enchanting Lillian Gish; Richard Lamparski, of the *Whatever Became Of?* books, sharing an apartment on East Thirty-ninth Street with an enormous shaggy dog called Baby Dumpling; Morton DaCosta, gay director of *The Music Man*; and the critic Elliott Stein, who one night took me out with no less than William Burroughs, creator of *The Naked Lunch*.

I had expected Burroughs to be a wild-haired, dressed-down, staring-eyed, madman-genius; instead, I met a somber, aging man with the look of a tired bank manager, dressed of all things in a gray woolen suit, a white, well-starched shirt, and a plain blue tie of the kind favored by presidents. Even more amazing, this guru of the sexually bizarre expressed shock at finding erect penises in gay magazines. Where had he been?

One night I came home late from dinner with Nicholas Benton and his adorable wife, Kitty. The wine, gossip, and in-jokes had flowed wonderfully and I was in the best of moods. But when I arrived at the wrought iron gate and the glass front door I felt something was amiss.

When I found the door open I knew I was right. I walked into the living room and saw Perry, very pale, being held at gunpoint by a youth of at most seventeen. The boy said that the sporting idol had promised him blackmail money and he hadn't been paid. Where, he asked me, was the safe and the combination to it?

Perry said he had protested we didn't know and I seconded the statement, and truthfully. I also mentioned that there had been numerous phone calls at night from others to whom the house's owner owed sums of money. I added that we too were looking for the cash, and that was the real reason we were house-sitting.

The youth, warning us not to move, began searching shelves and behind screens looking for the safe. Finally, he gave up and, evidently believing our story, left. He told us not to call the police, and we didn't. After all, the cops and their sons were probably fans of our host.

We stayed on for a time. There was no device to switch off the phone ring, and I dared not disconnect it as the *Times* and Time-Life might call at any time. The answering machine was crammed with more threats, but nobody else broke in. I toured Chicago and Detroit for *Hollywood at Sunset* and continued research for *Ziegfeld,* then returned to Rochester for more films while Perry returned to Los Angeles.

My diary of that year fails to tell me the date of a horrifying shock. Perry, restless at our apartment, had flown to Oklahoma City to visit his parents. There, he apparently took up with a boy several years his junior; then he disappeared. A relative called me and asked if I had seen him. I said I had just returned to Los Angeles after two months back East and had not. A few days later someone called to say he had been found dead. He had been strangled, sewn into a canvas sack, and dumped into the Oklahoma River. The murderer was never found.

I was dazed, unable to function properly for several days; and yet somehow I had to continue working. I interviewed the famous film composer Max Steiner, who greeted me outside his hillside residence in white silk pajamas at three in the afternoon, smoking an enormous cigar, and brought me into the house to hear his lilting score for *A Summer Place* that, his wife complained, he played day and night and "never wanted to hear anybody else's music." "They're all hacks," he said, cheerfully ignoring his extensive borrowings from other composers (the *Now, Voyager* theme was from Borodin).

As if I didn't have enough to do, I had some time before preparing for KPFK, a radio program in which I would appear with my *Times* colleague Stephen Farber and the film industry specialist John Mahoney, talking of current movies. The only sour interviewee was the director

John Schlesinger, a British snob with fake proletarian sympathies who complained because in our cramped studio space he had to sit next to me, not facing me, at the microphone. John Wayne was, by contrast, magnificently unfussy. Despite his politics, to the right of Mussolini's, and his support of the Green Berets in Vietnam, I found him exactly as I wanted him to be: so huge I could stand behind him and not be seen, a sweet-tempered, genial American giant.

I interviewed him for the Time-Life history of Westerns at Universal, where he was shooting a picture. He was in an air-conditioned trailer, the heat outside 110 degrees. Concerned that the hum of the air conditioner would affect the recording, he turned it off. He had us both take off our shirts, and we conducted the interview as if in a Turkish bath. And a magnificent interview it was. I had nothing to do except listen.

Lew Ayres, star of the great *All Quiet on the Western Front,* was my first subject for the Time-Life war movie album. He had been a pacifist in World War II so the choice seemed ironically apt. Although, he said, he had been shocked into his belief when he studied the horrors of the Western front for his part in the film, he admitted to me for the first time off tape that he knew he could never kill a man. It astounded him that young boys who were scarcely out of high school could actually plunge a bayonet into another man's belly or blow his brains out. Too kind and gentle for this world, he was happily isolated in his Brentwood house, all chintz and fumed oak and thick carpets, muffling him against the harsh realities outside.

Ayres's former wife Ginger Rogers would, we hoped, introduce the disc devoted to musicals. We located her at the pleasantly alliterative Rogers Rogue River Ranch, Route One, Oregon. I called there to ask if I might speak to the star.

A pleasant woman's voice answered. She introduced herself as Leila, Ginger's mother, who had appeared with her memorably in Billy Wilder's *Lolita*-ish comedy *The Major and the Minor.* She had infamously been the right-wing bell ringer of the J. Parnell Thomas Un-American Activities Committee, and I hoped she hadn't seen my book *Hollywood at Sunset,* which treated her accordingly. She hadn't, of course, and she proved cordial.

She said that Ginger was in transit and rattled off a detailed schedule, as if she were living it herself. She said that Miss Rogers had been in Chicago, staying at the Ritz-Carlton Hotel until just one hour before the present conversation, and that she was now at O'Hare Airport, where an

American Airlines flight would take her to New York for a gathering of J. C. Penney executives whom she would address at the Waldorf Astoria Ballroom (she was JCP's chief proselytizer). First she would check into a Towers suite and the address would take place at exactly 8 p.m., followed by a banquet. At precisely 11 p.m., she said, Miss Rogers would return to her suite, and at 9 a.m. she would be wakened by her secretary and maid and would proceed to sign photographs at the headquarters Manhattan store before lunch. Her voice retaining a low-pitched monotonous flatness, Leila, the terror of Communists, went on for half an hour until she had her daughter in Washington. As it turned out, Time-Life Books never did manage to get Ginger to sit still for a taping.

Fred Astaire, her partner in the delectable camp musicals of the 1930s, was available. A neighbor of Danny Kaye, that scourge of backstage hands and taxi drivers, widely hated in the business, he was housed in an all-white mansion on San Ysidro Drive in Beverly Hills. Armed with an assistant, Dan Price, and a tape recorder, I turned up there one sunny afternoon.

As we walked into the high-ceilinged entrance hall, I saw a frail, ghost-like woman appear at a balcony and gaze down at us, then disappear into a room. I was correct in guessing that she was the star's mother, seldom mentioned in reference books and biographies.

Astaire was surprisingly nervous, shy, and diffident. He was a reluctant interviewee, to say the least. No sooner had Dan and I settled in than I saw out of the corner of my eye a very attractive woman in late middle age walking on her own by the swimming pool. Instinctively, I knew who it was, and we asked Astaire if she would join us. She was Adele, his sister, married long ago to a British aristocrat and retired from the stage; they had as a couple been the toast of New York in the late 1920s.

As she came close to the French doors, Astaire said she wouldn't be part of any interview. She heard him, laughed, and said she would be delighted to be of help. Whereas he was fussy and introverted, she was a mensch: straightforward, down to earth, jolly, uncomplicated. She "made" the afternoon work.

After we were done, Astaire said he had something to show us. He took us to a broom closet that held a high pile of copies of *The Films of Fred Astaire,* an innocuous picture chronicle of his career. "I bought up every copy I could," he said. "Not because I like it but because I wanted nobody else to read it."

I asked what he found offensive in it and he showed us that in each copy a passage was blacked out. I wondered silently if the words were libelous, charging him with homosexuality or at least professional throat cutting. Then he said, "The author wrote that Adele and I crashed Long Island society in the 1920s. We didn't crash society, we were part of it, and were very welcome indeed." Could self-protection go any further?

He showed me an issue of a magazine, *Films in Review,* so obscure I was astonished he had even heard of it. He read us a passage in which a certain Tatiana Balkoff Drowne, reviewing the recent 1971 Oscars, had described him capering across the stage in a red wig. "I didn't caper, I danced, and the hair is my own," he said, and tugged at it to prove his point. He said he was going to write to the editor, Henry Hart, to demand a retraction and who was Hart anyway? I said that Hart *was* Tatiana Balkoff Drowne, and Astaire laughed for the first time that afternoon and said I could be his friend for life. He agreed to narrate the Time-Life musical disc in place of Ginger Rogers.

I found Dame Judith Anderson in a rural estate with a large, well-tended vegetable garden, her pride and joy, in Santa Barbara. As formidable in real life as she had been as Mrs. Danvers in *Rebecca,* she was annoyed that her passel of dogs had to be locked up in a place off the living room as they were making too much noise, sniffing and scratching on tape. She told me one story I would never forget.

In *Rebecca*'s final scene, Mrs. Danvers was burned in the fire she started at the mansion of Manderley. Naturally, gas flames that don't burn were used, but in a couple of shots Anderson had to be seen walking, with the roof caving in, and it could not be wholly faked. She refused, not, she said, because of fear of fire, but because of an instinct she had. The double used in the shots got sparks in her eyes and was blinded for life.

Jimmy Stewart, as gangly and warmly hospitable as I hoped; Busby Berkeley, vicious and snarling as he sat on a hot radiator at the downtown Biltmore Hotel; Joel McCrea, beaming and bucolic at his ranch near a mental home at Camarillo; Sam Peckinpah, who announced that he had the night before crushed a man's rib cage with hobnailed boots in the same bar where we now enjoyed scotches—all of these men were memorable in different ways. Jean Negulesco, Romanian-born director of such notable films as *Johnny Belinda* and *The Mask of Dimitrios,* gave splendid cantinas at weekends, where I met the greats of Hollywood; only the celebrated Dr.

Prinzmetal, cardiologist to the stars, was placed in his wheelchair in a corner, away from the conversation. I alone talked to him; the handicapped were a living contradiction of Hollywood glamour and were shunned.

While work continued on *Ziegfeld*, and *The Art of the American Film* was scheduled for publication by Doubleday, I began planning a biography of Cecil B. DeMille for the avuncular and respected publisher Charles Scribner Jr., who received me with glowing hospitality at his oak-lined office over his today sadly vanished bookstore on Fifth Avenue. Approved by him, I flew back to Los Angeles and drove to DeMille Drive in the Los Feliz district to see Cecilia de Mille Harper, the late director's daughter.

Mrs. Harper approved me chiefly because I could talk to her about horses, her favorite topic, as I had been raised with them. She approved me, and her father's secretary, Florence Cole, long the devoted servant of the epic-making master, now the keeper of the flame, gave me a grand tour of the house.

Miss Cole took me downstairs to DeMille's cellar archives. The first thing I saw was a glass case containing three shrunken heads used in DeMille's adventure-comedy *Four Frightened People*. I dubbed them Cecil, Jesse (Lasky), and Adolph (Zukor). The dungeon room was crammed with artifacts of the films: armor from *The Crusades*, togas from *The Sign of the Cross*, Northwest Mounted Police uniforms from the film of that name, paintings of the giant squid from *Reap the Wild Wind*, and hundreds of other items. Miss Cole showed me a dim, 60-watt lightbulb encrusted in grime. "It is not to be replaced," she said firmly, as if it were the ruby eye in an ancient Indian statue. Other commitments delayed my starting work for months, and I soon realized that I would not be able to write the biography Miss Cole and Mrs. Harper wanted. DeMille was a wonderful hypocrite, religious yet orgiastic, with a foot fetish so extreme that he made a movie, removed by the estate, called *Feet of Clay*, that was dedicated to the perversion. Meanwhile, I completed *Ziegfeld* and, following its successful publication, left on a talk-show tour with Goldie.

11

The book tour was pleasant, and it included appearances in Toronto, where the local celebrity Brian Linehan proved the most gracious and well informed of television talk-show hosts. Back in Los Angeles, I was glowing from the good reviews when Time-Life's Nicholas Benton sent me to interview Fritz Lang, the celebrated director of *M, Fury,* and *Hangmen Also Die,* at his home in a mountainous area near the Pacific Ocean.

A new driver, I had a difficult time negotiating the many hairpin bends over unfenced cliffs and sudden plunges of landspill and rock, and I arrived in a somewhat shaken condition. Lang, with his leonine head, black eyepatch, massive physique, and powerful liver-spotted hands, growling "I am ze last of ze dinozauers," was a formidable presence but the interview went well. At the end of it, some four hours later, he invited me to stay to dinner, a rare and welcome compliment from so difficult a man.

Time-Life required him to sign a clearance after he read the transcript. I sent both to him, and waited. A week went by; no word. Then, very late one night, the phone rang.

Lang's mistress, secretary, and later wife, Lily Latté, a contemporary and former classmate of Marlene Dietrich's in Berlin, was on the line. Talking in a theatrical whisper, she said she was terrified of being overheard. She had lost the clearance form. If Lang found out, he would certainly beat her, and she was old and frail. I must come at once to her rescue, bringing another form.

She had prepared a scenario worthy of one of the director's melodramas. I was to appear at the house at 6 a.m. when he would certainly be asleep. I was to rap three times on the door and she would open it a crack and take the clearance from me.

Since we needed the form signed, I had no alternative. To be sure of being on time, I set off at 4 a.m., with only three hours of sleep. I was drowsy and fearful I might drop off at the wheel. To add to the difficulty of reaching the house, there was a heavy ocean fog and my high headlights weren't working.

I arrived at five thirty and waited outside, surrounded by damp and swirling mist, and hoped in vain for a glimmer of dawn. At precisely six, I knocked three times. The door opened a fraction and a hand slipped out and grabbed the clearance. "Thank you!" In German, the voice said, "I will do anything for you." And I drove home.

If Lily Latté had been young, I might have taken her up on her offer; as it was, I couldn't imagine what she could do for me. Years later, I met her at a party at the home of Forrest J. Ackerman, agent and creator of the magazine *Famous Monsters of Filmland*. Not only didn't she recall the promise, or give so much as a hint of gratitude, she turned on me in anger over dinner because I had placed her in the same class with Marlene at the Berlin Gymnasium for girls in 1912. "I was there years after her," she said. I handed her an envelope containing the class list. She never forgave me.

No less bizarre was my encounter with Maria Rasputin, once billed in a circus, à la Mae West, as a lion tamer: THE DAUGHTER OF THE MAD MONK WHO RULED RUSSIA TAMES JUNGLE BEASTS. The suggestion that I should meet her came not from the *Times* or Time-Life but from Patricia Barham, daughter of the former general manager of the Hearst Press, who wanted me to write Maria's first authorized biography.

I visited Rasputin at a humble apartment near a railway siding, the walls shaking as trains went by. Her paintings and photographs of her father, the epitome of evil ambition, were presented in niches with candles flanking them as if they were holy objects. The interview continued at Patricia Barham's elegant house in the Rossmore district, a stone's throw from Mae West's apartment building.

With Guido Orlando, a famous promoter, Barham, and Maria, I sat for long hours listening to a sanitized version of the life of the chief influence on Czarina Alexandra and Czar Nicholas of Russia, following his apparent suspension of their son's incipient hemophilia.

Toward the end of a session, Barham announced that Maria had something very important to tell me. She fetched a cedarwood box, beautifully inlaid with gold, and asked Maria to say what was in it.

"My father's penis," was the reply. Ready for anything, I kept silent, hoping I looked impressed. "He was killed by Prince Youssupov, who envied his manhood because he himself was a fairy. When he poisoned him and it didn't work he stripped father naked and personally cut off his member. He hoped by possessing it he would become a man. He didn't."

"How did *you* obtain it?" I asked. After all, Rasputin was poisoned, shot, beaten, and drowned. "I searched," Barham said, "all over Europe for years, spending a fortune, until at last I found it in an obscure antique shop in Paris. If you agree to do the book I will let you see it."

The prospect was uninviting, even if the penis had been embalmed, but I said I would think about it. Next morning the phone rang and Barham was on the phone. She said that thieves ("Communists no doubt") had broken into her house and taken the sacred box.

I canceled the idea of writing the book. And I felt that the object concerned would probably have turned out to be a fossilized, very old black banana.

For a recorded history of the silent film, Time-Life asked me to interview the once celebrated star Corinne Griffith, whose squeaky voice had doomed her at the outbreak of talkies. I called her at her home in Beverly Hills and she said, "I am *not* Corinne Griffith. If you wish to see her you must visit an unmarked grave in Mexico."

"May I ask who you are then?"

"I am *Mary* Griffith. Her twin sister. Let me explain. She, Corinne, was starring in a film in Mexico in 1920. She was stricken by a mysterious local malady and died suddenly at age twenty-four. Mr. Adolph Zukor, head of Paramount, called me in person and told me I must save the day; a cancellation of the picture would be a disaster for the studio. He told me what had happened; I cried and cried. He said I must pull myself together: there was a million dollars in it if I would become my sister. I had never acted and didn't want to act. But I couldn't resist the money, and I felt Corinne would want me to help. So I went to Mexico and took over, and nobody knew the difference. From then on, I was Corinne Griffith."

$\mathcal{I}$ was busy now with the DeMille biography, working in the cellar archive. Every time I heard a footstep on the stairs, I had to put back the sacred, fly-specked, 60-watt bulb, which I had replaced with a 100-watt, clear, crystal equivalent. I tried on a Royal Canadian Mounted Police uniform when nobody was about and was delighted to find it fit perfectly. One afternoon, I was going through some scrapbooks when a note fluttered to the floor. It was a blackmail letter from gangsters in Chicago wanting money to hide the fact from the American public that Gloria Swanson was having an adulterous affair with the famous movie director Marshall Neilan. Notes between the studio boss Jesse L. Lasky and DeMille showed that the money was paid—at midnight at a deserted intersection in downtown Los Angeles.

In the midst of all this work, my *Art of the American Film* appeared. It was approved by most critics and set for college courses across the country. There were memorable social occasions. For a Friends of the Library Banquet at USC honoring the late Moss Hart, I took Mae West as my date. That evening, in a play scene, Truman Capote portrayed Sheridan Whiteside, the irascible Alexander Woollcott-like central figure of *The Man Who Came to Dinner*; Debbie Reynolds was the nurse, a part acted in the film by Mary Wickes, who, with my friends Joseph and Patricia Cotten, was at our table. The surviving members of the cast of Hart's patriotic *Winged Victory,* led by Edmond O'Brien, sang from a rigged-up World War II air force canteen, and Garson Kanin talked so long that our table in chorus shouted to him to sit down and he did. At the end of a very long evening, Kitty Carlisle Hart, the honoree's widow, unforgettably sang "My Ship," from *Lady in the Dark.*

No less memorable was a party at the home of David Bradley, irascible creator of such Hollywood Hall of Shamers as *They Saved Hitler's Brain* and *Twelve to the Moon.* The silent screen actresses Mae McAvoy and Carmel Myers arrived at the same time. Myers said to McAvoy, "Mae, I thought you were dead." To which McAvoy sweetly replied, "Carmel, I thought you were alive."

Rouben Mamoulian, director of *Blood and Sand* and *Summer Holiday,* that favorite of the Lindsay Anderson–Tony Richardson axis in London in the 1940s, arrived with his wife, Azavia, painter and department store heiress. She slipped and fell in a mink-clad group of silent stars, all seated on the floor to see themselves on the screen as they were forty-five years before.

He pulled her up and pushed her outside to the veranda where we heard the unforgettable words: "YOU HAVE DISGRACED THE NAME MAMOULIAN!"

Christmas 1972 was no less weird. Bradley's lover at the time was an evil gnome named Tom Webster whom Bradley had picked up years before at a beach. Webster looked at him whenever his back was turned as if he would like to stab it. On this occasion he was dressed as Santa Claus and had fixed up the table not in a Christmas fashion but as if it were Halloween, with plastic skulls as candle holders. He went out to the kitchen to carve the turkey and at that moment Bob Hope's sister arrived. We heard a scream; she cried out that this demon intended to kill her. We ran in and indeed Santa Claus had pinned her to the refrigerator with a carving knife. "If you do anything to me, you will have Bob Hope to answer to!" she cried, and the thought of this most futile of threats had us all laughing. We overpowered Webster and locked him up in the master bedroom.

In the midst of all this activity, Seymour Peck called to ask if I would interview Lucille Ball for the *Times*. She was shooting the musical *Mame* at Warner Bros. and I was to visit the set, then talk to her at her home.

Apart from my conversation with her on Orson Welles, I had seen her on a visit from Australia in the 1960s when she had been working on her hour-long *Lucy Show*. In a sequence in which she learned to parachute, with Rex Reason, she had insisted on plunging from the top of the sound stage herself, doing it over and over again with manic intensity, screaming at everyone, including her leading man. It was more like seeing an actual air force training course than the fashioning of a comedy episode.

On set on *Mame,* she was dressed up as Santa Claus, mouthing to a recording of "We Need a Little Christmas." When her red, fur-lined cap fell off during a take, she stalked off grimly and shouted at her milliner, whom everyone called the Mad Hatter; this time the cap must be glued on. The Mad Hatter pointed out that if it was glued, her wig would come off with it when she removed it. She shrugged, took a break, and clutched my arm.

"I died last night," she said. I felt like saying, "In Pomona?" but resisted the impulse. Puffing away at a cigarette, she announced that her esophagus had failed and she had turned blue from head to foot. She walked back to the set and went into a dance routine, niftily using a leg that had been broken in a skiing accident a year before. The cap stayed on. I caught up with her days later at her leafy, very feminine home in Beverly Hills. Lucy limped into the living room, in brown tunic and hot pants. She launched without being asked into a detailed account of her various accidents. ("I'm a Leo, so my limbs snap like matchsticks.") The first mishap was when, at eight, she shot a neighbor's child with a gun supplied by her grandfather; her second was when she was famous and her car ran into a snowdrift in a blizzard in Central Park. ("What's that?" said the driver of a snowplow to his companion. And the man replied, "It's Lucille Ball in a snowdrift.")

Other accidents were frequent, and Lucy listed them all. A horse stepped on her foot in *Fancy Pants*; an alligator chewed her leg on *Roman Scandals*. Bitten by a bear on one episode of *The Lucy Show*, she was gored by a bull's head mounted on a dolly in a fake bullfight scene in another. William Holden lit up her fake nose in still another *Lucy* and it caught fire; she dunked it in the Irish coffee.

She said she was skiing one year at Aspen when she shot through open french doors into somebody's living room. ("The old couple was watching me on the box. They saw my reflection behind them and the man said to the woman, 'We'd better call a technician. We're getting a double image.'")

She called her son a "faggot"; he wasn't and isn't gay, and I had to remind her this was a family newspaper and that the statement was libelous. She lied he was sleeping with Dino Martin, Dean Martin's equally straight son, later to be killed in a plane crash. She tore into Patty Duke, insisting paradoxically that Patty had a baby with Desi Jr. out of wedlock; when Duke appeared on her doorstep with the child, she turned them away until Duke told her there were fifty photographers around the corner waiting for a signal to film her act of rejection. She had to let Duke in, but she rejected Desi's girlfriend Liza Minnelli's seven dogs. ("I told her, 'Every time a dog drops a litter, you can't dump them on me. I've got five already!'")

Grim, cheerless, albeit a genius of television farce, Lucy was astonishingly a disciple of Norman Vincent Peale, the proselytizer of optimism. She seemed more like a disciple of Strindberg or Hieronymus Bosch. She left me with a problem. Next day, she said, she would be appearing in a fox hunt scene. "How can I avoid it biting me and giving me rabies? I have to turn the damn thing over and tickle its belly. And if it's a mechanical one it'll break off a fingernail. Look, there's one on the floor!"

My article appeared unchanged. Ball was furious I had quoted her, even though I had warned her repeatedly that she was on tape, and I had cleaned up many of her remarks. She sent me a letter on pale blue stationery, her name spelled out at the top with tiny red stars placed through the blue letters. "How could anyone so young [I was forty-two] be so cruel?" she wrote. I replied with a two-line poem: "If you would keep your house in order / Don't talk into a tape recorder." I heard from her no more.

Mame opened and bombed. In New York soon after the premiere, I met the projectionist at a party; he told me that fifteen minutes into the screening, Ball had invaded the projection room and demanded to know why the picture was out of focus. "It's in your contract," he told her. "It takes *hours* off your age."

*H*aving always admired the films of Roman Polanski, I was delighted when Seymour Peck asked me to interview him, and especially when I found him in an appropriately Raymond Chandler-ish house, owned by George Montgomery, star of the Chandler movie adaptation *The Brasher Doubloon,* on a day of fog and drizzle—Polanski weather. Nor did he disappoint in person: tiny, unsmiling, restless, and self-conscious, he paced about his rocky hillside garden, disappearing troll-like into a cave to turn on the tap that activated a waterfall. The water was brown.

It symbolized perfectly his worldview, expressed to me in the dismally lighted house, with various Lolitas engaged in a game of pool, of the hopelessness of existence. The sister of his murdered wife, Sharon Tate, called him within minutes of my arrival to say she was hemorrhaging, ill, alone, and frightened. He said he had stopped believing in God or the devil when he was twelve. ("We are born; it means nothing. We die.") He hadn't believed in any part of his film *Rosemary's Baby*; witchcraft and devil worship seemed to him mere manifestations of human folly. He said that *Chinatown,* which he had just finished, in its picture of a corrupt Los Angeles in the 1930s, quite supported his view of mankind's venality. But evil? That was as pointless a word as *good,* and I didn't have the courage to ask him if he even knew the difference.

He revealed his nature as I left. We had gotten along quite well because I had read and admired his favorite authors, Bruno Schultz, Kafka, Sartre, Camus, and had liked the plays of Samuel Beckett. As I got into my car, he noticed that my headrest had somehow been turned inside out. "Not only won't it cushion your head if you get rear-ended," he said, "but it will decapitate you. Good-bye!" And with that, he was gone.

I had been feeling lonely and bereft after Perry's murder and moved restlessly from one apartment to another, unable to shake off my grief. I remained celibate for months, my sexuality frozen, devoting myself to work, the best of all salves. Then, while living on Kings Road in West Hollywood, I realized I had to live again.

Disliking the somber, chilling and silent, dark atmosphere of Hollywood pickup bars, so far removed from their jolly and noisy Sydney counterparts, I began haunting bathhouses. In this pre-AIDS era, they were crowded around the clock. Labyrinths smelled pungently of amyl nitrate, with narrow underlit rooms down long dark corridors, each room equipped with no more than a bed and sometimes a basin, like prison cells. Orgy rooms were set aside, so pitch dark it was impossible to tell whom one was having sex with: a boon to the ugly or overweight, but those of us who were neither preferred to see what we were getting. Not for the first time I was impressed by the physiques of young Americans: lean, defined, and seldom, to my relief, bodybuilders.

These silent and ruthlessly unfeeling sexual encounters were never satisfactory; I needed a lover. Laughing at myself, I enlisted with a gay dating bureau run by a picturesque hunk out of an office in West Hollywood. The man I met was Al Banks, about my age, handsome, thin, financially independent, and good natured. We moved together to an old German settlement of Hollywood Knolls, overlooking Burbank, where the great director William Dieterle had once lived. The houses were designed by the architect Richard Neutra, who provided steel as opposed to wooden frameworks, a protection against the ubiquitous termites of Los Angeles.

It was (probably still is) a beautiful house, even though it brought me some of the most frightening experiences of my life. Built into a hillside, it had a stone-flagged entrance hall, a redwood den with a fifteen-foot ceiling, and three bedrooms framed around a curving staircase that led to a sunken living room and dining room. The attic was an artist's studio with a bed placed at the top of a tall ladder, directly under the ceiling, and there was a back staircase once used as a servant's entrance, running up two floors, which I would always keep locked because I remembered that David Niven's wife, Primula, had fallen down similar stairs when she missed her footing in a game of hide-and-seek at their Beverly Hills home many years before.

Soon after Al and I began to move in, I received a call from Nick Benton at Time-Life to interview Floyd Crosby, cinematographer of *High Noon,* for the Western history disc and for his classic work on *Tabu,* the South Seas semidocumentary made by Robert Flaherty. His son was David Crosby, of the popular band Crosby, Stills, and Nash.

I drove to Ojai, a California country town reputed to have magical properties and strong literary antecedents. Iris Tree, celebrated aesthete and daughter of the British impresario and actor Sir Herbert Beerbohm Tree, had for years run a salon there to which the greatest writers came.

Beautifully proportioned, the Crosby house stood high above a green valley shaped like a punch bowl, which many painters and poets had admired. Crosby and his wife were warmly welcoming, the interview went well, and they asked me if, instead of making the long drive in the dark back to Los Angeles, I wouldn't prefer to stay the night? I happily agreed and called Al to explain.

After a delicious dinner and hours of pleasant chat, I went to bed in the guest room close to midnight. Moonlight streamed through my windows as I fell into a peaceful sleep. Then, suddenly, as if someone were tugging at my arm, I woke up, drenched in sweat.

There rose beside my bed a tall pillar of smoke, all the way to the high, white ceiling and fully visible in the pale glow of the quarter moon. I was paralyzed, unable to move, feeling my soul going down into the earth beneath the house. Although I saw nothing inside the smoke, I knew in my inner being that a Native American was standing there, hidden by the black cloud, watching me intently. I asked him silently to go away; he didn't.

I lay for hours, still fixed in position; I couldn't even reach out for the light. Then as dawn came, with a rustling of trees outside, the smoke dissolved and the dark pillar was gone.

Unlocked, stiff, my limbs hurting, I managed to walk to the bathroom and take a shower. But I was still limping and drained as I came down to breakfast.

"You look like you've seen a ghost," Floyd said.

"I *have* seen one," I replied.

"Oh, not again," was Mrs. Crosby's comment. She told me that the house stood over an Indian graveyard; that the Native Americans buried there didn't like the idea of houses built over them; and that many guests had fled my room never to come back. Others saw nothing; I was one of the few who had stayed. I explained that even if I had wanted to leave I couldn't, that I was rendered paralyzed. I asked my host and hostess why they hadn't warned me what to expect. "You'd have thought us mad if we had," they said, almost in unison.

In the year 2000, I called Mrs. Crosby to see if I had imagined the whole episode. She assured me that I had not; and that recently a Dutch woman importer, who was notably unimaginative and pragmatic, had quit a guest house on the property because she saw several pillars of smoke moving around and that her son, an athlete, and his girlfriend had also moved out; they had, like his mother, no belief in ghosts, but saw the same phenomena.

Back at the Hollywood Knolls house, I again crossed the Borderline. The locked rear staircase echoed all night to the sound of a child running up and down, laughing and crying. I could hear a woman sobbing, and even on the rare hot nights the house grew chilly. On the staircase outside my room, a padlock to the attic was open every morning after being locked the night before. One afternoon I heard the front door creak ajar. I looked out of my den and saw that it was shut. Nobody was there. A man's heavy footsteps trod down the stairs; I could see the man in my mind's eye, young and somber, just below me, listening.

That night I gave a party. One of the guests, the television writer Walon Green, was halfway down the steps when he said, "Lance is here." He said he was aware of the presence of his dead friend Lance Reventlow, son of Barbara Hutton, who had been killed in an accident not long before I rented the house.

He told me he remembered how Lance had told him about this hide-away, that he loved the attic room, and I described the padlock hanging open each morning. "That would be Lance's little joke," Walon said.

We held a séance with glasses and letters set in circles, with a medium, the eccentric Hollywood character Samson de Brier, in charge, to determine the identity of the child on the back staircase. We rested our fingers lightly on the glass, looking at each other to make sure nobody would push it; it refused to budge. Samson felt someone was blocking the vibrations and we took our fingers off one by one. When Al Banks removed his, the glass rushed about. He confessed that in 1951 he had had a lobotomy, which his aunt had ordered to remove him from his inheritance. It was clear that the desensitizing of parts of his brain (he suffered from grand mal seizures, which I witnessed at the Knolls and in Palm Springs, and at times had dissociative speech patterns) prevented anything coming through.

We asked about the footsteps on the stairs. The glass spelled out that a ten-year-old boy thought he was still climbing the hill some eighty years after he had fallen to his death, long before houses were built, and we heard Samson talk to him in the kitchen telling him it was time to move on. There were no further disturbances.

One night, very late, I returned from a party to see, on the hillside behind my house, a young man of perhaps eighteen scything grass in the moonlight. "An odd time for this," I said with a laugh. He smiled, turned around, and vanished.

My life with Al Banks was becoming strained; our never very satisfactory relationship had evaporated. And then I met Richard Palafox, a young and handsome Filipino nurse, and everything in my life was turned upside down.

12

My relationship with Richard, which continues to this day, was triggered by a circumstance in New York. In town for briefings at Time-Life Books and the *Times,* I went one night to the Everard Baths, known in gay circles as *The Everhard.* It was a Grand Central Station of sex. One entered the place, paid a fee, and, if lucky, survived a tough looking-over by a custodian; passed as fit, one undressed, put clothes in a locker, and then wrapped a towel around a waist that was by requirement fat free and defined.

There were numerous rooms with slightly open doors; the men inside were naked, often erect and waiting. The swimming pool was green and inviting under a brilliant array of light, and as one slipped into it, mouths would consume genitals under water; the suppliers of pleasure were seldom seen.

In an orgy room, I joined a young, handsome dark man from Manila. He came to my hotel, the Waldorf, and spent a passionate night with me, followed by several more. He was sweet, not bright, a plumber by trade who could never have shared a life with me. We parted, and he cried helplessly, touchingly; he said he was in love with me.

I arrived in Los Angeles to receive a phone call from David Bradley. He told me that a young Filipino nurse was pursuing him but he wanted only Caucasians. He passed Richard on to me, and we began an affair.

Richard was far removed from Ramon, my New York lover. He was aristocratic in bearing, fierce and gentle in shifting moods. He came from a line of Spanish grandees who had settled in the Philippines in the eighteenth century and had married scions of rich local families. World War II had shattered the world of refinement and luxury in which his parents had grown up. The Japanese took their lands, their house, their money. In desperation, the parents farmed out their children, including Richard, in nursing, engineering, and farming.

He obtained a medical degree at the University of the Philippines, cooking and waiting tables to pay for his course. Norine was also a nurse, as I have written, and they were similar: devoted, unpredictable, romantic and sentimental, yet tough and controlling. Fate took a hand: at the same time that Richard and I decided to live together, Norine died in a hospital in Sydney of stomach cancer and intestinal blockage. And my stepmother, Jill Deacon, also died, due to an accident during heart surgery in London.

I moved into the apartment block called Fountainview West, today Westview Towers, on La Cienega Boulevard in West Hollywood. It turned out to be a halfway station for celebrities moving between Los Angeles and New York who had not yet bought a home in the West.

Gene Hackman, sour and distant, was often seen in the elevator clutching a bag full of groceries; James Coco was a chubby sweetheart; Broderick Crawford, who lived across the corridor from me, was genial and warm, far from the terrors he portrayed in pictures, and we became friends.

Despite Richard's presence in my life, my fickle spirit needed other replenishments. I met a young painter and we enjoyed a torrid, brief romance. He was overjoyed when I introduced him to Phil Ochs, the rock star, soon to die; then he drifted away. I advertised for "intellectuals only" in the classified ad pages of the gay weekly the *Advocate,* which specialized in physical descriptions; I was surprised to receive several replies, only one of which worked out. The schoolteacher I will call Brent was exactly my type: slight, defined, his well-arranged muscles supple rather than overdeveloped. He also had a brilliant mind.

The problem was that, even while we shared nights of intense sex and long, drawn-out talks afterward, Brent couldn't get work in Los Angeles and told me he would have to leave town. Thus I settled on Richard instead, and, after writing Brent a brutal note of dismissal, I saw Richard place it with a flourish in the mailbox outside the House of Pies.

I had spent one late afternoon and evening at Mae West's apartment. Our friendship had deepened, encouraged greatly by her manager, Stanley

Musgrove, whom I saw often at the gay Roman Holiday Baths in the San Fernando Valley. Christopher Isherwood was cold toward me; Don Bachardy's innocent and nonsexual interest in me he misunderstood and was visibly upset about.

When we went down in the elevator I saw a look that could have killed in the famous novelist's eye. That night, Richard and I slept in separate rooms. At an early hour of the morning, perhaps 2 a.m., a fire broke out in an apartment building on Fountain Avenue across the street. I woke up to see Isherwood standing facing me inside the curtains that were red with a fiery reflection; he himself seemed to be a creature from hell.

I could see the window through his body, and the fire beyond. I was voiceless; paralyzed as I had been in the presence of the Native American at Ojai.

As if in answer to a silent prayer, Richard walked in; his simple, uncomplicated goodness acted as a grounding device and Isherwood dissolved.

A check of the morning news showed that Isherwood hadn't died. I called Curtis Harrington and asked him what the experience might have meant. He told me he had had the same one years before.

Staying with the hostess Iris Tree at Ojai, he had shown an interest in a young man Isherwood was dating. In the night, Isherwood's double image came to him and threatened him, the wallpaper and door visible through the writer's form. Later, I found in a biography of the novelist a similar incident recorded by another man who had wanted one of Isherwood's boyfriends.

Years later, after Isherwood died, Don Bachardy held an exhibit of his paintings of him at Santa Monica, showing him in flames exactly as I had seen him. Youthful beforehand, Bachardy had aged into a replica of his dead lover, and a book he brought out of profiles and photographs of great figures of the screen was marked with Isherwood's demoniacal wit. Dwelling on every physical flaw, it had no resemblance to anything that Don would once have written or said.

There were more earthly events in 1973. Mecca Graham, veteran walker to the stars, asked me if I would be Marjorie Main's escort at parties; I was happy to agree. I loved the immortal Ma Kettle with her hair in a knot on top of her head à la concierge, a style affected also by Katharine Hepburn. One evening I took her to the garage apartment occupied by the Broadway producer Arthur Whitelaw. She had asked Arthur to screen *The Women*,

George Cukor's version of Clare Boothe Luce's famous all-female play, as she wanted Groucho Marx, Arthur's close friend, to see her performance in it. Though both were under contract to MGM in the 1930s, she had never met Groucho.

He arrived glowering, in the company of a young female companion, Erin Fleming. At one stage he deliberately dropped his meal on the floor and made her scrape it up from the carpet. (She was given a bad deal and deprived of all his money when he died, but in truth she was a martyr.) The film began on Arthur's rigged-up screen. Marjorie's big scene at a dude ranch for rich Reno divorcees in which she played a Stetsoned proprietor was a long time in coming, and Groucho, though I tried to stop him, groaned and walked into Arthur's bedroom. I ran in to bring him back; Marjorie was upset. I found him watching *The Best of Groucho* on television. When I tried to budge him, he hailed me with four-letter words. Remembering Marjorie's tears, I haven't been able to watch him on-screen from that day to this.

Richard was working as nurse to Wally Cox, friend and alleged lover of Marlon Brando. Night after night the phone would ring and Brando's purring, sibilant voice would murmur in my ear that he wanted to see Richard and make love to him. He offered him a Mercedes and a house in Tahiti if he would go to bed. Richard told Brando he already had such a car (he didn't, until 1981) and that he didn't like Tahiti (he had never been there). Finally, I told the star of *The Godfather,* whom I had interviewed on the set and found so boring I couldn't write a word on him for the *Times,* to get lost.

In the midst of this drama of unrequited love, Guy Flatley of the *Times* called me with an unforgettable question, delivered as calmly as if he were offering me the chance to write a piece on a friend. Would I like to interview Katharine Hepburn?

I tried not to show a degree of excitement but instead asked Guy when that would be. It turned out that after many years of refusing all interviews, Miss Hepburn had consented to talk to the *Times,* to promote a screening on ABC television of Edward Albee's *A Delicate Balance,* in which she starred.

Eunice Chessler of ABC was in charge of the arrangements. The two *New York Times* interviewers in Los Angeles were Aljean Harmetz and myself. Hepburn had asked if Aljean was a woman. The answer was in the affirmative, and Miss Hepburn had said that in view of that she would see Mr. Higham.

This was lucky for me, but not surprising. Female stars, even those few who were as realistic as Hepburn, were afraid of women reporters, as they noticed wrinkles in face, neck, and hands and were not always averse to describing them.

Not an admirer of Alexander Graham Bell, Hepburn preferred to conduct arrangements by formal letter; she would not have appreciated the advent, years later, of e-mail. After a series of written exchanges with Miss Chessler, she agreed to see me at the unusual time of 1:30 in the afternoon, when one would normally be at lunch.

Eunice told me that the star would tolerate no lateness and that I must be exactly on time. Fanatically punctual myself, that was no challenge to me in a city where almost everybody was always fashionably late. But I still checked with the time on the telephone before leaving Fountainview West and arrived early, crossing the few feet to the Hepburn house north of Sunset only when the radio announced the half hour.

The door flew open and there she was, looking at her watch. "You're punctual," she said, as sharply as if I hadn't been. She looked very hard into my eyes and seemed to like what she saw.

She led me into the living room, which had once been Spencer Tracy's; a fire crackled cheerfully in the grate on this damp, chilly foggy afternoon, and she showed me a Christmas wreath she had just finished making, saying she was prouder of it than of anything she had done. I stood for a moment admiring the beautiful Dufy-ish watercolors of oceanside scenes on the wall: white houses, white sails, blue sea, anchors, ropes. I knew instinctively who had been the artist. "You can say anything you like about my acting," she growled behind me. "But don't say a word against my paintings." I told her how much I admired them and she said she had done them in Cuba when Tracy was shooting a film. She curled up in a large, black leather armchair—Tracy's—and our rapport was instantaneous.

She was very much part of the room: it had the unpretentious, oak-paneled look of a retired sea captain's, with its well-scrubbed brassware, comfortable worn-down furniture, and Indian rugs.

She had a sense of proportion about her career and Hollywood I had not encountered in any other performer. When I brought up an unlikely subject, Australian lyrebirds (I recalled she had been looking for these rarely seen avians during her antipodean tour in Shakespeare in the 1950s), she described seeing them dance, something very few have done, with great intensity and accuracy. And she could laugh when she quoted a review of her Portia in *The Merchant of Venice* in the Melbourne *Age,* which stated that it was obvious she was all washed up as an actress, otherwise why would she be reduced to playing in Australia?

Others would have harbored resentment for the comment but not Katharine Hepburn. She had a complete sense of the unimportance of her career when compared with that of great doctors, scientists, and saviors of the poor. ("Acting's just waiting for a custard pie, that's all.")

The wonderful stories she told me are included in my authorized biography *Kate: The Life of Katharine Hepburn,* but one must be retold. When she was appearing in the musical *Coco* on Broadway, the Uris Theater was being built nearby, and on Wednesday and Saturday afternoons the blasting and hammering could be heard in her theater. At a matinee she stopped the show and informed a delighted audience that she would put an end to the racket. She walked out through the stage door, in high heels and a Chanel creation (with hat), and made her way to the Uris. Then she took a workman's elevator to the top girder and walked across it, when a slip could have sent her plunging to her death.

She said she told the foreman who she was and that he must stop the work on the afternoons of Wednesday and Saturday. He replied, "You didn't have to say you are Katharine Hepburn." She descended, returned to the stage, told the audience what she had done, and received a standing ovation. Then she went on with the performance. She got her wish. Construction stopped at each matinee.

We talked until nightfall—four hours of glorious listening for me— until she realized she must prepare for guests who were coming for dinner. She insisted—no other star would have done this—on guiding me down the slippery steps to the street, and to my car opposite, in the rain without an umbrella. I drove off in a glow of joy and wrote the best article I ever did for the *Times.*

Both Seymour Peck and Guy Flatley were good enough to say that they loved the piece, and from then on my assignments were far more regular than before.

Publication of the article resulted in many phone calls and letters of congratulation. With several love affairs going on at once, I was in a state of extreme narcissism, much too healthy and a little crazy. Several publishers approached my New York agent, the gentle and devoted Jane Wilson, to see if I would be interested in writing a Hepburn biography. Jane forwarded the letters on to me, and I read them carefully, one by one.

The best offer came from Sheri Huber, a senior editor at W. W. Norton, a publisher I didn't normally associate with popular biography. I felt that Hepburn would prefer a distinguished imprint, and in conversation with Huber I found her to be not only an ardent fan of the star, but an intellectual: cultivated, well informed, though quite unfamiliar with the motion picture industry.

I called Jane Wilson and said I had made my choice. But I also explained to Huber that I couldn't consider embarking on the book without Hepburn's authorization.

It wasn't so much a moral decision but a practical one: she had very few friends, and none, I knew, would speak to me unless she gave them permission. And, I felt, rightly so. I didn't understand the kind of writer who could pester a subject, put a foot in a door, or embark on forms of coercion to secure an interview.

Knowing Hepburn's dislike of the telephone, I wrote to her saying, in complete honesty, that I wouldn't go ahead with Norton unless she agreed to help me with the book. She wrote back to say that she had never agreed to an authorized life, but that we had had a most interesting afternoon, my article was the only one written about herself that she had been able to finish, and that she would see me that Friday, at 1:30 p.m. as before.

As soon as I arrived on this second visit, she cast me a sharp, almost threatening glance from Spencer Tracy's black leather chair, saying that many had asked her for the opportunity. I didn't quail, and that seemed to impress her. She said she was certain that I would go ahead with or without her permission. So as not to seem sycophantic or ruthless, I said nothing. I could see she liked that; she took it to be a display of honesty. She told me she had two tests for me, and the results would determine whether she would help me or not.

The first was preceded by the statement that everyone she had worked with in her early days in Hollywood in 1932 was dead. So there would be nobody to talk to. I unrolled a sheet of butcher paper, similar to that given to me by Barbara Stanwyck's companion Helen Ferguson. On it I had written the names of Hepburn's many still-living colleagues.

"What's that?" she snapped, and I told her. "This is perfectly horrifying! Just read two names."

"Victor Heerman and Sarah Y. Mason."

"The writers! They saved my *Little Women*! They can't be alive."

"Oh, but they are, in a cobweb castle, a haunted house on West Adams Street downtown." She was amazed and delighted; I could interview them.

The second condition was tougher. I must tell her the greatest of all love stories. Of course, I thought of the obvious: Antony and Cleopatra. Abelard and Heloise, Romeo and Juliet. Then I recalled a recent conversation I had had with my friend the great director King Vidor a few weeks before.

King and the silent screen star Colleen Moore had worked together on a forgotten 1922 movie, *Sky Pilot*. At parties, they performed a mentalist act; he would stand on a platform, blindfolded; Colleen would move through the crowd and take various objects from their owners—a ring, a bracelet, a scarf, a cigarette case. She would ask Vidor what she was holding in her hand; by phrasing the question in a prearranged form, and accenting certain syllables, she would then "tell" him in effect what the item was. The code never failed.

They fell in love. Their affair continued on and off for years until at last she gave up her career and married a Chicago stockbroker. Decades later, in 1964, King was walking down the Champs Elysées when a woman's voice behind him said, "What is this that I have in my hand?" and without turning round he said, "A lady's bracelet," and of course it was Colleen. Their affair resumed in their sixties and was continued as warmly as before.

As I spoke, Hepburn exclaimed that this was indeed the greatest love story ever told. Then she said, "Of course I'll help you. But on one further condition: I won't have to read the book. Oh, and there's another. You must find and interview Jed Harris, who directed me on the stage."

Jed Harris! The brilliant and erratic producer-director of *The Front Page* and *The Heiress,* among countless other hits, had disappeared. The most hated man in theater history, with five successes on Broadway at one time, he was the model for Laurence Olivier's malevolent monarch in the film version of *Richard III.*

Nobody in Manhattan theater circles could tell me where Jed Harris was: neither the imperious, detestable Elia Kazan; nor the genial Lincoln Center archivist Paul Myers; nor my brilliant editor Seymour Peck; nor the charming actor Cyril Ritchard, lunching with me at the Peacock Room of the Waldorf Astoria, where I was staying; nor Laura Harding, Hepburn's oldest living friend; nor yet the legendary stalwarts of the Theater Guild, Lawrence Langner and Armina Marshall. Nor even the great musical star Alfred Drake in his somber office at III West Fifty-seventh Street.

And I clearly must find Harris. But first I had to return to Los Angeles for a memorable interview for the *Times* with the great Western director Raoul Walsh, who, as if it had been staged for me, was, on my arrival at his home in California's Santa Susanna Mountains, mending an eagle's broken wing. Further delay was caused when, at lunch at the Beverly Hills Hotel Polo Lounge, I overheard a woman at the next table tell her friends that Mercedes McCambridge, Oscar winner for *All the King's Men,* was furious that she had been denied a credit for providing the demoniacal voices in *The Exorcist,* generally attributed to the teenage Linda Blair.

I at once went to the table, introduced myself, and said I would be happy to help. I called Sy Peck, who agreed to a story. The same afternoon, I was at Mercedes' apartment, high in an impersonal building in the Wilshire corridor. She showed me a long line of red Seconals on her bathroom shelf and said she would take them all—or embark on a world cruise.

I advised her to do neither and that I would make sure she had screen credit. She told me of drawing the devil's voices from her nights at Bellevue Hospital in New York, when she heard others suffering from the dt's, and she swallowed rotten fruit and eggs to further bring off the effects. My story was published, she was given the credit she so richly deserved, and we became friends.

The article was about to appear when I received an invitation to Chasen's restaurant to Linda Blair's birthday party. A Warner Bros. publicist flourished the "blue" pages, the *Times* proofs of the piece, in my face and asked me what I thought I was doing. I told him that I knew what I was doing, and how had he managed to obtain proof pages that were locked up and out of bounds? Then I walked out.

It was time now to find Jed Harris. Back in New York, the celebrated New York producer Jean Dalrymple told me that Charlie Abrahamson, Harris's manager, would be able to answer my question on his whereabouts. I went to see him at his permanent residence, the Royalton Hotel, then unrestored and shabby, little better than a flophouse, opposite the also unrestored Algonquin (is it perverse to miss the romantic squalor of New York in the 1970s?).

Abrahamson's rooms were a long way down a corridor lined with a faded, badly swept carpet and a grimy window at the end. Small, balding, and pale, but sturdily built, he invited me into a cluttered, dimly lit room smelling of stale tobacco and sweat. His office room was cramped, with a Grand Rapids rolltop desk straight out of Jed Harris's *Front Page*; papers, yellow and brittle with age, stuffed into pigeonholes; a revolving chair; and play scripts, letters, and contracts stacked up, also yellow, on the old Chinese rug. He didn't invite me to sit down, but I did.

The conversation was difficult, starting with my repeating the statement made on the telephone that Katharine Hepburn had authorized the book; it left him unimpressed. He jigged his left knee up and down, swung in circles in his chair, took phone calls and made them, offered coffee in a cracked china cup that contained none, scratched his head, and at last sat still as I threatened to leave.

"What are you here for?" he asked.

"As I mentioned several times, to arrange an interview with Jed Harris."

"He'll only see you if you pay him five hundred dollars and the bus fare from Atlantic City." The former New Jersey resort was, in those pre–Donald Trump days, a pathetic run-down shadow of its former self.

"What on earth is he doing there?"

"He's flat broke and living in a tenement. Normally he wouldn't talk to anyone but he's desperate for money; he could be evicted."

"But he is one of the most famous and successful figures in the history of Broadway."

"He's such an egomaniac he would only put on shows with his own money. The profits were never enough."

I heard Abrahamson out. I told him that I had never paid for an interview before, but Miss Hepburn was adamant I must see Harris. I agreed to pay the bus fare one way, and half the payment, the rest on completion of a satisfactory interview. "You know your villain," Abrahamson said. "But I have to hold the balance in escrow or he won't do it." On that understanding, I handed Abrahamson the full amount.

Feeling I had wandered into an early Warners talkie, where brutal bargains were struck with gangsters who talked out of the corners of their mouths, I left as, without bothering to show me to the door, Abrahamson was busy making another phone call.

I went back to the Waldorf and waited. And waited. Afternoon, evening I stayed in, the black rain beating on the windows, the night made bearable by a hot date in a white raincoat. Deciding finally that Jed Harris wasn't going to bite, I went out next day to Ardsley-on-Hudson to interview the charming Joseph Anthony, who had directed Hepburn in *The Rainmaker*. When I returned to the hotel, there was a message from Abrahamson that Harris would meet me by the Waldorf lobby clock at 12:30 that Sunday, April 21.

It was easy to spot him in the crowd. Already, the New Casualness had taken root: in this formerly exclusive hotel, where once nobody would be seen without jacket and tie, or dressed in a tuxedo for dinner in the Peacock Room, an army of tourists were milling around in T-shirts, shorts, and sneakers, shouting cheerfully at each other.

Harris was a lone, formally dressed figure. He wore a wide-brimmed black caballero hat; his white face resembled a semianimated skull, with burning red-rimmed eyes and a wicked slash of a mouth. Over his bony shoulders was slung a heavy black wool overcoat that had seen better days, worn like a cloak, as if he were a road company Mephistopheles in *Faust*. To add to the melodramatic picture, he wore a loose-fitting parson's suit, David Belasco clerical collar (but with shoestring tie). His chest was sunken, his legs very long and spindly, his patent leather dress shoes, size maybe fourteen, surprisingly well polished, but probably not worn for a long time.

I offered him my hand. "How did you recognize me?" he snarled, not shaking it. Surely, I thought, he can't be serious. Even if he hadn't resembled a scarecrow in a nineteenth-century country field, wouldn't he assume I had seen his photograph? He looked at my tape recorder. "That's very cheap," he said.

"I only use the expensive one for important people," I replied.

He smiled; a smile of death. "I like rude people," he told me. "Takes one to catch one, Mr. Harris," I replied.

I invited him up to my room. Looking around, he said he had expected a suite. I wanted to remind him he lived in a tenement, but I remained silent. "This isn't the Waldorf," he said.

I looked at him hard; maybe he was senile, and I had wasted the bus fare. He added: "The real Waldorf was pulled down in 1931 to make room for that phallic symbol, the Empire State building." I was careful not to say that 1931 was the year in which I was born.

I began by asking Harris about his direction of Miss Hepburn in the play *The Lake,* in 1934.

"Dorothy Parker said she ran the gamut of emotions from A to B. She didn't get as far as B." He paused. "During rehearsals, she came up to me and threw her arms around me in front of the whole cast. It was shockingly unprofessional of her. She said to me, 'I have loved you, I love you now, and I will always love you.' I replied, 'You haven't acted, you aren't acting now, and you will never act.' I told her to put an ice pack on her head, lie down for three hours, and then come back and give a performance. She came back. She did *not* give a performance."

I asked Harris if he had seen Hepburn in *A Delicate Balance* on ABC TV. He said he had, but that she was "still acting as badly as ever." When he had by mischance seen her in recent telecast films, he had been appalled to note she was still using the defunct Delsarte acting method, leaning against doorjambs and pressing handkerchiefs to her forehead to express despair. I didn't have the nerve to say that she had never acted like that; at least, not on the screen.

Several times, he picked up my tape recorder and walked to the window, looking out into the driving rain and stating he would drop it onto Park Avenue. I warned him that if he did he might hit, and kill, a pedestrian. And wind up in the electric chair in Sing-Sing. ("Not a bad idea. At least I'll get free board and lodging.")

He closed by saying I was a "nice man" but his tone implied I knew nothing about the theater. I finally asked him why he was broke. "I financed my own shows. I needed complete control. When I went to Mrs. Martin Beck at her theater, she wanted to run everything. I paid for all the plays I did for her." There was something grandiose and splendid about the old bastard's boast. At the end of the afternoon, I actually liked this *monstre damné*. After he left, I called Charlie Abrahamson and told him to pay him his second $250 and bus fare. Luckily, Hepburn never asked me about the interview.

There was an even ruder man in New York, Michael Bennett, Hepburn's choreographer on *Coco*. He lived at 145 West Fifty-fifth Street, in a pop art apartment done out in what I would call abattoir modern. The sofa I sat on was a pair of cloth lips; facing me was a table in the form of a heart; nearby, another table was formed like a human liver.

The lean, bristling, brilliant, and uptight young Turk of the American musical theater was starkly unwelcoming. "I don't believe this interview is authorized," he said. "Hepburn would never cooperate with any writer."

"If you don't believe me why did you agree to see me?"

"I like to meet con men and frauds."

"Why don't you check with Miss Hepburn herself?"

"Where is she?"

"At her home in West Hollywood. Here's the phone number."

"You'll pay for the call?"

"Send me the bill when it comes in. Specify the charge."

"Five bucks in advance."

"Here it is."

He picked up the phone. "I'll say this for you. You've got a fucking nerve."

"Just place the call."

He did. He handed me the extension phone so I could hear Hepburn's cry of denial.

I think: This guy is a fucking idiot. Wouldn't I have given up by now if I wasn't authorized?

Hepburn's genteel companion Phyllis Wilbourne came on the line. Bennett said: "There's some hack here, Charles Higham, says Kate authorized a book."

"She did. Wait. I'll fetch her on the phone."

Bennett glared at me. I desperately wanted to punch him on the nose.

I heard Hepburn's voice, growling from a cold. "Yes, he's all right," she said. "Just *don't tell him any good stories.* I'm saving them for my book."

Thanking her coldly, Bennett hung up. He spent the next two hours attacking Hepburn viciously; his account of the production of *Coco* did, however, have an authentic ring. I used most of it in my book.

There were more bizarre encounters. My friend the critic Elliott Stein introduced me to his pet tarantula. George Rose (*Coco*), a specialist in effeminate stage roles, lived near Fourteenth and Ninth in Greenwich Village. When I entered his apartment, I heard a roar and a snarling puma appeared, held insecurely by the actor on a long leash, and it bared its teeth

153

at me. Asked to stroke it on my lap, I refused, not wishing to have it bite my balls off. Not long after that, Rose was murdered by gay thugs in the Caribbean, like the composer Mark Blitzstein long before him.

Kate was a joy to write, and Sheri Huber's editing was inspired. Norton was delighted with the finished result and the book went onto the best-seller lists even before it was published. It was clear that this was my break-through book. The reviews in *Publishers Weekly* and the *Los Angeles Times* were ecstatic; of the others, only *Time* struck a sour note.

The *Today* show's excellent producer Patty Nager called, and I was booked to appear the next morning. I left Los Angeles for New York with Broderick Crawford and his friend Johnny Mercer, one of my favorite lyricists ("Tangerine" remains my favorite song). We were preceded aboard the plane by the Who; they occupied most of first class, pushing Brod and Johnny into business class with me. My more affluent traveling companions were nice enough to say that they preferred that.

We took off in the morning on a supposedly nonstop flight with plenty of time for Brod and Johnny to meet their New York appointments to discuss, respectively, a movie deal and a new musical. (The Who were booked for Madison Square Garden.) Then, as we flew over Chicago, the pilot announced that we had lost an engine and might lose another: FAA regulations called for the announcement and we were warned that a severe electrical storm, which had been causing us heavy turbulence, was raging below us and that no clearance could be obtained to land in other cities. We would have to make an emergency landing at O'Hare. The captain said the risk involved was considerable; not because the TWA 747 couldn't fly on three or even on two engines but because we would have to dump fuel with lightning about and there might be a fire.

The cabin went almost completely dark, emergency lights glimmering like sick glowworms from the bulkheads. As when I almost drowned, I felt separate from my body, watching myself and the scene of tense, pale, almost paralyzed passengers. A woman began to sob.

Brod said to me, "Charles, I don't think we're gonna make it." I replied, "It's all very well for you. You'll be on the front page and I'll be back to the crossword puzzle and the chess problem." "Not with The Who on board," Johnny said with a laugh. "Brod and I will be back there with you." No more piercing a remark could be made by the Old Music about the New.

Roger Daltrey and his manic crew invaded business and economy class, ignoring the rules and setting our nerves on fire with a screeching, pounding performance that in the circumstances didn't even win a cheer from the young people on board. Most people around me were heard saying that it was horrible to think this was the last music we would ever hear, that they wished the band would return to their seats. Following a tussle with the flight attendants, the group returned to first class and quieted down. I was told later that they had wanted to make us feel more relaxed, like, perhaps, the string orchestra on the *Titanic*.

We circled for hours through black, beating rain and flashes of lightning, and at last were told we had lost only one engine and were able to land at O'Hare. When we stepped out into the storm, a crowd of reporters and photographers were waiting. Brod said correctly, "They're not for us," which was a great relief. As the reporters besieged Daltrey and his group we were able to answer just a couple of questions and rush to the washroom to try to make ourselves look presentable.

Another plane was produced and we all took off again into the same storm and turbulence. At last we touched down at Kennedy at 4:30 a.m. A cab got me to the Waldorf by six and I now had one hour before the studio limousine picked me up to take me to *Today*. I showered, shaved, did push-ups and sit-ups, ran up and down the corridor, and at exactly seven, with no breakfast, I was at the reception desk in the lobby to greet the uniformed driver. Still not exhausted, and glad to be alive, I gave the best interview of my life to *Today*'s genial Gene Shalit, a combination of Lewis Carroll's the Walrus and the Carpenter, whose face I suspected, under its heroic display of shrubbery, was probably small, twinkling, and childlike. He was a big fan of Hepburn and of my book.

There were eight more interviews that day—radio, press, television; all went well. Then at 11 p.m., ready for a tour of other cities, I fell into a much-needed sleep at the hotel. I had seldom been happier, and the tour, with *Kate* an instant smash hit, went extremely well.

13

*Y*ou're a big best-selling author now," said Ross Claiborne, the enchanting editor in chief of Delacorte Press over lunch at the Madrigal restaurant in New York. "We can't possibly afford you." Sweet words indeed, and one day he did.

What was I to write next? The obvious temptation was to find subjects of equal magnitude: Bette Davis perhaps, or Joan Crawford. But I felt, in my snobbish heart, that my literary reputation was imperiled, that if I kept writing pop biographies, no matter how successful, I would no longer be taken seriously as critic and poet.

I decided to strike a compromise: I would write a biography of a writer for Norton. I settled on Sir Arthur Conan Doyle, creator of Sherlock Holmes, and my editor Sheri Huber enthusiastically agreed with the idea, along with her excellent boss Starling Lawrence.

I needed to have the support of Conan Doyle's only surviving child, Lady Jean Bromet, commander in chief of the British Women's Air Force. The ink scarcely dry on the contract, only two weeks after the *Kate* talk-show tour came to an end, I was on my way by British Airways to London with Richard, who had never been to England. I hadn't been there since 1954, twenty-two years before.

It was intoxicating to be back, not as a parcel packer, struggling book-store clerk, or publisher's assistant, but as a best-selling author. Instead of a seedy flat, I now had as my address the Dorchester, to this day my favorite hotel. The Grill was in those days an alluring replica of a Spanish dining room, more Hollywood than Madrid, with heavy purple velvet curtains, and Philip II chairs; Michael Caine and his wife were regularly installed at a corner table near the window.

Now I could enjoy my childhood favorites: summer pudding, prepared a day in advance, steak and kidney pie, roast beef sliced on the joint, sherry trifle, and an entire trolley load of the finest English cheeses. Even the weather was sunny, the streets filled not with the wan and wasted figures of the war years, but with apple-cheeked and bustling crowds, the young dressed pleasingly. The city was leavened agreeably by the foreign elements of which the old were heard complaining from nearby tables at breakfast: a feast of porridge and brown sugar, poached eggs, lashings of toast and Dundee marmalade, Cornish or Devonshire cream, and freshly boiled eggs.

So as not to hurt Richard, I avoided the places that he might have guessed Norine and I had frequented; I even avoided Hatchards, where I had been humiliated by the manager Ellic Howe, now filled with my books on display tables.

It was a steamy July, and going to un-air-conditioned theaters every night meant being drenched in sweat in seats designed not for men of my height, but for midgets of an earlier age. It didn't matter; we enjoyed everything. My British agent, Felicity Brian, was a pretty, sweet-natured hostess; just showing Richard, a royalty buff, Buckingham Palace from the outside was a joy. Giving lunch at the Dorchester to Penelope Houston, editor of *Sight and Sound,* who had published me when I was young and struggling, was delicious in its display of power. A socialist to the core, she still enjoyed the smoked salmon and pâté de fois gras like a child.

Lady Bromet and Sir Geoffrey, her elderly husband, gave me lunch at the Royal Air Force Club, and they had me to tea at their home at 72 Cadogan Square. Lady Bromet acted swiftly, asking me to go to Switzerland to retrieve some valuable Conan Doyle manuscripts of Sherlock Holmes stories that, she said, her late brother Adrian had maintained there, but had vanished after his death. I was now, to my great delight, a latter-day Holmes myself.

The Lausanne Palace Hotel was a dream of luxury. On the edge of a paradisal lake, it offered us, and we took, night after night, free boat trips across the sparkling moonlit waters to the town of Evian. Our lovemaking was unstinting and joyful, the lunches and dinners on the grand terrace delicious and impeccably served. Life, we agreed, couldn't be much better. But soon there were problems.

So often, in obtaining authorization to write a life story, I had been forced to bring unwelcome news to heirs and friends, and this was no exception.

I found out that Adrian Conan Doyle had been lent by the Swiss government the fabled twelfth-century Château de Luçerne, for a peppercorn rent of one pound a year, in return for supplying a Sherlock Holmes museum as a tourist attraction, a replica of the Holmes flat at 221B Baker Street in London, with the usual accoutrements from drug needle to Turkish slippers.

The museum was a disaster. Desperate for money, Adrian turned out to be a latter-day Moriarty; he offered the château for sale for a million dollars to the University of Texas in Austin as a European campus without benefit of ownership, a criminal act of which Lady Bromet knew nothing. Finding that the title deeds were forged, Texas withdrew. During the subsequent investigation, Adrian, conveniently for the family's honor, died.

Where were the papers? I was alarmed to find that they were not in the Lausanne bank vault where Adrian had told Jean they were deposited; instead, he had sold them illegally to an autograph dealer, the House of El Dieff in New York, whose irascible owner, due to my miscalculation of the time difference, I awoke by telephone at his home at 2 a.m. In anger he confirmed what I feared: not one of the precious manuscripts and letters survived in a library or museum; all had been disposed of privately at high prices.

I found that Denis Conan Doyle, Sir Arthur's younger son, had an even worse reputation. Courage and chivalry were the outmoded watchwords of the family. Adrian had staged medieval jousts on bridges in England during World War II, dressed in a full suit of armor, and Denis, to outdo him, had embarked on a Bengal tiger hunt in India. Unhappily, he ran away from the advancing beast and died of a heart attack.

His widow, the Princess Nina Mdivani, married a certain Anthony Harwood, who posed, without bothering to correct the spelling of his name, as a Harewood, a royalty-connected family in England. After he was murdered by motorcycle hustlers at the Stanhope Hotel in New York, Nina was put away in a mental institution. So much for the legacy of Sir Arthur, the strictest of Victorian moralists.

I made the original discovery that Sir Arthur had found the basis for the Holmes stories in his youth. On his early visit to London, from Scotland in

1874, a murderer named Moriarty was on trial, Oliver Wendell Holmes was in town on a lecture tour, a violinist named Sherlock was appearing at the Wigmore Hall, a Dr. Watson was his Uncle John's friend and next door neighbor, and so forth. Madame Tussauds Chamber of Horrors catalogue, surviving in the British Library, gave accounts of murder cases on which the author had based his tales. Later, the first scholar to do so, I found dozens more.

By coincidence, Conan Doyle's best friend, Robin Sanders-Clark, lived only a mile from me in Los Angeles, and the greatest collection of Doyleana, including the *Beeton's Christmas Annuals* in which the Holmes stories first appeared, was just five miles farther on, at Occidental College. Thus my chief sources were in my own backyard.

I decided to open up the chronicle to give a full account of Sir Arthur's addiction to spiritualism. Along with my belief in the supernatural, well supported by experience, I didn't believe in most mediums, spirit photographers of course, or those who claimed to have found fairies in the backyard. A field ruined by quackery had been affected by the skepticism evoked.

How had Conan Doyle, creator of the master of deductive logic with his deerstalker hat and magnifying glass, succumbed to such charlatans? The reason was touching: his favorite son had died in World War I and he couldn't accept the fact. Not psychic himself and therefore unable to be assured of the boy's survival from direct experience, he relied on crooks who provided the son's voice, dressed up as his dead mother, and produced "ectoplasm," which was made out of butter muslin.

Although Lady Bromet, to whom I sent the transcripts, was not displeased by the portrait of her father as a man, she was unhappy with the statement that he was buried in secret in a laundry basket to avoid press coverage and that I was "fairly obviously skeptical" about spiritualism. When reporters called her for her comments, she would make none. Another potential friendship, dissolving in truth, ended for good.

But I had compensations: long and enthusiastic reviews by John Fowles in London's *New Statesman* and by the usually difficult Paul Theroux in the *New York Times,* and the *Times*'s selection of *The Adventures of Conan Doyle* as a Book of the Year.

Sheri Huber and I realized we must now come up with something more commercial. The glow of good reviews couldn't compensate for loss of income and an uncertain financial future, especially since I was house hunting now with Richard.

I decided that Marlene Dietrich would be the ideal choice. I knew her well and therefore could give an account of her, personally and firsthand. I also knew many of her colleagues: her directors Josef von Sternberg, Billy Wilder, Fritz Lang, Curtis Bernhardt, and Tay Garnett, among others; her writer friend Walter Reisch; and some of the actors she had worked with, including James Stewart, Cesar Romero, and John Wayne.

The tall and cheerless Cesar Romero was my first interview. The most closeted of gay stars, he was a cold antithesis of his warm, macho, Latino personality on the screen. His memory of making *The Devil Is a Woman* with Marlene was quite vivid: The director von Sternberg told him to walk down a staircase one hundred times and say one word, yes. After the hundredth time, Romero was ready to kill. His voice filled with contempt, von Sternberg said in front of cast and crew, "I now call upon Mr. Romero to say yes for the one hundred and first time." Romero said no and walked off the set, to general laughter and applause.

My close friend Sam Jaffe played the demented Peter; he told me that von Sternberg was furious with him over the way he acted a scene, and Sam gave him the finger sign. "Don't you realize," von Sternberg said, "I have five million disciples?" "How nice for you," Sam said. "Christ only had twelve."

I found von Sternberg at his Westwood townhouse, at 4 p.m., sitting in a chair under a skylight through which the late afternoon sun conveniently bathed him in a single beam of light. He was leafing through a book of poems of Hafez in ancient Persian, pretending to read a language with which he was not familiar. He led me downstairs to a study, where I was surrounded by primitive carvings obtained from his travels. Every time I asked a question he countered with "next please" until at last, ready to leave this talented fox in his art deco lair, I asked him how, at a time when Paramount Pictures was on the ropes, 1934, he had managed to have big crowd scenes in *The Scarlet Empress*. "Ernst Lubitsch, who ran the studio, called me in to berate me," he purred, sucking at a tobaccoless pipe, his pale, mustachioed plump face stamped with disagreeable self-satisfaction. "I told him he had only himself to blame: I had taken his own crowd scenes from his silent movie *The Patriot*."

As for Dietrich, "I found a key in her back and I wound it and off she went." The insult reminded me of Hitchcock's comment on Ray Milland in *Dial M for Murder*: "I wound it up, I put it on the floor, and *it didn't work*."

I found Risa Royce, von Sternberg's American wife at the time of his first affair with Marlene during the shooting of *The Blue Angel* in Berlin. She told me that, furious at his many absences from the Hotel Adlon (she found out later that he made love to Dietrich on a tiger skin under a mirrored ceiling), she told him to break off the marital relationship and marry Marlene. "I'd as soon share a telephone booth with a cobra," was his reply.

John Lodge was Marlene's leading man in *The Scarlet Empress*. Powerfully built and strikingly handsome, he had left acting (not his forte) for a distinguished career in politics. Grandson of Henry Cabot Lodge, he was first congressman, then governor of Connecticut; later, he was successively ambassador to Spain and Argentina. I found him at his home in Westport.

When I arrived too early on a chilly April morning, I was surprised to see trestle tables on the veranda covered in picture books on Marlene. Apparently, I was supposed to look at the competition in an icy wind with a threat of rain and no umbrella while waiting for admission at 11:30 for conversation and lunch. Irritated, I rang the doorbell.

There was no response. Suddenly, I heard a stream of abuse in Italian directed by some imperious woman at more than one servant; I knew enough of the language to determine that the help had failed in their domestic duties.

At last a maid opened the door, and I caught a glimpse of a dark and impassioned grande dame with her hair in curlers, wearing a black silk robe over a lace negligee. I recognized Francesca Bragiotti, a favorite movie actress in Italy before World War II, who had married Lodge many years before.

Lodge proved to be an entertaining host and had the grace to ask me to lunch, even if he did describe my newspaper as "that pinko rag." Those at the table were right wing, business figures whose conversation was directed against liberals, faggots, and Hollywood movies.

Over an excellent Italian meal, Lodge, in his resonant voice, told of how on one visit to Madrid he had stayed with Isabel and Juan Perón. Going to the bathroom one night, he had taken a wrong turn and walked into a room where his host and hostess were sleeping. At the foot of their bed was a glass coffin containing Evita, long since dead of cancer and maintained, in an embalmed effigy, as a permanent traveling companion. A manicurist and hairdresser were taken along for the ride.

Lodge added that Isabel Perón was presently under house arrest in Buenos Aires by an anti-Peronist regime. He said he had airlifted Beluga caviar, pâté de fois gras, and Dom Perignon champagne to her by helicopter after bribing her jailers.

Richard and I flew to Europe so that I could talk to Marlene's former German and Austrian associates. In one city, armed with an interpreter supplied by the British consul, we visited the home of a leading collector of Dietrichiana who, while producing photographs and scrapbooks of rare interest covering the Berlin years, gave Richard a drug in his tea that sent him to sleep while he made a violent overture I rejected without difficulty; as a result, we left empty handed. On our way to Vienna, there was an incident straight out of a Hitchcock thriller: Richard's Filipino passport and American visa didn't qualify him for a brief stopover in a border town that mysteriously didn't seem to fall under German, Austrian, or Italian control, and he was taken by the police off the train. I was told not to follow.

Released at the last minute, Richard leapt aboard the moving train, almost falling under the wheels. The unsympathetic passengers merely stared, except for one man who told me that I hadn't needed to lose my nerve. I saw the chilly side of the German temperament and was too upset to eat lunch.

The Sacher Hotel in Vienna, with its famous chocolate torte and easy access to the opera house, where we saw an unforgettable *Flying Dutchman,* and Martha Graham in her dotage, was a delight and so was Marlene's former friend and director Karl Hartl, a man of the greatest sophistication and charm.

He told me an unforgettable story. His early patron and mentor, Count Sascha Kolowrat, of Sascha Films, was dying of cancer at forty-two at Semmering, near Vienna, when he told Hartl he had one unfulfilled wish: to see Marlene's legs once more before he died. Hartl went backstage where Marlene was appearing in the play *Broadway* and gave her the message. She smiled and nodded. Next day she took a car and driver and went to the hospital. She walked into Kolowrat's room, raised her skirt, wished him well, and left. The count called Hartl at once and said, "Now I can die happy." And he did, the following day.

It was wonderful to see Marlene's early films, so hard to obtain in America, thanks to Peter Jubelka of the Austrian Film Institute and his go-between, the enchanting Lisl Neumann.

In Los Angeles, a friend, the director Tay Garnett, said that when Marlene met him for the first time at the Universal Studios commissary to discuss *Seven Sinners,* in which she would appear under his direction with John Wayne, Wayne ambled in wearing chaps and a cowboy hat. "Daddy," Dietrich said to Garnett, "buy me that." And sure enough, he did.

The director Jean Negulesco told me that during World War II, Marlene had lived in the house, later belonging to Negulesco himself, that had once been Garbo's, on North Bedford Drive in Beverly Hills, with her lover, the great French star Jean Gabin. Every night at dinner, they saw a mysterious, black-leotarded, and masked figure flitting past the french doors; when they went out to investigate the figure was gone. They dubbed it Fantômas, after the famous figure of French silent and sound films, a ghostly mass murderer who terrorized Paris in sinister black garments and hood.

They set a rabbit trap, and one night after the figure flitted by, they heard a scream. They ran to the spot and stripped off the hood and cloak. The trapped, sobbing visitor was Garbo, eager to see what she could of the Gabin-Dietrich affair in the home she had once occupied. They let her go with a caution, and a bandage for her ankle.

Negulesco told me Marlene hated dogs but Gabin insisted on having one (she also hated cats). The dog barked incessantly day and night, greatly annoying Garbo, who lived up the street. One night the dog went missing. Gabin offered a reward, posted on every tree in the neighborhood; no response. Finally, Marlene had an idea. She told Gabin to climb Garbo's garden wall. He did, and found the dog muzzled into silence and chained in the yard. He let it loose and carried it out by the gate. Marlene decided against telling the press, thus avoiding another headline: GARBO DOGNAPS FRENCH STAR'S POOCH.

*L*ife continued at a good pace, and my relationship with Richard deepened, but 1976 was marked by a very unpleasant surprise. Seymour Peck called to tell me that he had been fired.

This was shocking. He was my mentor, the man who had changed only one word in all of the many articles I had written; I was still in America because he had given me a career and arranged a green card for me; he was the inspiration of my life with his good cheer, support, and deep admiration.

So far as I could determine, he had assumed more autonomy than certain figures in the *Times* hierarchy had found tolerable, and his unshakable influence had jarred less unequivocal spirits. When I flew to New York to see him, his corner desk in the big Sunday section office was showered with sawdust; his replacement's room was being built behind him (he had never had an office of his own).

I found him, unbeaten and cheerful, in striped shirtsleeves in a small boardroom where a year before he had given a party in my honor. Now he was an obscure figure on the *Times*'s Sunday magazine, given little work to do. I asked him if I should resign; he urged me not to. Perhaps it was cowardly of me, but I stayed on; I couldn't leave the most important job in my field.

And there was no indication I would be fired, nor were my *New York Times* Los Angeles colleagues Stephen Farber and Aljean Harmetz. In fact, I scored a coup that gave me four more years on the paper. I had been working desultorily on a piece about violence in movies that seemed to me dull and obvious, a moralistic filler assignment of the sort I tried to avoid. Wanting to impress the bosses, I called the great Erich Fromm at his home in Zurich, to obtain his comments on the subject. I was sure he hadn't seen a movie since *Birth of a Nation* but I also guessed he would be eager to indulge in a flight of interpretation in the *New York Times*.

I was right. Incredibly, he was listed in the Zurich telephone directory and couldn't wait to talk. His words made little sense, but such abstruse reasoning from so eminent a source would dazzle certain bigwigs at the paper. It did, and his comments appeared inside a special border inside my piece; I lost count of the congratulations. How could I possibly have found such a person, and even more incredibly persuaded him to talk? I made up a story of a prolonged search and struggle, and the piece secured my future for four more years.

14

*O*ctober 1976 found me in New York, talking about Dietrich with the director Joshua Logan; the publicist Viola Rubber (who kept the autographs of the famous on her broken leg's cast); Betty Comden, the gifted partner in musicals of Adolph Green; Al Hirschfeld and his wife, Dolly Haas; Marlene's schoolmate Elli Marcus; and the journalist and editor Leo Lerman. There were lunches and dinners, at Lutece with Jeanie Luciano and Lisl Cade, Sheri Huber at Barbetta's, the publisher and author Robert Giroux at the Players Club, and dinner with a friend of earlier years, Dudley Field Malone, and his lover at their elegant apartment on East Fiftieth Street.

Back in Los Angeles, I formed a new friendship with the talented director Robert Stevenson (*Jane Eyre*, *Mary Poppins*) and his psychiatrist wife, Ursula. Their home in Burbank overlooked a branch of Forest Lawn, and I asked Robert why. He replied that it would save heavy transportation charges to take him to the main cemetery in Glendale when his time came.

In February 1977, as if I weren't busy enough, I was possessed by a story about a changeling in Ireland: the young daughter of a California couple on vacation disappears and is replaced by an evil spirit, an exact copy of herself. I had never given thought to such a subject and knew nothing of Irish folklore, but for a week, working from dawn to dusk with my secretary, Frances Mercer, I dictated the entire novel without notes, leaving us both exhausted. Accepted at once, *The Midnight Tree* was published successfully by Pocket Books without a word changed.

I received a call from Alana Ladd, daughter of Alan Ladd, inviting me to her mother Sue's house, to discuss a possible life story. The family was obviously looking for a hagiography as they showed me a shrine with Ladd's screenplays bound in leather, candles, and photographs. Though I was touched, and admiring of the late star, I knew the subject wasn't for me.

Evenings with Mae West became more fun than ever. We would go to, of all places, the Los Angeles warehouse district, literally on the wrong side of the tracks, with an actual railroad yard not far away, to Man Fook Low, the vaguely obscene-sounding Chinese restaurant she favored. On our arrival, the staff lined up against the wall as if she were Catherine the Great at her imperial palace; she had played the part on stage and relived it now, sweeping in royally, resting on Paul Novak's arm, to the high dais where the table was set out for us, seating twelve.

Following her step by step—she could hardly move—we, her retinue, sat at the table and remembered to say something flattering every few minutes. Normally, such sycophancy would have stuck in my throat. But one wasn't admiring a human being; this was an ancient and lovable Minerva. Mae West and reality had nothing to do with each other.

I was in the group that took her to the hundredth birthday party of the grand old monster Adolph Zukor of Paramount Pictures. It was held at the Beverly Hilton ballroom, and almost everyone in Hollywood of any note was there. Bette Davis arrived early and, according to the hotel staff, had a tape measure drawn to the exact center of the reception room floor, where she planted herself for an entire hour until the banquet began. By contrast, Barbara Stanwyck almost hid in a dark corner; when I spoke to her, she said she wished the ground would open and swallow her up. As at our previous meeting at the Park La Brea Towers, I was amazed by her recessiveness: the boldest, the most fiercely extroverted of stars in such films as *Union Pacific* and *Ball of Fire* was a shy, uneasy wallflower.

A moment occurred that could never have taken place anywhere else. One of the most famous unsolved mysteries in the history of show business was why George Jessel, the dazzling star of *The Jazz Singer* on Broadway, hadn't repeated his role in the first Warner Bros. talkie, thus securing himself a permanent place in legend. Al Jolson had taken over and become world famous overnight.

For once in a lifetime, Jack L. Warner and Jessel were on the same spot;

I was told they hadn't spoken in the almost half century that had elapsed since *The Jazz Singer*'s premiere.

"Now," I said to them, "that you two gentleman are together for the first time in memory, Mr. Jessel, would you say why you didn't get to play in *The Jazz Singer*?" "Because," Jessel replied, "this son of a bitch gave me five dud checks in a row."

"Is that true, Mr. Warner?" I asked. "Like that other George, this one never told a lie," Jack replied, winked at me to indicate Jessel was in fact lying, and walked away.

Elsa Lanchester, a specialist in eccentric movie characters, from the manic surrealist painter in *The Big Clock* to the bulldog-defying maid in *The Spiral Staircase,* called me one winter afternoon and asked to see me.

I had been struck by the anomaly of her marriage to the great Charles Laughton, whom Sir Laurence Olivier considered the finest actor of his generation. Since Charles was gay and Elsa was not, it seemed strange that they had stayed together all those many years, he starring so often in vehicles unworthy of him, she providing comic relief in some surprisingly good pictures. It was clear to me that to have a career as his wife, Elsa had given up a chance of marrying and, until a certain age, having children.

I arrived at her house on North Curson Avenue in Hollywood in heavy rain. Small, with dyed red hair, a plump figure, and the familiar clownish face, she greeted me then and later with a sweeping bow, accompanied by the flourish of removing an invisible feathered hat, as if she were a seventeenth-century cavalier, a comment on what she took to be my patrician manner.

She told me that she had been through several writers, looking for a man who could manage an authorized life of her late husband, who had died in the same house; she told me that these authors had disappeared into bars on drunks, and/or run off with other men. Would I take on the assignment? In a weak moment, I agreed, and lived to regret it. For months almost every day over tea and Dundee cake with marzipan, scones, or crumpets and lashings of tea, served by her energetic housekeeper, she told the story. From the first she spoke of Charles's adultery with a rent boy soon after their marriage in London and how she had sold the couch on which the sex took place when Charles was out. She offered me a look into a large filing cabinet in which she had stored private detectives' reports on his various goings-on with hustlers, and, repelled, I refused the privilege. It was easy to see that consciously or not she was out to revenge herself on Charles, that instead of divorcing him (as his wife she got more work as eccentrics in pictures) she had held up to him the evidence of his predilection for youths capable of performing with a man who was unattractive physically and hated himself for it. I wrote a book about his career with little reference to his private life, and I'm not sure she was pleased with the result, *Charles Laughton: An Intimate Biography*.

*M*y brief career as a party giver began in 1977 at Fountainview West. Among my frequent guests were the great producer Pandro S. Berman; the remarkable patron of the arts Justine Compton (Mrs. Harold Clurman, described in more detail later); the legendary Jean Howard, bisexual mistress of Louis B. Mayer; Miliza Korjus, imposing star of *The Great Waltz,* banished from Hollywood after only one picture because she was taken for a Nazi spy; Norman Lloyd, memorably the sly villain of Hitchcock's *Saboteur,* falling at the climax from the Statue of Liberty; Sam Jaffe and Bettye Ackerman Jaffe; the Robert Stevensons; Joel Greenberg; and Anna Sten, the ill-fated Sam Goldwyn discovery unaffected now by her failure as a star, an enchanting Russian to her fingertips.

Later that year, I secured a contract from Ken McCormick at Doubleday to write a life of Errol Flynn I had been planning for over a year. My first inkling that this might be a problematical work, that it would be far removed from the lightweight tale of an antic adventurer I had planned, was when, with the help of the Mexican star Dolores del Rio, I was able to conduct a very rare interview, her first since 1940, with Flynn's first wife, the French movie actress Lili Damita. Long since retired, she had married a dairy millionaire, Allan Loomis, and divided her time between Fort Dodge, Iowa, of all unlikely places, in the summer and, much more appropriately, Palm Beach, Florida, in the winter.

She wouldn't see me in person but agreed to a telephone conversation. She solved a mystery I was not to make public until after she was dead; I kept the promise and reveal it now for the first time.

The disappearance of Sean, her famous son with Flynn, is unsolved to this day. The handsome actor was on a mission for various magazines and photographic agencies in North Vietnam, posing as a resident of Ireland, which was not involved in the war. He had vanished, leaving no trace. Damita said she had kept his room at their house in Miami cleaned and ready for him for years; even his suits were maintained in a closet, as she was certain he would one day return (she had been Jack Kennedy's nurse after the PT *109* incident and had continued part-time work as an RN in order to survive until she married Loomis).

Finally, she told me, she snapped; she called her old friend Walter Cronkite, certain that of all people he might know the answer. He looked into the matter and with his extraordinary influence was able to extract the facts from the CIA before the Freedom of Information Act was ratified in 1978. He called her and told her he didn't think she should know the truth; she insisted, and he was forced to give her the report. Sean had been caught by the Vietcong and had been punished as a spy; he had been pegged to the ground in a jungle clearing and trampled to death, his rib cage smashed by hobnail boots. Devastated, Damita closed Sean's room forever and gave all of his clothes to charity.

With the Dietrich and Laughton books published and doing well, followed by Bette Davis's stormy chronicle, and money at last, after a prolonged struggle, released from my father's estate following my stepmother's untimely death, I had enough to buy a house for Richard and me to live in together after five years at separate addresses. And we found a beauty.

The architect had created a handsome Spanish-style villa, similar to others he had built in the then unfashionable Los Feliz district. It had a commanding view of Griffith Park, the largest municipal park in America, and the Sierra Madre, snow capped in winter and echoing with memories of Humphrey Bogart and Walter Huston; on clear days one could see all the way past Century City to the Pacific Ocean. Two and a half acres of hillside grew wild plants and flourishing trees; inside the house, the high ceilings and ceramic and platinum tilings created an attractive impression.

At first it wasn't for sale, but I kept going back to look at it. It had all the earmarks of a house designed as a place the architect intended to live in. Happily, just as it was finished, the architect's wife decided Los Feliz was beneath her; she preferred to live in the more upscale Encino, in the San Fernando Valley. I bought the place at once and resisted several offers to buy it from me, even before we moved in.

We had hardly done so when Patrice Wymore, Flynn's third wife, who ran his plantation at Port Antonio, Jamaica, called to say she was in town for a few days and would see me. I took her to lunch at the Bel Air Hotel and she proved to be a keeper of the flame, charming and still beautiful but uselessly naive as an interview subject. I found his final mistress, Beverly Aadland, who was fourteen when Flynn first met her, living in Palmdale, a depressing small town in the high desert, swept by icy winds. She had married a used car salesman, and all she had left of Flynn was a battered, black iron trunk, with a few mementos in it. Her history after Flynn's death proved to be fascinating: unable to accept that he was gone, she bizarrely became the mistress of his double, Paul MacWilliams; there were stories of her parents' quarrels, with one parent pushing the other under the Angels Flight railway car, and a shooting of a sailor in self-defense that had her languishing unfairly in Juvenile Hall.

Next day, I talked to Jack Warner about Flynn at his office. He autographed his memoirs with a flourish and the initials CBE after his name. Knowing he was not a Commander of the British Empire, I didn't bite when he asked me to identify the letters. "Consolidated Bullshit Enterprises," he said with a smile.

Flynn's second wife was Nora Eddington Black. I took her to lunch at Scandia, preliminary to having her drive me to the Flynn house, where she had lived with him high up on Mulholland Drive. After her third old-fashioned, irritable that I didn't drink (I pretended I had suffered from hepatitis and she expressed annoyance rather than pity), I got the measure of this touchy, feisty woman. The drive up into the hills was perilous indeed, her black Mercedes spinning alarmingly close to a fenceless cliff edge, even though she was still sober.

The sprawling house was alive with gospel music being played loudly on a pipe organ. Nora rang the doorbell; neither of us had any idea who lived there. The door flew open and a woman stood there; we told her the reason for our visit and she let us in. Her husband, she said, was Stuart Hamblen, many times platinum disc winner, creator of the enormous hit "This Ole House." Nora looked at me with raised eyebrows: the home of the most wicked and irreligious of stars had become the shrine of a religious pop composer.

Hamblen greeted us warmly. The orgy room, where Flynn staged sexual derbies, men mounting women from behind and pushing them on all fours along the floor while others watched though a two-way ceiling mirror, had become a chapel. The aquarium, where he had painted enormous male genitals on the walls while fish swam about, had become a shrine. Hamblen showed us around, cheerfully oblivious to the provenance of the rooms.

I delivered the Flynn biography, a steamy but not surprising and quite apolitical chronicle, to my editor Ken McCormick at Doubleday, who accepted it overnight. But then something happened that changed my life forever.

15

$\mathcal{I}$ received a phone call from a man in New York of whom I had never heard, who said he was making a small, independently financed documentary on Flynn and wondered if I had solved the mystery of two characters in the actor's best-selling memoir, *My Wicked, Wicked Ways*: a man named Schwarz and another named Koets, the first an American filmmaker in New Guinea in 1931 who had used Flynn's pearling boat, and the other a Dutch explorer in the same region.

I replied that I had not, that I felt it was a weakness in my book that these two people couldn't at this stage be found and were probably dead. The caller said he had the answer: Flynn had divided a close lifelong friend into two, creating these fictitious figures. Schwarz and Koets in fact were a certain Dr. Hermann F. Erben, a Nazi agent who, in 1946, had turned state's evidence at the Shanghai trial of the German spy ring working for the Japanese in China: the notorious Bureau Ehrhardt.

It was a simple matter to obtain the trial transcript from the National Archives in Washington. It confirmed that Erben was the spy and stool pigeon who caused the Ehrhardt group to go to prison. He himself didn't escape; reneging on a plea bargain, the United States military authorities, led by Colonel William E. Williamson and Colonel Frank Farrell, both acting for the OSS, had him shipped off to a prison camp in Germany.

What, I asked myself, was Errol Flynn up to? Why had he lied about his friendship with Erben, disguising him by splitting him into two fictitious characters in what purported to be an accurate autobiography? Obviously, he was determined to hide the association, and it was mandatory that I explore the matter further.

I called Ken McCormick at Doubleday, who said that he was willing to hold up the book's publication so that I could follow the lead. But he could give me no more money; I had been paid the balance of the advance and from now on I was on my own. Luckily, I had saved up from my previous books and decided to commit all the cash I had to the new exploration, wherever it might take me.

The Freedom of Information Act had just been ratified and files on World War II espionage were open for the first time. I flew to Washington and put up at the Madison Hotel, leaving behind Richard, who was busy working at his hospital.

The forbidding National Archives building, huge, gray, and chilly, took some exploring but at last I found the appropriate file room; it resembled the interior of a submarine, windowless, with open pipes rising from floor to ceiling. Long rows of filing cabinets set against the walls had seldom been opened in sixty years, and then only by members of the staff.

These drawers contained thousands of tiny cards, brittle and often browned by age, on which the names of suspected enemy agents were typed. I began with Erben, Herman J. There were dozens of cards on him marked PSA (Possible Subversive Activities). And then I found more on Errol Leslie Flynn.

From these I gleaned that Flynn acted as Erben's cover for years; that he stepped in time and time again, when Erben, a naturalized American citizen, was threatened with deportation as an enemy agent; that he hid him aboard his yacht, the *Sirocco,* and took him into Mexico in defiance of the authorities in 1940, when Flynn's country was at war with Germany, an act of treason. And that Erben had joined the Abwehr, German military intelligence in Mexico City.

I returned to Los Angeles in a daze. Espionage was not my field, and Flynn had been my boyhood idol; the St. Peter's School outing to see *The Private Lives of Elizabeth and Essex* was the high spot of the early 1940s. At the same time Flynn made the film, he was, I now knew, assisting a Nazi spy and perhaps was one himself.

It became necessary to obtain the State Department files, which would cover a mysterious trip to Spain by Flynn and Erben during the 1937–38 years of the civil war in that country. The State Department had a strict rule that if anyone was alive the files could not be released. But my good luck worked for me again.

In 1934, in a device worthy of an Alfred Hitchcock thriller, Erben had faked his death on a train in Austria to escape detection as a Nazi agent. He had arranged with fellow spies to be carried out of the railroad station in a flower-bedecked coffin; once he was on the way to the morgue he jumped out and fled. Whoever read the thousand pages of documents at the State Department on Flynn and Erben saw the death notice in a 1934 newspaper clipping and had clearly not read on, or he would have seen hundreds more references to Erben, up to 1969. As a result, a mass of evidential pages was sent to me by mistake, and I was able to determine the nature of the Flynn-Erben operation in Spain, California, and elsewhere.

U.S. consulate files showed reports from Spain that Flynn and Erben, posing as benefactors of the Loyalist government cause, in opposition to General Franco's revolutionary, Nazi-backed forces, went behind the lines and reported on the activities of the Thaelmann Battalion, the German volunteer force that had left Hitler to assist the Barcelona government. As a result, the families of these men were killed in the concentration camps.

This was an important intelligence mission; later, it was possible to establish that Flynn took many reels of films of the Thaelmann soldiers and handed them over to the Nazis in Paris via the German agent Bradish Johnson, correspondent for *Newsweek,* for transmission to Berlin.

This spying mission was as important as Kim Philby's for the Communists in Spain, but completely unknown. How was I to find Erben? His citizenship revoked in 1940, his journey from China to Europe in 1946 poorly charted, was he still alive thirty-three years later?

I figured that this rascal would still claim to be a member of the American Medical Association abroad thirty-eight years after he was stricken from the records. And indeed I found him in the AMA's Vienna listings, which gave his home phone number.

I called repeatedly but had no reply. Then, I tried one more time. A woman's voice answered in German. She said she was Erben's sister, Hilde Schnirch, that she came in once a month for ten minutes to pick up the mail, and that I was very lucky to catch her.

I asked for Erben's whereabouts. Her reply was dramatic: he was in a leper colony at Sagata in the Philippines. Not as an inmate, she added hastily, but as a doctor there. She said the colony was for obvious reasons out of bounds to outsiders and that there was no point in my going; she said the place had no telephone and that Erben never answered his mail.

I contacted the Filipino consulate in Los Angeles and they sent me a list of English-speaking journalists in Manila but warned me that whoever I chose would not be able to conduct the interview at the colony under health regulations.

Some instinct made me pick out a name from the list: Marcos Agayo. I called him and he astonished me by saying he could indeed go to Sagata as his mother was Dr. Erben's assistant and he had grown up there. He left at once and sent me thirty-six hours of unforgettable tapes, all far more revealing than Erben intended. He even confirmed that Flynn had transported him across the border to Mexico in 1940: an act of treason.

Before and after *Errol Flynn: The Untold Story* was published successfully but to a predictable chorus of skepticism led by my former friend Walter Clemons in *Newsweek,* many more witnesses came forward. One episode I have not recounted before because of the pain it would have caused all concerned; the participants are now, and sadly, dead.

The actress who called herself Margo was famous for *Lost Horizon,* as the woman whose youth had been mysteriously preserved in the Tibetan lamasery of Shangri La but the moment she leaves she ages horribly and dies. She was married to Eddie Albert, and they had for many years lived next door to my haunted house in the Hollywood Knolls. She was a friend of mine, part of a liberal group including Sam Jaffe and Bettye Ackerman Jaffe, Stella Adler, Mary Anita Loos (niece of the creator of *Gentlemen Prefer Blondes*), and the actress Evelyn Scott.

She called me late one night to say she was shocked at the public skepticism and could categorically state that she was aware of Flynn's Nazism and would go on any talk show or speak to any journalist to confirm it. She said that Eddie had been in intelligence in Mexico in World War II and that when he worked with Flynn on the film *The Roots of Heaven* in Africa in 1958 he had asked Flynn about his political civilities, of which he had more than an inkling.

Flynn said he had been given a year to live at best and felt that Albert should know the truth. He gave him a complete account of his work with Erben as a Nazi collaborator. I thanked Margo and hung up; then, at dawn, she called me again, crying out hysterically that I must forget everything she had said; that Eddie, who was on location, had warned her he would kill her; that if I went ahead with it he would publicly call me a liar; and that he would lose the popular bank commercial in which he was now appearing if the story got out.

I called Bettye and Sam, and they said that Margo had also rung them, terrified that her husband might shoot her. Until Eddie Albert died in the year 2005 I couldn't reveal the fact that by hiding Flynn's treason he was himself a traitor to America. Now with Margo and their son, Edward, both dead, I feel the veil of secrecy can be lifted.

The new version of the book was completed in the fall of 1979. The picture was clear: Flynn had first been initiated in the Nazi philosophy by Dr. Erben, aboard the German freighter SS *Friderun* from New Britain to Marseilles in early 1934 (a letter surfaced later from Flynn to Erben, sent from England to Vienna, saying that Hitler should be brought to the United Kingdom to get rid of the Jews). Flynn gave Erben every assistance as a Nazi agent in America and interceded at a level as high as Eleanor Roosevelt to protect him when he was threatened with deportation. He helped him to expose the anti-Hitler Germans in Spain; he got him to Mexico City to join Nazi military intelligence; he kept in touch with him through neutral mail drops when Erben acted as an informer in the Japanese Pootung Assembly Center for allied prisoners, reporting on their plans for escape and seeing to it they were tortured to death. When the war was over, Flynn sent Erben ten thousand dollars, a very large sum in 1946, at a prison camp of the American army in Germany. Later, Flynn tried desperately to import this declared and condemned war criminal and traitor to the United States via the New York congressman Sterling Cole.

My ill-fated intention was to have a detailed set of source notes establishing all the facts from Washington documents and an index, as well as an exhaustive list of individuals who had helped. The top-secret work was leaked to the *New York Post* by a painter I had confided in unwisely. Hence, at the outset of 1980, "ERROL FLYNN A NAZI SPY" hit the headlines, and the publisher rushed the book out over my protests, anxious to cash in on the story and thus losing me a degree of credibility.

One person after another came forward to confirm my findings. The first of these was Jane Chesis, Flynn's private secretary for several years.

When she worked for him in Rome in 1951, there was a filing cabinet in his apartment that was never to be opened; Flynn told her he had the key. One day, he left on an appointment and she found it open. Unable to resist, she looked inside.

She was shocked to see letters with Nazi insignia on them sent to Flynn before and during World War II. Letters seeking money were signed by Germans from locations in Mexico, Brazil, and Argentina. It was clear that Flynn had given financial assistance to America's exiled enemies in these three countries. He caught her looking, swung her around, and hurled her to the floor; documents were scattered everywhere. Drunk, he failed to strangle her and she fled downstairs. When she came back that night, the cabinet and the papers were gone.

I was on the locally popular Owen Spann radio show in San Francisco when Spann, who was giving me a hard time, took outside calls. One of these was from a British-sounding woman, Mrs. Anne de Chutkowski, née Anne Lane, who lived in the Bay area.

Much to Spann's annoyance—he was clearly a fan of Flynn's or felt sure that members of his audience were—Mrs. de Chutkowski said that she could confirm my findings firsthand. She had, she said, been working at MI5, British Intelligence, at 4 Curzon Street, London, during the immediate postwar period, under Sir Percy Sillitoe; she had been in charge of the Flynn "Most Secret" files.

Spann wanted to cut her off, but I insisted she leave her telephone number and she did. The men in the control booth waved at me; they were pleased for me, and Spann glowered at them. I longed to punch him on the nose.

As soon as I was back at the St. Francis Hotel I called Anne, who gave me more details. She told me that the files showed that Flynn had been under watch order as a Nazi sympathizer and enemy of Britain since 1934 and that a massive espionage dossier had been assembled on him ever since. She said she had asked Sillitoe if this was "the" Errol Flynn and he replied, "Sadly, yes it is."

As a record keeper she had not been allowed to be privy to every report in the concertina folders, tied with red ribbon, nor had her sister Nanette, now living in South Africa, who refused to cooperate with me because she considered herself restricted by the British Official Secrets Act.

I was reflecting on the development when the phone rang. A colleague of Gerry Brown, the well-known London *News of the World* roving correspondent and a specialist in Irish terrorism, wanted me to give Brown an interview. I agreed, saying that Brown would score the coup of his career if he could find the file that had been in Anne's charge.

He was to call me on Monday at the Waldorf Astoria in New York before I went on *Good Morning America*. He did, and told me, in his James Bondish Scots voice, that he had found the file.

It was, he said, at the Ministry of Defence; two public relations men, Tony Brooks, connected to MI5, and Brigadier Guy Watkins, PR officer for the army, confirmed it was there. He was permitted a briefing by Brooks; the main file, exactly as Anne had described it, was of beige manila, concertina-style, tied with a red ribbon, and crammed with intelligence reports. Among other things it showed that Flynn was indeed under Watch Order from 1934, as Anne had seen; that he had gone to Spain and Germany on secret missions; and, most important of all, that he had, at a meeting at the Railway Hotel in Madrid in 1937, arranged for Sean Russell, quartermaster general of the Irish Republican Army, to move the IRA from Communist support to Nazi. Flynn was registered in the file as a major supporter of the IRA.

In addition, a meeting in Paris was monitored at which Flynn, the Duke of Windsor, Reinhard Heydrich, and Rudolph Hess, among others, met to discuss a British deal with Hitler. Gerry had meantime contacted Irish intelligence in Dublin under its leader Colonel Dan Bryan, whom he later flew to interview; Bryan confirmed the Flynn-Irish-German connection.

A few days later, Gerry called from London to say he had been denied direct access to the files. Sir Francis Pym, undersecretary for defense, had insisted they be sent to the Home Office, and they were. Tony Brooks, speaking to me from Berlin, confirmed the situation. From that day to this, the Home Office and Ministry of Defence have denied any knowledge of the existence of the files, and even a direct application to former prime minister Tony Blair elicited no help. A massive cover-up has taken place.

Professor Kemp Niver, chief preservationist of early pre-celluloid paper films, called me and invited me to lunch. He told me that if I were to print what he was about to say, or mention it to press, TV, or radio, he would have my legs broken. He had Mafia connections, he said, and I actually took him seriously.

He said he had been the cabin boy aboard Flynn's yacht the *Sirocco* in 1940; he was first-generation German and spoke the language fluently, as did Flynn, who had learned it from Dr. Erben. He overheard Flynn conspiring in his skipper's cabin with the Nazi architect-spy Hans Wilhelm Rohl, who had worked with the Japanese and not only had built much of Pearl Harbor's installations but had given the specifications to Tokyo. Flynn was—the conversation revealed—the contact with the spy Ulrich von der Osten in New York, who had transmitted the information through the Japanese and German consulates.

I received a call from a fan of mine, a student at USC who had referred me to a book by Caryl Chessman, the famous death row criminal at San Quentin who had fought for years against his execution. The memoir, *Cell 2455 Death Row,* contained a chapter in which Chessman described escaping from Chino, the minimum-security farming prison in California (the date, which can now be established from newly declassified FBI records, was August 1943).

He described how a Yugoslavian cellmate had told him of a cache of documents that the cellmate had stolen from a house that exactly answered the description of Flynn's, high up on Mulholland Drive, along with money and valuables in the safe.

The Yugoslav hid the papers in a secret place near the Hollywood post office and was captured. He told Chessman that these papers, implicating a major star, would be perfect for blackmail. Chessman escaped and decided to obtain the documents. Later, he told his San Francisco attorney George T. Davis that the star was Errol Flynn.

In his memoirs, Chessman dubbed Flynn Mr. Christopher, a sly reference to the character of the Nazi spy leader in the movie *The House on 92nd Street,* who used that pseudonym and was in fact a cross-dressed woman—a reference to Flynn's bisexuality. Chessman obtained the documents and made his way to Flynn's house. Flynn took him on as a Nazi sympathizer and flew him to Mexico City to meet Hitlerians in exile. This fit Jane Chesis's picture of assistance in the form of money to prominent Nazis in Latin American countries. Chessman's agent Joseph Longstreth confirmed that Mr. Christopher was Flynn, and Davis said that Chessman had given all the facts to him in the death-row cell when Flynn died in 1959 ("Now that the traitor is dead I can tell the truth").

As the evidence mounted, confirming my findings at every level, my own newspaper, the *Times,* had to break its rule against featuring its own writers in a major piece, and the editor in chief sent Sharon Johnson, assistant West Coast correspondent, to my house to examine the documents and interview tapes. She said that a major conflict had developed among the Rosenthal and Sulzberger *Times* ruling families; some believed me, knowing my reputation for accuracy, and others, who had been boyhood fans of Flynn, refused to accept the story. I said that I was appalled that after ten years without a blemish on my record, and scoop after scoop established as correct, I would be doubted by anyone. But of course, I agreed, Sharon had a job to do, and the paper's own reputation could be involved.

She had planned to come for two days but left after only four hours, saying I had enough to hang Flynn several times over. She filed her piece, some twenty-five hundred words confirming everything I said; then silence.

Weeks went by. No *Times* assignments for me; no story. I called her. She was on the verge of tears; she said the story had been killed at a very high level. I knew my days at the *Times* were ended, and I returned the latest of many calls from the rival *Washington Post.*

I said I would give the *Post* access to all the facts, that I had been betrayed by own paper, and that the documents and tapes were ready. Cynthia Gorney, a respected California correspondent of the paper, flew from San Francisco and came to the house. She also planned to stay two days; she also was gone within four hours. And she ran a very long article in the Style section on March 18, 1980, that totally confirmed every word I had said and written.

A major support in the Flynn affair was the Australian film director Philippe Mora, who believed in me from the first and took an option on the film rights. But nobody in Hollywood agreed to go ahead with the movie, and at a meeting with Alan Ladd Jr., son of the star and now a major industry figure, Ladd told Mora he was horrified by the evidence and didn't want to know about it.

And now another person came forward to confirm my Flynn determinations. Carl Schaefer, head of Warner Bros. foreign publicity since 1940, called me for a secret meeting at the downtown Los Angeles Public Library where, he said, nobody would expect to find him. The cloak-and-dagger tone of his voice was appealing and I guessed the meeting would have to do with Flynn, whom Schaefer had handled for the foreign press for many years.

I wasn't disappointed. He said that it might cost him his job if he were to be given as my source; only now that Schaefer is dead can I write of what he told me. He said that in 1942, after Pearl Harbor, Jack Warner called Schaefer and told him to "get his ass to Acapulco" on the next plane and that there he would find Flynn at the Hotel Reforma, in or out of bed with the Nazi spy Hilde Kruger. Schaefer found Flynn and Kruger in a bar and ordered Flynn to return to Hollywood at once or his Nazi connections would be publicly exposed. Flynn flew back to Hollywood with Schaefer.

This revelation led me into a new exploration of Nazi agents in America, led by Hilde Kruger. She was the mistress in succession of Donald Flamm, Jewish head of radio WOR New York; J. Paul Getty; Fritz Wiedemann, Hitler's World War 1 commanding officer and now contact consul in San Francisco; Flynn; and, later, two presidents of Mexico. I found that Allied Artists (a British group of agents headed by Alexander Korda, Victor Saville, the actor Edward Ashley, and the writer Charles Bennett) arranged for Reginald Gardiner, the on-screen effete comedian of *The Man Who Came to Dinner* and *Born to Dance* and in fact a vigorous womanizer, to go to bed with Kruger to determine the facts about her: she was acting as a courier between Mexico City, Acapulco, Los Angeles (where the hard-core Nazi George Gyssling was consul general), and Wiedemann. When the musical star Miliza Korjus (*The Great Waltz*) was mistaken for Kruger, Korjus's career was ruined.

In the midst of all this, Melvin Belli, the famous ambulance-chasing, self-styled protector of the underdog and chief rival at the San Francisco bar of Chessman's lawyer George T. Davis, filed suit against Doubleday and myself for libel of Errol Leslie Flynn.

No such thing as libel of the dead exists. In France, charges of syphilis or madness of the deceased can be the basis of suits by families under the Napoleonic Code because these are inheritable. Belli, acting for Flynn's daughters Deirdre and Rory, spurred on by their mother, Nora Black, and a press agent, Warren Seabury, said I was guilty in Quebec and Tasmania. It took me exactly one hour in a Los Angeles law library to find that these unlikely locations had no such statute, and, of course, neither plaintiff nor defendant was resident in either place.

This cockeyed nuisance suit could have cost me dearly but for the fact that my contract with Doubleday allowed me to use my own lawyers or theirs in the event of a suit. Since I used my own lawyer, the brilliant

Michael Harris, and they did too, it would have been a conflict of interest for them to carry out an idle threat that they would withhold my verified royalties, pending a verdict in my favor, and they were forced to release the money.

Martin Clancy of *20/20* was a powerful enemy. He set out, as he said, to "get" me, totally ignoring all the evidence, failing to examine my documentation, taking no account of the *Post* piece, and instead came up with a feeble program, in which he interviewed a snarling Dr. Herman Erben, now in Vienna, a badly made up Jane Chesis, and not, as I had urged him, Gerry Brown. He called me gleefully just before the program aired to tell me he had "done me in." I told him he hadn't and couldn't and that I had never seen *20/20* and wouldn't watch it now. "You mean you won't turn it on?" he asked. "No, Mr. Clancy, I will not," I repeated, and I didn't.

Scooped by the *Washington Post,* the *Times* became desperate. Sharon Johnson resigned, disgusted by being censored and suppressed; a belligerent, shrill-voiced Robert Lindsey, of the West Coast bureau and author of *The Falcon and the Snowman,* arrived, ready for the kill.

I behaved calmly, sat him down in my living room, and brought out piles of documents. Aghast, he said he couldn't believe all this was my evidence. I told him I was aghast that he would disbelieve me after ten years as my colleague. He read everything I showed him carefully and said he was very impressed by my documentation. Then he filed a confirming piece that said Flynn had served the Nazi German cause before, during, and after World War II. But the article was not what my opponents at the *Times* expected. Unable this time to cancel it, they ran it in an obscure place on page seventeen next to a Bloomingdale's advertisement.

At last the libel suit, in which Warren Seabury obtained maximum publicity for his clients, and in which the producer Ronnie Shedlo also played a part, finally came to court. I had an ace in the hole. My lawyer Mike Harris read from the responding brief I had helped prepare—the answer to plaintiff's charges mandatory in all litigation—a passage I had found in a book on defamation that said there could be no libel of the dead; if there were, there would be no history. The court listened to this and then, on my instruction, Harris delivered a bombshell. "The author of this statement," he said, "is none other than the attorney for the plaintiff, Melvin Belli, in his book *For the Plaintiff.*" Everyone laughed, even the judge, and the case was thrown out of court.

Later, Belli showed his true hand. In an article in the *Los Angeles Times,* he stated that he thought Flynn was not homosexual—another element of the libel suit—but had had an affair with Tyrone Power. Had I been put on trial, I would have had him on the witness stand; he had told me this long before. Further, he said that he knew Flynn was mixed up with Nazis, but only "for the fun of it." The article was cause for disbarment but by this time I had had enough. And then Belli died.

Perhaps my finest hour was when Colonel Frank Farrell, Dr. Erben's OSS control in China at the time Erben turned state's evidence at the Ehrhardt trial, invited me to address the OSS veterans in New York. I stood before hundreds of men, who might have been thought to boo and catcall me, as they had been Flynn's worshippers as boys; instead they gave me a standing ovation and talked of my courage, and many announced they had seen Flynn at Yorkville, the Nazi stronghold in New York, with enemy agents. I asked why none of their official reports had been attended to. None could answer that. It seemed insufficient, but how could I argue with so astonishing a crowd that accepted me as one of their own?

Next night at dinner Farrell told me that Flynn had made a deal with the CIA to obtain retrospective immunity after the war by agreeing to spy on Castro in Cuba. This made sense; Flynn was a friend of Batista, whom Castro overthrew, and he had made a film that ostensibly was propaganda for the Castro regime, *Cuban Rebel Girls,* which contained many images of Castro's defense and troops, an exact duplication of Flynn's mission in Spain during the civil war. Later, Farrell confirmed that this was indeed the case, but too late for any *Flynn* editions as the book slid slowly out of print in the mid-1980s.

The Flynn affair brought not only attacks on my reputation, but an attempt on my life. I had left my rented car overnight outside my garage because of a problem with my electric door opener. When I started the vehicle on my hillside, it went inexplicably in reverse; someone had tampered with it. The brake refused to work. Even the emergency brake had been tampered with. Luckily I had the presence of mind to steer the Toyota into a neighbor's house, breaking the walls and almost bringing down a valuable collection of china and glassware on the other side; had I not managed this, I would have gone over the cliff and been killed. It took me weeks to recover.

When the paperback edition of *Flynn* appeared in 1981, Dell Publishing, headed by my good friend Ross Claiborne, decided to send me on a nationwide tour of some twenty cities. Certain the trip would be very taxing—no proper sleep, food, or chance for exercise, and a succession, surely, of skeptical fans of the late star battering me verbally—I decided to pay for the trip myself and go by train. Despite the bad state of Amtrak, with roadbeds that made it almost impossible to stand upright in a compartment and meals that would disgrace a skid row kitchen, I enjoyed the journey and managed in the long stretches between cities to actually get some rest—with good books and frequent dozes between walks the length of the train. And I discovered Minneapolis, a magnificent and unsung city, with its glorious millionaire suburbs, elegant restaurants and hotels, and overhead walkways allowing the lucky citizens to go to market without facing the elements—not to mention the sister city of St. Paul, with its fine art galleries and business offices decorated exquisitely with Alexander Calders.

Back in Los Angeles in July 1980, I found yet another confirmation of my findings on Flynn. Bettye and Sam Jaffe invited me to a lunch party in Altadena, a leafy Los Angeles suburb, at the home of their friend the painter Joe Mugnani. The party was held under a fine spread of oak and eucalyptus trees, on trestle tables outside the house. Both the food and the company were superb.

Someone piped up with a question for me on Flynn's Nazism and I summed up the significant details. A distinguished-looking man, Dr. Joseph Ford, of the faculty of California State University in Northridge, began to speak and held all of us spellbound.

He said that during World War II he had been, as a scholar fluent in Japanese, engaged as chief decoding clerk at the San Diego naval base, intercepting messages between German, Japanese, and treasonable American spies, and the name that came up most frequently was Errol Flynn's. Flynn, he said, was a liaison between all parties, and was the lynchpin of the enemy operation in California. Ford had been shocked and filed his detailed reports to the Office of Naval Intelligence and the FBI. Nothing was done. Several guests asked him, why the protection? Because, he said, as others had, to reveal that Flynn had been involved would have caused not only a loss of public morale, at the time after Pearl Harbor, but that evidently someone in a high place suggested to Warner Bros. that instead of being tried he should be used as a propaganda weapon, fighting Nazis on the screen. It was much later that I found out Flynn had been protected by a pro-Nazi element in the State Department, that J. Edgar Hoover of the

FBI was in the pay of Warner Bros., and that the Office of Naval Intelligence reports were passed to the immigration department, whose head was the Nazi collaborator Major Lemuel Schofield, and buried there.

How could I follow this book? If anything emerged from writing it, it was that Flynn could never have avoided ruin had there not been a powerful element of protection in government by those who not only opposed the war but profited from it by trading with the enemy. That gave me the title of my next work, *Trading with the Enemy,* and I embarked on a journey of discovery that went beyond anything I had experienced in the chase after Flynn.

The advance on the book was small. Delacorte had doubts whether it would sell (it is still in print and selling in 2009), so I had to finance it, reluctantly, with another star biography. With great impatience, I put together a life of Bette Davis that, surprisingly enough, turned out to be a book I was proud of: feisty and fast moving, filled with new material drawn from the Warner Bros. files at the University of California. *Bette* was a Book of the Month Club selection and received very good reviews, especially by Rex Reed. It was a success, though not as big as *Kate,* and had many diverting elements.

Miss Davis herself was not involved; she was furious when the book appeared. There was one dramatic incident I must recount. I was addressing a women's club in Los Angeles when a fierce-looking woman in a blue dress, pushing ahead of the long line of autograph-seeking book buyers, told me to general stupefaction that I was a liar. I asked her calmly what she was talking about. She denied that her late husband, Harmon Nelson, once married to Bette when he was the bandleader at the Blossom Room, had bugged Bette's house to obtain a record of her nocturnal love making and subsequent conversations with a sexually challenged Howard Hughes. She demanded to know my source for so scurrilous a charge. I replied that the source was none other than Bette Davis herself.

She stormed out, everyone sighed with relief that she was gone, and I went on signing books. This onslaught was very small potatoes. And in fact Mrs. Nelson did talk to Bette Davis, and Miss Davis confirmed that she had told me the story and that it was true.

Then matters became sticky and strange. Davis embarked on her own book, *This 'n' That,* with my former editor Bill Whitehead, now at Dutton. To give advance notice of it she went on talk shows and was asked to confirm my account of the bugging incident. Now she said it wasn't true, that I had made it up—an act of slander, but if I sued her who would expect a jury to find in favor of me over Bette Davis?

Whitehead had signed her to the contract on the basis she would tell that story among others. She called him to say that he must remove it from the pages; he refused and she threatened and finally it was cut, along with the story of her killing her second husband, which I was compelled by lawyers to alter myself. Similarly, in the *Flynn* book, I had to disguise Hilde Kruger as Gertrude Anderson, because Kruger was then still alive, leading some of my critics to say that no such person existed, thus undermining my credibility. And other names had to be changed as well.

My favorite Davis story was this. She had been chairman of the Tail Waggers Society of Hollywood when a pooch took a bite out of her nose, and she returned to New England to nurse it. Her correspondence with Jack Warner turned out to be hilarious, the epic of a proboscis equivalent to that of Cyrano de Bergerac. When she returned to the set of *The Man Who Came to Dinner*, her costar Monty Woolley said to her, "Don't worry, Bette. In our scenes together, you can play with your back to the camera and nobody will see anyone but me." She backhanded him so hard he fell off of his chair.

Her melodrama *Deception* was dubbed "Conception" on set because she was visibly pregnant. On *The Corn Is Green*, a grip had tried to kill her by dropping a "barn door," the metal cover of an arc lamp, on her head; this time (it had happened before) someone tried to blind her with acid in her eyewash. She called a union meeting, unprecedented in Hollywood history, to complain about Jack Warner. From that moment her days at the studio were numbered and when she finally left there was no farewell party, just hot dogs with the electricians on a bench; even the studio car was denied her and she had to send home for her station wagon.

Work began on *Trading with the Enemy*. Under the Freedom of Information Act, I obtained throughout 1981 a substantial mass of documents, thousands in all, that showed beyond doubt that the great American corporations continued to do business with Hitler during World War II. Both Ross Claiborne at Delacorte/Dell and his brilliant editor Jeanne Bernkopf (the inspiration of Joseph Wambaugh, James Clavell, and other best-selling authors) gave me approval to go ahead; Jeanne's only caveat was that I must prove collaboration after Pearl Harbor, and I agreed.

I found that in Basle, in neutral Switzerland, from Pearl Harbor to VJ Day, the Bank for International Settlements had an American president, Thomas J. McKittrick, and German, Japanese, and Italian vice presidents. All were involved in obtaining the gold contents of the spectacle frames, cigarette lighters and cases, and teeth fillings of thousands of murdered Jews and shipping them to aid in the German cause in Geneva. McKittrick was given an SS Police escort to Berlin for conferences with Hitler's banker Dr. Walther Funk, then allowed to sail to America aboard the neutral Swedish ship the *Kungsholm,* where he reported to the Federal Reserve Bank, not holding back words on the ingots fashioned from the Jewish victims.

From this point of departure, appalling in itself, I went on to find that Standard Oil of New Jersey fueled German U-boats in the South Atlantic and that the Chase Bank of Manhattan kept open its branch in Nazi-occupied Paris for the duration of the war, financing the German operation there—treason that was authorized at Rockefeller Center, the bank's headquarters. I found that Henry Ford and his son, Edsel, authorized the building of German armored cars and tanks at Nazi-occupied Poissy, near Paris, also for the duration, resulting in the deaths of many American and British troops.

ITT built the rocket bombs that devastated London through authorized contacts sent via Sweden to German firms; RCA supplied information on American ship movements to German Telefunken with subsequent loss of life; William L. Batt, head of the American War Production Board, authorized shipments of secret formulas to Berlin via Sweden while urging Americans to save bicycle tires and scrap from old automobiles for the united war effort.

I delivered the chronicle to Jeanne Bernkopf, who with her customary skill edited it into readable form. The reviews of *Trading with the Enemy* were the best I had received. Even my own *Times* in the wake of my unhappy departure declared it one of the important books of the year. Then something happened.

I was on the NBC morning news when the host announced that a surprise guest would take me on, charging me with falsehood. The accuser was Kenneth Mills, vice president of the Chase Manhattan Bank, who handled their public relations.

I said that I looked forward to a face-to-face confrontation, whereupon the host announced that I would be talking to him on remote: from the boardroom at Rockefeller Center. I called him chicken, and then we saw Mills, on screen, who said that I was wrong about his bank; in saying it had aided Germany during the war, I had overlooked the fact that it was only to protect its French customers. This was an admission that it was open with authorization for the enemy, and I replied that the only customers the bank protected were those who collaborated with the German government; that the bank confiscated the Jewish accounts the moment the Maginot Line collapsed, and before the Germans asked it to.

All Mills could do was repeat his prepared statement. In short, he was sunk. Several Jewish employees were said to have resigned the same day.

I was picketed by neo-Nazis in some cities when I went on my train tour but I ignored them and saw they were mostly shaved-head punks with nose rings and nothing better to do. Then I reached Portland, Oregon, and a new piece of information.

I was enjoying a beer and a snooze in the dark brown, elegantly upholstered bar of the Benson Hotel when a tall man and a younger one he introduced as his son shook hands with me in congratulation.

The man said that there was another book he would like to see written: "Trading with the Other Enemy," the history of American collaboration with the Soviet Union from its formation through the cold war and beyond. He said that he and his son, both Marines, were unwillingly involved in shipments to North Vietnam during the Vietnam War, and that they had refused to proceed only to be threatened with charges of mutiny and court-martial. When they landed supplies in enemy areas, they were taken in hand by a grateful Vietcong and proudly shown gas stations with American oil company insignia.

I followed this up in Los Angeles, but the records were not to be found (for obvious reasons), and without documentary support I couldn't go ahead. I also heard charges from various confidential sources that Ford trucks had been used to carry the Russian army of invasion into Afghanistan. I was told that American banks made a secret billion-dollar deal in Moscow to sell satellite technology to the Russians. I also was led to believe that the Bank for International Settlements arranged for interest payments on American loans to Russians in the cold war, to be paid by adjusting the gold accounts, to avoid bullion being detected at customs in New York. Again, all these were allegations, and without documentary proof.

I needed a break in the form of a more lightweight project, and even before I had finished *Trading with the Enemy,* I embarked on another star biography, the life of Merle Oberon, with the capable if contentious assistance of the writer Roy Moseley. My chief reason was that I had found Miss Oberon to have been a World War II courier of secret messages to and from London and Los Angeles, working with her husband, Sir Alexander Korda, whom I recalled with pleasure from our brief meeting in London when I was eighteen.

If there is a single mandatory requirement of a biographer, it is surely that he knows the place of his subject's birth. According to reference books, Oberon was born in Hobart, Tasmania, also the birthplace of Errol Flynn and the capital of the beautiful island state of Australia that lay to the south, the last stop before the South Pole. She herself had lied in interviews that her father was killed on a kangaroo hunt and that she had been adopted by the governor of Bombay.

I wrote, as I had on the subject of Flynn, letters to the editor to every newspaper in Australia, seeking information. I had received many answers on Flynn, none of them flattering. This time I had only three replies.

In the first, the writer stated that she was the midwife when Merle was born, and that just as the baby was delivered a blackbird flew through the window, whereupon Merle's mother decided to name the child Merle, the French for blackbird. The second letter stated that Merle had been born two hundred feet down in a tin mine and had been brought up to the surface black as soot. These letters seemed to me nonsensical, but the third emphatically did not.

The writer stated that if I thought Merle Oberon was born in Tasmania, then there was no further need for correspondence. If I did not think so then she would be happy to give me some information.

Her name was Mrs. Freda Syer, and she lived on Dunk Island in Australia's Great Barrier Reef. I called her on the telephone and a grocery store manager answered; he said she had no direct line, but he would have a boy fetch her to the telephone by bicycle.

I waited for thirty minutes on the line until at last Mrs. Syer turned up. She said she was pleased to hear from me; she had never received an overseas call before. She said that it was a fluke I had found her because she almost never went into the town of Cairns on the mainland but had gone there to shop and by chance had picked up the newspaper the *Australian,* which she almost never read. It contained my letter—my luck again.

She had been Merle Oberon's sister's neighbor in Bombay for thirty years; I had never known Oberon had a sister. She said that Merle was born in that city, not in Hobart, Tasmania; she had been raised in the Girgaum district in great poverty, her mother a laundress for the red light district; and Merle's sister was dead, but her son, Captain Harry Selby, was very much alive, living in Bombay as Indian manager for Corning Glass.

The coincidence of a long-term Bombay resident I probably would never have found turning up on an obscure Australian coral reef island and just happening to see my letter staggered the mind; it was as astonishing as finding the lost *It's All True* at a vault in Paramount because I was mistaken for a stock footage buyer in San Jose. I thanked Mrs. Syer profusely, and decided at once to put a call through to Bombay; she had given me Selby's telephone number. That proved to be no easy task in those presatellite days: a call had to be booked at least a day in advance, and one was required to remain by the telephone round the clock until a call came through saying that the required party was available to speak to me.

I received many calls in the course of a day, so I was forced to install a new line and a new instrument, cut off my regular phone as I might be interrupted, and stay within reach, as the response could come at any time. For the next twenty-four hours, Richard served me my meals by the phone and I didn't sleep. And I waited. And waited.

At last, at four o'clock in the morning, the phone rang and I snatched up the receiver. I heard a shrill babble of voices as if I were talking into a giant birdcage. Several operators screamed at once and I could barely make out that if I waited a moment, they would connect me to Captain Selby. Fearful I would be cut off (I had heard that many were), I heard his warm and welcoming voice on the line. He confirmed that Mrs. Syer was right, expressed amazement that I had found her, and him, and said that he was in fact Merle's nephew and that his mother was her sister. He said his mother had lived and died in miserable circumstances, jealous of her movie star sibling and tortured by the fact that she had to beg her for money. Later, Selby told me that his mother had sent a young man to Hollywood to try to extract funds from the producer Sam Goldwyn, who had Merle under contract, on the threat of revealing Merle was Eurasian, and had been told to leave town or find himself in the foundations of an extension of an early freeway, with cement riding boots.

I asked Selby to come to Los Angeles and he agreed, provided of course that I paid the fare and put him up at a hotel. His next requirement was not as easy: he insisted I take him to Disneyland.

I told him to be sure to bring a record of Merle's birth and he said he had none; I at once sent him a list of churches copied from Baedeker's guide to Bombay, in this case for 1908, the year, he said, of Merle's birth. Nonbaptism at that time was unthinkable; a child could go to hell. I was certain a baptismal record existed in a church and would also show the birth date.

He found the record in the twenty-fifth of the numerous churches listed in the guide and arrived in Los Angeles in the best of humors, twinkling, sweet natured, lovable, and loyal to his family.

He said that Merle, when she went to England in the early 1930s, had to pretend to be white; that her mother, who was Indian and very dark, had to pose as her maid in London in a frilly cap and apron, and serve meals to guests; that this made her mother miserable; and that when the old lady died, it was from a broken heart. Because her death had to be hidden, as it might reveal her racial origin, she was buried in the family vault of one of Merle's aristocratic friends, her tomb marked as if she were a fifteenth-century duchess.

Korda was dead by the time I started work, as was Merle's second husband, the cinematographer Lucien Ballard, whom I had known and luckily interviewed; he had been killed in a freak accident coming off a golf course. Her third husband, Bruno Pagliai, was too ill to talk; but his brother, Ferro, was cooperative.

Roy Moseley was instrumental in obtaining the cooperation of Merle's last husband, Robert Wolders, through the good offices of Merle's beloved friend and dress designer, Luis Estevez. The hypersensitive Wolders was a problem, chiefly because of an incident that had occurred in Merle's later years.

She had received, he said, an invitation from the Lord Mayor of Hobart to dedicate a National Trust blue plaque on her alleged birthplace, a pleasant house in a wealthy suburb. They flew there together, and at the luncheon to announce the dedication she collapsed in the middle of an autobiographical speech and couldn't go on. He was worried about her but didn't suspect anything. He also said that on a world cruise the ship stopped in Bombay and she wouldn't go ashore.

I explained the facts of her birth and he was furious; Merle, he said, had never lied to him. He declared Captain Selby a fraud after money, and he contacted the U.S. ambassador to India John Kenneth Galbraith, in an effort to discredit him. But I had obtained FBI files that proved the facts of Merle's birth, and in great distress Wolders admitted after reading them that I was telling the truth.

Then he admitted another example of Merle's lying. He said that she and Bruno Pagliai had pretended to their unrelated adopted children, both of whom had been found in separate ruins in an Italian earthquake, that they were in fact their own offspring. One night watching Robin Leach's *Lifestyles of the Rich and Famous* on television, the kids learned the truth; shocked, they ran from the house and vanished for months. Pagliai's men and the Mexican police located them living in poverty and brought them home.

Later, after *Princess Merle: The Romantic Life of Merle Oberon* was finished, something tragic occurred. Bruno Jr., or Little Bruno, as he was known, had given me interviews. He was handsome, moody, dark, and obsessed with fast cars; he had five Porsches at his home in San Francisco's Bay Area. When he heard after a year of waiting that Bruno had left him a vast fortune, and that the will would be read in Mexico City, he raced one of his automobiles direct to Mexico, too impatient to wait and take a plane. As he was driving through Mexico City's crowded outskirts, he crashed head-on into another car and was killed instantly. Just turned twenty-one, he would have inherited $150 million.

There were many stories of Merle's life in Acapulco with Bruno. It was said that she was greatly annoyed, and so were her neighbors, when an Arab millionaire built a tower that blocked the views and also offered the shrill sounds of the muezzin's chant, which greeted the dawn each day. There was a violent explosion; one of the residents had dynamited the tower, and the singer in it.

At this time, my agent made a deal with Coward-McCann for a dual biography of Olivia de Havilland and Joan Fontaine titled *Sisters*.

It was a rich subject: the lifelong rivalry of sisters, internationally famous stars and Oscar winners. I had met them both. My friend Ross Claiborne, the editor of her proposed but never completed memoirs, arranged for me to meet Olivia at the Polo Lounge of the Beverly Hills Hotel to discuss the possibility that she might want me to do an authorized life. But the fact that I didn't drink annoyed her; albeit sweetly, she made it clear that my failure to join her in a cocktail was not what Her Majesty sought in a courtier, much less a subject. And there was something stubborn, humorless, and saintly about her that finally put me off.

Joan was much more fun. I was in New York, attending the first (and last) night of a play about a talking tree; she sat next to me with her escort of the evening, and I introduced myself. She invited me to join them at "21" for supper; we left the play at intermission and made our way there, the scene of many lunches of my childhood and recent years.

I dared to ask Joan whether she heard from Olivia; I expected to get hot coffee in my face but instead she laughed. "What do you know of her?" she asked. "That she's preaching from the pulpit every Sunday at the American Cathedral in Paris." "She always was a lousy lay . . . preacher," Joan quipped cheerfully.

I realized that Joan, who had written her own autobiography, *No Bed of Roses,* and the endlessly procrastinating Olivia would not cooperate, and indeed to talk to both sisters would be impossible; neither would agree unless she alone was interviewed.

So I proceeded apace. I began with the sisters' origins. I found that their father, a lawyer and author of a textbook on patents, had settled in Japan. When he took a mistress into his house, his wife, Olivia, and Joan set off for California and settled in the small town of Saratoga. I drove there in an effort to find the boardinghouse where they lived.

The place had been run by a Mr. and Mrs. Lundblad, from Sweden, and their married daughter Hazel Bargas, when the exiles from Japan arrived in 1920. They had a popular houseboy, Jimmy. I was sure no trace of that family could still be found after sixty-three years, and the boardinghouse must long since have been closed.

I arrived in the middle of a thunderstorm; putting up at a local inn, I began asking around, and finally rang the doorbell of a tiny, green, painted wooden cottage not much larger than a kennel. The young couple who opened the door and asked me in delivered a bombshell. They said that the Lundblad boardinghouse still stood, and they pointed to a crumbling Victorian structure covered in Algerian ivy and Virginia creeper that stood just directly across the street. The windows were blinded by high brown wooden shutters, and the porch was made of green, painted collapsing clapboard; a rat scurried about.

I rang the doorbell, which gave a faint sepulchral chime. No reply; I tried again.

Then the front door opened a crack and a wizened Filipino face peeped out. To my amazement, he introduced himself as Jimmy, the original houseboy of 1920, and said he had been working there ever since.

I asked if he knew what had become of Hazel Bargas, daughter of the sisters' landlady, and he astonishingly said she was in the kitchen and would I like to meet her? I followed him as he gave me a tour. He showed me the dining room, where the upright piano still carried the group song-book he said the girls had used at parties; on a table thick with dust lay copies of *The Water Babies, The Forest Lovers, Ivanhoe,* and the *Alice* books that still carried the sisters' bookplates.

Hazel Bargas, just turned ninety-three, sat warming her rear at the 1908 Franklin stove, like Aunt Fanny in *The Magnificent Ambersons.* Her high black wig was like a Kabuki actor's, her black dress with puffed sleeves dating probably from 1938. Her wedding ring had bitten so deep into her finger that it would have taken a saw to remove it.

Bargas said that Olivia and Joan were opposites: Olivia was sweet, cheerful, loving; Joan sour, rude, and hostile. The origins of their lifelong conflict was clear: Olivia, editing the high school magazine, set a competition for the best last will and testament of her fellow pupils; she won her own competition with the words, "I bequeath to my sister the ability to win boys' hearts she does not have at present."

I was able to trace the growth of that enmity over some sixty-two years. I was also able to describe the story of Joan's adoption of a Peruvian girl, Martita, who gave me a very rare interview during a thunderstorm at her home in Portland, Maine. On the verge of tears, Martita told me that she had been born and raised in Machu Picchu, the famous ruined Inca city high in the Peruvian mountains; that Joan on a goodwill tour, the Holly-wood star bestowing her charm on the unfortunate, had spotted her sitting outside a stone hut in rags and decided on the spot to adopt her and turn her into a lady.

Joan, Martita said, paid the family five hundred dollars and whisked her off by plane to Los Angeles; the child was horrified at being taken from her parents, terrified by the flight, and miserable on arrival. She had never seen a bathroom or even a door; she had never seen fleecy towels, indoor toilets, bedsheets, blankets, carpets, ice cream, candy, or a kitchen.

The moment she came of age, Martita fled her foster mother and hid in the home of a protective lawyer and his wife in Pennsylvania, which had no law extraditing children to parents when they didn't want to go. Joan told the lawyer that she had a document from the Roman Catholic Church authorities that Martita should be deported to Peru as an undesirable alien, but Martita stayed on.

There was a memorable scene when the sisters took their father's ashes to the Channel Island of Guernsey to scatter them over his favorite cliff. Their mother, Lilian, accompanied them. When Joan and Olivia tossed the ashes into the wind, they blew back into Lilian's face. He had always hated her.

The sisters made no comment after the book was published successfully in New York and London; when my colleague Stephen Farber asked Joan over drinks at the Polo Lounge what she thought of it, the response was typical: "It's a lovely day today." This was different from Marlene Dietrich's response, which, according to a friend of hers, was to throw my biography *Marlene* that someone sent her that year for signing out of the window of her apartment on the Avenue Montaigne in Paris; it struck a potted geranium on the windowsill and the two objects crashed down on the head of a woman, said to be married to an Argentinean diplomat, who was so badly injured that Marlene had to pay a colossal hospital bill. I wrote Dietrich a note suggesting that next time someone sent her my book for signing, she should consign it to the incinerator chute.

One day in 1983 I picked up a copy of *Newsweek* and saw an item that upset me very badly. Herman Abs, chairman emeritus of the Deutsche Bank, had, I read, been appointed head of an investigative council set up by the Vatican to look into allegations that the Holy See was behind certain money-laundering and drug-dealing operations, through the Calvi Bank of Milan.

From my research for *American Swastika,* a sequel to *Trading with the Enemy,* I knew something that *Newsweek* had chosen to ignore: Abs had been on the board of, and a principal figure in, the I. G. Farben Buna rubber factory at Auschwitz, where thousands of Jews died, and he had been the employer of the present pope, who had been a poet and a factory worker for I. G. Farben in Warsaw.

I called Rabbis Marvin Hier and Abraham Cooper at the Simon

Wiesenthal Center of Holocaust studies in Los Angeles and told them of my shock and dismay. They summoned me to a meeting later that morning; I brought with me much damning documentation on Abs, but more was needed and, without wasting a moment, the rabbis called Tom Bower, an authority in the field, in London, and he at once couriered a full-scale dossier. This was fortunate, because the same Abs records had mysteriously (or not) vanished from every American archive or library in which they had been stored.

It was clear to all of us that Abs had to go. To that end, the rabbis called a press conference at the Holocaust museum where, surrounded by the photographs of Auschwitz, I joined them in addressing a hundred members of the world's television and radio networks, satellite and cable shows, and the press. Rabbi Hier spoke on the moral issue; I spoke on the political. For two hours beforehand, from 6 a.m., I gave an exclusive to my own former paper, the *New York Times,* and to the *Wall Street Journal* correspondent.

The story was suppressed everywhere. The *Wall Street Journal* filed a long article based on my documents and it was killed outright; the *Times* piece was cut from 2,500 words to 250 and was totally innocuous, tucked into a world news survey; only ABC of the three American networks ran the story, and then cursorily, and no foreign network did anything about it. It seemed that nobody was prepared to take on either the Vatican or the continuing existence of Hitler's principal financial backer as the pope's employee.

The rabbis left for Rome with my own and Tom Bower's dossiers, but when they arrived at the Vatican they were asked to table the matter, as relations between Israel and the Holy See were greatly improving. Soon afterward, the Vatican issued a statement to the effect that in view of certain aspersions being cast on the appointment of Herman Abs, the committee investigating the Calvi Bank would be discontinued. It was a Vatican solution of which Machiavelli would have been proud.

It was at this time that my social life assumed great intensity, and would continue at that pitch for over a decade. June Levant, widow of the famous wit and musician Oscar Levant, invited me one night to her apartment in the Sierra Towers in West Hollywood, where I met Vincente and his wife, the British-born Lee Minnelli, whom I had interviewed for the Merle Oberon book. They adopted me as a kind of mascot, Lee introducing me to everyone as a great-great-grandson of Sir Arthur Conan Doyle, a fantasy of which I never disabused her.

The parties of the mid-1980s were unrivaled since the 1930s, and have not been surpassed. Perhaps the most lavish host was David Murdock, the hotel broker, who at his magnificent house at Christmas greeted over one hundred guests with thirty carol singers in medieval livery, and then placed us under the stars at tables decorated with orchid trees and served by an army of white-tuxedoed waiters.

His chief rival was Della Koenig, widow of a German Mexican industrialist, who also placed her guests under the trees, with musicians to play for each table.

Jules Stein, head of Universal Studios, and his enchanting wife, Doris, from Kansas City, were often my hosts at their hillside home on Angelo Drive, bought later by my former boss Rupert Murdoch, who sensibly changed not a stick of furniture when he moved in. Night after night, they entertained the world of society; one memorable day they threw a lunch party for the friends of Venice, Italy, designed to raise funds to prevent the city sinking in the sea. Fritz Ingram, the New Orleans billionaire, also gave superb parties at the former home of Blake Edwards and Julie Andrews.

Of all my women friends of that time, I especially valued two, Stella Adler and Anna Sten. Stella, the great and glorious acting teacher and gifted thespian, scion of the royal family of the Jewish theater, was beautiful, tall, imperiously sweet, and presided over a galaxy of famous friends at Los Angeles parties given by the actress Evelyn Scott. Anna was Russian, unpunctual, earthy, sturdy, her career overexploited and ruined when Sam Goldwyn tried to make a Dietrich of her in the thirties. Now, when I would often meet her in New York, she was learning to act, after many Hollywood films, at the Actors Studio, utterly devoid of bitterness and overjoyed when I told her how wonderful she was in the Russian *Girl with a Hat Box,* about a young and innocent girl adrift in Moscow in 1929. Enjoying the women's company was like warming one's hands at a roaring fire after a long hike through winter snow.

Judy Garland, 1960s (Bison Archives)

Cary Grant, 1960s (Bison Archives)

Merle Oberon, 1960 (Bison Archives)

Walt Disney, ca. 1961 (Bison Archives)

Katharine Hepburn, 1967 (Bison Archives)

Roman Polanski, 1970 (Bison Archives)

Bette Davis, 1973 (Bison Archives)

Orson Welles, 1974 (Bison Archives)

Francis Ford Coppola, 1982 (Bison Archives)

Lucille Ball and husband Gary Morton, 1984 (Bison Archives)

Marlon Brando, 1995 (Bison Archives)

Charles Higham at a beach in California, ca. 1994

Charles Higham with partner Richard V. Palafox in Mexico, 2007

16

*A*s usual, I was busy on several books at once. *American Swastika* was the most important of these: a companion volume or sequel to *Trading with the Enemy,* it was an account of the collaboration not just between American corporations and Nazi Germany during World War II, but by members of the American government in the supposedly unblemished Roosevelt administration.

I had believed the story that immediately after the Japanese attack on Pearl Harbor, Congress voted for war with Germany, which was of course part of the Axis and therefore in partnership with both Japan and Italy. But a preliminary investigation showed me that in fact nothing of the kind took place: Germany declared war on the United States, and had it not done so, it is far from certain that Roosevelt would have entered into an open conflict with Hitler, then or later.

I discovered that Roosevelt had, at the outbreak of the European war, drawn up a plan, without benefit of Congress, and, in utmost secrecy with certain generals, a provisional Victory Program, code name Rainbow Five, which called for an invasion of German-occupied territory in 1940 and the defeat of Hitler: D-Day long before the event.

Such a plan was illegal and it is far from certain that it could have been implemented. When I contacted its chief architect, General Albert C. Wedemeyer, he couldn't answer when I said that a declaration of war before Pearl Harbor and the ordering of a U.S. invasion of Germany was surely a fantasy.

He explained to me Roosevelt's true purpose. The president, he said, in fact had this phantom plan to get his country into war, to end the Depression by ensuring full employment, support Winston Churchill, and wreck Hitler's chances of engineering a joint attack on America with the Japanese. The plan was to force Hitler into declaring war himself.

Wedemeyer told me that Rainbow Five, the size of the Manhattan telephone book, was stolen from a safe at the War Department, wrapped in a brown parcel, and that Roosevelt had arranged for the safe to be unlocked. A marine in presidential employ carried the plan through security ("The equivalent," Wedemeyer said, "of that in the average chicken coop") and took it to the home of Senator Burton K. Wheeler, the leading isolationist and Democratic opponent of Roosevelt.

Wheeler, seeing the plan as a breach of neutrality and proof of Roosevelt's illegal and supraconstitutional behavior, in turn took the plan to another isolationist, the fiery Colonel Robert R. McCormick, owner and publisher of the *Chicago Tribune,* who at once published it on the front page.

Simultaneously, McCormick sent the plan to Hitler by Western Union. Hitler met with Joachim von Ribbentrop, his foreign minister, and asked him if the existence of the plan called for immediate action.

Ribbentrop replied that American ships were sinking German vessels in the Atlantic (the opposite was also true) and that Roosevelt's supplying of bombers and manpower to England was a breach of neutrality. Hollywood in movies since *Confessions of a Nazi Spy* (1930) and *Escape* (1940) had already declared war on Germany. Thus, Hitler had no alternative: he must declare war himself.

He did, and in that declaration of war gave all the reasons, starting with Rainbow Five and the undeclared war in the Atlantic. Delivered a few days after Pearl Harbor, the speech was published all over America with the reasons omitted, so that it would seem that the declaration was merely in support of Japan.

In fact, as Ribbentrop explained to Hitler, the terms of the Tripartite Pact between Germany, Italy, and Japan didn't call for any one of the partners to join in an attack if the other partners were themselves assailed. If one partner entered into a state of war, the others didn't have to; indeed, Italy had come in very late after Germany against England in 1940.

Hal B. Wallis, one of the greatest Hollywood producers, wrote to me with what I later found to be a characteristic succinctness: would I be interested in writing his authorized biography, or help him with a memoir?

I decided on the latter; and I went to see him at his office in Beverly Hills. He was thickset, with powerful shoulders, and a very strong stare that could charm or intimidate, according to his mood. Effectively retired, he wanted to set his record straight; realistically he expected no large sale, as he would not be dishing up scandals, but we wanted his circle of friends to have something in their hands he could be proud of.

It was flattering that the creator of *Casablanca* had chosen me, and I accepted, although ghostwriting was something I probably never should have considered. But he would take no share of the advance, and there were always bills to pay.

Writing the book, *Starmaker*, was a very strange experience. Wallis had forgotten everything of his best years at Warner Bros., when he was the spearhead of the studio's policy of realism—news stories snatched from the headlines. I drew from the studio files preserved at USC by the excellent archivist Ned Comstock, and brought Hal, week by week, an account of the movies. He remembered no details of making them. He signed off on everything without a murmur and was happy to do so.

The story of *Casablanca* was appealing; almost everyone in the movie had to be brought in from another studio at hair-raising expense.

As a result, Dooley Wilson, a hasty replacement for Ella Fitzgerald as the singer-pianist at Rick's Café, who famously rendered "As Time Goes By," came in from MGM at a higher salary than Ingrid Bergman, who was under contract to David O. Selznick. Peter Lorre, borrowed from Universal, was paid almost as much for a very small part as Humphrey Bogart in the lead. Wallis had no recollection of any of this. It made the best chapter in the book, and he was praised by everyone for his vivid memories.

His greatest boast was that he had developed the career of Elvis Presley from musical idol to movie star. One night at his house in Holmby Hills Hal was rummaging through a trunk for photographs of Presley when a 35 mm color transparency fell to the floor. He tucked it guiltily into his pocket. His charming wife, Martha Hyer, told him to show it to me; he refused. Blushingly, he pulled it out after a gentle scuffle. It showed Hal with his arm around a fifteen-year-old girl. It was just his greeting of an Elvis fan, shot at Waikiki, but he must have feared it would have sinister connotations, and he snatched it back and destroyed it.

Martha was surprising. Night after night we ran the movie he had made starring his alleged mistress Lizabeth Scott; she made no complaint, but urged him constantly to spice the book up with accounts of Scott and the other women in his life and he refused. How many wives would have taken that position?

One night at the couple's Trancas Beach house, we were enjoying dinner with a view of a sunset-reddened sea. The meal was a fish concoction cooked inside a pastry shell with a fish's face on it. The Chinese husband-wife team of help, a bonded couple from Hong Kong, stood waiting for instructions after serving coffee.

Hal said, "There's nothing like *Japanese* servants." Remembering this was the ultimate insult, I frowned, and Martha said, making it worse, "Chinese, Hal, Chinese."

It was in that year that I again crossed the Borderline. I was a guest one evening of the director Alexander Singer. He had made one of my favorite bad movies, *Love Has Many Faces,* with Lana Turner and Hugh O'Brian, which contained a very funny exchange: Turner, playing a rich, frustrated wife looking for men in Acapulco, meets a beach bum, played by O'Brian. Turner to O'Brian: "You're 90 percent rat and 10 percent man." O'Brian to Turner: "Any time you want the 10 percent . . . just reach out and grab." Turner to O'Brian: "I'd break my arm first."

I had written my appreciation to Singer, who invited me to dinner with his wife and the writer Leonard Spigelgass. When I arrived at the house and was asked to sign the guest book, I looked at it—a large, ivory, bound volume—and felt a shock of electricity run up my arm. I opened the book to an early page; I saw the date of 1936 on it; clearly, it had remained in the house through many successive ownerships.

I turned at once to a certain page. There I found inscribed: "CHARLES HIGHAM. SO MUCH ENJOYED MY VISIT HERE." I had never known that Father had been in Hollywood, and the look on my face brought conversation to a halt for a very long time.

I was reminded that night of a similar experience in 1971, when I first settled in Los Angeles. I had a strong impulse, inexplicable and strange, to call Betty Compson, a star of the silent film *The Docks of New York,* who hadn't had much success in talkies.

I found her telephone number (I forget how) and called her. She said she was retired long since, and that she was now the Betty Compson who hand-painted a personal brand of ashtray. She didn't want to be rude to an Englishman so she would take down my number, but I wasn't to expect her to call.

I spelled out my name and she took a deep breath: could I possibly be related to Sir Charles Higham? I said I was his son and she burst into tears. She told me to come to her at once.

She opened the front door of her modest pink stucco cottage in Glendale, holding a photograph in her hand. It was a picture of my father, signed "For Betty. May all your dreams come true. Your loving Charles," and under his name a long line of kiss-crosses.

She said that they had met for the first time at a banquet at the London Advertising Club in the late 1920s; father had slipped his address at Savoy Court inside her handbag when she wasn't looking and had written these words on the back: "Midnight, I'll be waiting."

She went against all common sense, and he greeted her in a Sulka dressing gown and pajamas, champagne cooling in a bucket. She didn't leave for a week. He wanted her to give up her career and become Lady Higham and she refused. Instead, he married my mother; and she married the director James Cruze (*The Covered Wagon*), who ruined her financially. Her Hollywood Boulevard mansion gone, she had only this tiny cottage, which, thank God, she said, she had given to her mother.

And now two more trips across the Borderline. With my close friend Gerald Turbow, I went to a fund-raising party for the Los Angeles Chamber Orchestra at Santa Monica, at the home of the philanthropist Royce Diener. I wanted to go because Cary Grant and Randolph Scott had lived there as lovers.

As soon as I arrived, I sensed something; I knew there was a place I had to see. I used the excuse of going to the bathroom to walk into adjoining rooms. In a corner of one of them, I felt a presence; I stood silently, unmoving, and at that moment my hostess walked in. "You're psychic aren't you?" she asked me. I didn't reply. "This," she said, joining me in the corner, "is where we have had visitations." And she said that Cary Grant, after splitting with Randolph Scott to live with Barbara Hutton for a time, had stayed on there; on the anniversary of Hutton's death every year, three loud knocks emanated from that spot.

I was at a party that year given by the actor Hurd Hatfield, a friend who had been memorable in *The Picture of Dorian Gray,* at a house in Beverly Hills. The downstairs bathroom was occupied so I walked to the one upstairs. I passed, down a long corridor, a children's playroom with flowered wallpaper and airplanes, toys, and dolls. As I looked, the room changed into a dark and threatening room, and I had the feeling it had been the scene of something horrible. I came down, shaken, and my host told me in a whisper, not wanting her guests to hear, that it had once been the scene of a brutal murder.

I was fond of Cornel Wilde, who had survived the devastating notices that greeted his performance in *A Song to Remember* as Frédéric Chopin to become producer and star of such notable films as *The Big Combo* and *The Naked Prey.* I had less rapport with his beautiful but neurotic wife, Jean Wallace, who had been most memorable in *The Big Combo* as a drug addict victim of Richard Conte.

I would spend happy days at their elegant house in Beverly Hills, where Wilde delicately maintained his flower garden and trellised vines with all the dedication of the ecologist he was, avoiding dangerous pesticides and other pollutants and advocating clean air that at last came to smog-smothered Los Angeles—a campaign that matched the Green movement in many ways. It was sad that at parties at the home of Marilyn Hinton, a pineapple heiress who had lamps in the form of Hawaiian pineapples, pineapple motifs in the wallpaper, and a palm tree smack in the middle of a pool in her Bel Air living room, there were bets to see whether Wilde or Wallace would be the first to throw the other into the water in fits of rage.

There were memorable meetings almost every week in those days. Evenings at the home of Richard Basehart, fine actor of *The Brothers Karamazov* and *Fourteen Hours,* were always agreeably civilized and Old World. His second wife, Diana, and her mother were enchanting hostesses, and Basehart, though deeply regretful that he had not had a big stage career (his dream was to play Lear) and contemptuous of most of his films, was alive with plans, which I strongly encouraged, for a Richard Basehart Theater in Los Angeles that were eventually fulfilled. He did reluctantly admit that he had given a good performance as Robespierre in Anthony Mann's *The Black Book,* about the bloodbath of the French Revolution.

Rex Harrison was a much less relaxing companion. I felt from our first meeting we could never be close friends. I recall the gala opening of a restaurant in Beverly Hills. A young and attractive male singer took up the traveling microphone soon after we were settled in and, no doubt with the best of intentions, came to our table and sang, fatally, and directly facing Rex, "I've Grown Accustomed to Your Face." Rex's response was typical: "I'm not accustomed to yours, so I suggest you go as far away as possible and sing something else." The unfortunate victim obeyed.

I would visit Alfred Hitchcock as often as I could, always enjoying his fake British cottage at Universal, his passel of well-trained white Sealyhams (which never barked when we were talking), and his wonderful staff, headed by Peggy Robertson (his daughter, Pat, owlish in glasses, would sometimes drop by). His favorite off-color story concerned Jessica Tandy in *The Birds*. "Hitch," she had said plaintively, "what will I do when two hundred sparrows come down the chimney?" "Just hold on very tight to your skirt, my dear," he replied. "And remember. A bird in the hand is worth two in the—"

Rod Taylor, brash and new from Australia, did the unthinkable on the same picture. Hitchcock had a little joke that when Taylor's character opened a refrigerator door in one scene, he would find a dead seagull inside it. Taylor opened the door and froze. Hitchcock went red with rage and the crew trembled. "The light doesn't go on when I open the door," said the star. "It's all wrong, matey."

After a prolonged silence, Hitchcock folded his hands over his belly and said, "We will now close down the picture for the rest of the day while our new technical advisor from Australia addresses us on the correct operation of American refrigerators."

Hitchcock loved to tell me this story but his favorite concerned the now forgotten but once famous London playwright and actor Frank Vosper, a friend of his, who appeared for him on the screen.

They were aboard ship crossing the Atlantic. Vosper was restless one night because he was convinced his lover was in bed with a ship's steward. Hitchcock's cabin was next to his. One night, he looked out of the porthole and saw Vosper kneeling on the balcony outside the neighbor's stateroom, hoping to surprise his companion by shining a flashlight into the darkened cabin.

When Vosper saw Hitchcock looking out, he was startled and slipped from his perch; he fell down a deck onto a metal davit suspending a lifeboat. He cried out, and Hitchcock wickedly called down, "Is that you,

Frank? Or a seabird?" The reply was another scream for help; Hitchcock's wife called the captain. But it was too late; the ship took a lurch in the swell and Vosper fell into the sea. The vessel circled for hours but no trace of the famous actor-dramatist could be found.

Someone I had always wanted to meet was Raymond Burr, memorable both as the sleepy-eyed but alert attorney of the excellent *Perry Mason* series on television and as the sleazy villain of such notable noirs as *Desperate, Crime of Passion,* and *The Blue Gardenia.* I asked a friend, a prominent agent who knew him, how a meeting might be arranged. I had heard on many visits to Fiji when working for the P and O Orient Lines that Burr owned an island nearby where delectable Polynesian and Melanesian youths surrounded his muumuued figure in a harem equivalent to Marlon Brando's in Tahiti, an alluring thought.

The agent, over drinks at the Plaza in New York, told me that he didn't recommend a meeting; he found Burr distinctly creepy, and now the man was in failing health. The epitome of urbane, impeccably dressed elegance, representing top authors, the agent astonished me by saying that in his youth he had been a Hollywood hustler, with a regular beat on Santa Monica Boulevard and La Brea Avenue. One night a chauffeur drew up next to him in a black limousine and asked him to hop in. When he was told there would be a fifty-dollar fee for his services at a house in the Hollywood Hills, good money in those days, he accepted at once.

The house was pleasant, and the youth was offered a drink and a seat in the living room; the chauffeur asked him to wait. He waited as requested . . . and he was still waiting an hour later. With no magazines or books to read, he had little to do except note the fact that the room had one peculiar feature. On a large, circular mahogany table at its center was an enormous bowl containing a pyramid of blood oranges.

He saw through the french doors that it was going to rain and decided he would leave. He was about to call out to the chauffeur when the man entered and asked him if he was ready. "Ready for sex?" was his answer. "Didn't anyone tell you?" the man said. "Tell me what?" the young man replied. "Mr. Raymond Burr likes to be pelted with those." The chauffeur pointed to the oranges in the bowl, and the visitor got up from his chair and left.

It was at one of David Bradley's Old Celebrity parties that I met a young man who told me a story so incredible it had to be true. Although her career was long since over when he reached his majority, he had a crush on the Austrian star Hedy Lamarr, famous initially for appearing in the nude in *Ecstasy* in 1933 when such scenes were forbidden, later for her radiant looks in such sultry vehicles as *White Cargo* and *Lady of the Tropics*. She was, not without reason, considered the most beautiful woman of her age.

The youth longed to meet her when she was retired and living in, of all unlikely places, Orlando, Florida, near Disney World. The young man, whom I will call Sultan, of Arabic background, had money and decided to hire a private detective to see how best he might approach the reclusive star. He found out that she would see only one man, whom I will call Madison, on a regular basis, and Sultan approached the man, who promised to do what he could.

The two fans met and pondered how to break though Lamarr's barrier of secrecy. When Madison asked if she would ever consent to receive anyone other than himself, she replied only if that person was unable to speak of her present looks and condition. One night, Madison and Sultan were watching television when the famous old movie *The Four Feathers* came on. Its central theme was that an Englishman in the war in the Sudan poses as a Sengali, a member of a tribe whose tongues have been cut out to obtain information.

Madison told Lamarr that like the Sengali, Sultan had been deprived of his tongue in an incident in Saudi Arabia. She was deeply moved and invited Sultan to her apartment. For months he took pictures of her and sat silent while she talked of her colorful life in Europe and Hollywood. Then one day, while he was filming her, an ashtray fell on his foot and he yelled, "Shit!" Horrified by his deception, she threw him and Madison out.

But later, she forgave them as they had gone to such desperate measures and they all three went out for a reconciliation dinner in Orlando. A number of elderly fans came up to her for autographs; she turned on them, saying she wanted to meet only young people. "Young people don't know who the fuck you are," an old man said. "Nobody under seventy does!" She ran out and Sultan returned to Los Angeles; at the end of his story he showed me the disturbing photographs of Lamarr she had forbidden him in perpetuity to use. Sadly, this was just as well: they were a tragic record of the disintegration of beauty.

I embarked, with the warm encouragement of my agent, Barbara Lowenstein, on the biography *Orson Welles: The Rise and Fall of an*

American Genius. Correcting a number of errors in my previous work on his films, I was able to trace his origins all the way back to the *Mayflower,* and to explain much of the inspiration for both his characterization of Charles Foster Kane and of Aunt Fanny in *Magnificent Ambersons.* He had based Kane, though never admitting it, on his fearsome great-grandfather, the powerful Wisconsin lawyer Orson Head, and Aunt Fanny on his neurotic and hysterical grandmother Mary Head, who practiced witchcraft while defying the Kenosha townspeople who condemned her for marrying a brewer by placing broken beer bottles in the façade of her home.

In dealing with Welles's life as a whole, I reread some of the autobiographical pieces he had written, and his interviews with, among others, the French critic and historian Maurice Bessy. I found him as I had indicated in the first book, a positive Baron Munchausen of liars.

As an example, he told Bessy that his father, Richard, had set fire to the family-owned hotel by falling asleep on a cold winter's night without putting out his cigar. The Kenosha fire department had to break the river ice to bring up enough water for the hoses to extinguish the blaze.

It took weeks of dogged trawling through the unindexed Kenosha newspapers to find the true story. The fire took place not in winter but in summer; the staff had been testing the flues for the coming cold of the fall by waving newspapers in front of the living room fire; these papers had burst into flames; and the home was rapidly consumed. Richard Welles escaped with his pet parrot and nobody was injured or killed.

After the book was finished, I sent Welles's devoted cameraman Gary Graver to his house with the genealogical chart, prepared for me by the Sons of the American Revolution, showing the *Mayflower* sailing through his ancestors' names. Welles was fascinated by it, and Gary fancied that for a moment the wounded genius softened in his hatred for me. But I suspect it was only a fancy.

When *The Films of Orson Welles* appeared in 1970, Peter Bogdanovich had taken the extraordinary step of writing to newspapers all over the world telling them to ignore my book, which of course had the opposite effect and insured for a marginal scholarly work the massive degree of attention that helped put me on the map. This time, sixteen years later, he didn't make the same mistake, but he couldn't resist giving interviews attacking me, which again insured increased sales. Again I wired him to thank him for doing so.

The book published, Richard and I took off for one of the many cruises we enjoyed in those days; I was still in love with the life of the sea and exotic tropical ports.

Delta Airlines (the letters stood for Don't Expect Your Luggage to Arrive) changed schedules and we were left stranded in Fort Lauderdale, Florida ("The ship, Mr. Higham, has sailed"), with twenty-seven other passengers, some of them influential with the line. All hell broke loose and we were flown to St. Thomas to join the ship there, with several days' accommodation at the Bluebeard's Castle Hotel.

I walked into the lobby looking forward to a welcome rest, but the desk clerk told me there were thirty messages for me and a television team was setting up cameras in the hotel lounge. I couldn't understand it; surely I must have been mistaken for someone else: a movie star perhaps?

No, the man said, and handed me the local newspaper. Orson Welles had died while we were in transit. One message was from my editor, Toni Lopopolo, at Macmillan: could I cancel the rest of the cruise and fly to New York for the *Today* show? I called to say I could not. I had promised Richard this trip for years; we hadn't had enough time together lately. Toni was furious and hung up in my ear. I gave interview after interview at the hotel; when the lounge was crowded we continued in our suite.

We went on with the voyage. We had become friends with Steve, the band's saxophone player; as late arrivals, we had been placed not with the other passengers but with the entertainers, which proved to be a joy as I could exchange talk of mutual friends in Hollywood and New York. Steve was a fine man and a very good musician, and he asked us to a rehearsal where we sat enthralled as he tooted away at Duke Ellington, Hoagie Carmichael, and Cole Porter.

And again I crossed the Borderline. Early one morning Richard and I were doing our daily three-mile walk around the deck when Steve came jogging past us. Overweight, he was out of breath and we warned him not to overdo it. Oddly, he didn't respond and I noticed his face was an unsettling gray shade.

He was missing from breakfast and I feared he had indeed overdone it. He was also missing from brunch and dinner and I asked his bandleader what had happened. The bandleader, very tense, referred me to the ship's staff captain.

The staff captain said in strictest confidence that the night before at midnight, that is to say, before we saw him jogging, Steve had been at the top of the ship's central atrium, drinking and chatting with friends as he sat on the brass railing. He had tilted too far back and had crashed down six decks. He lived for only an hour. The staff captain said that death on a ship was very bad publicity and would we say nothing. We didn't, and I haven't until now.

We were halfway through the Panama Canal when a voice on the ship's public address system summoned me from the swimming pool to the radio room. Through the crackling wires I heard, cutting in and out, the voice of my high-powered agent, Barbara Lowenstein.

She told me I was to come at once to New York where a fabulous book offer awaited me. I asked what it was; she said she wouldn't tell me until I got there. I said that I couldn't get off a liner in the middle of the Canal and that I would have to reach home before I could consider making the trip; I had no wish to disembark in Acapulco and change plans on a grueling trip and that (as I had said to Toni Lopopolo) I was not going to deprive Richard of a much-needed vacation.

She announced that the book would be the inside story never told, of the royal palace of Monaco, including the facts about the late Princess Grace's marrying Prince Rainier, her death in a car crash, and the sinister forces than ran the town. I said that I wanted to live out my lifespan and wouldn't risk myself or Richard's future. I had heard the rumors that Grace had been murdered. Impatiently, Barbara said she would talk to me when I was home, and she hung up.

Meanwhile, one pleasure did emerge from the Welles affair. I found on our return to California that he had featured me in his still unfinished film *The Other Side of the Wind*.

The story was of a certain Jake Hannaford (John Huston), a prominent director who, plagued by charges of communism and homosexuality, returns to Hollywood to pick up where he left off several years before. He makes an erotic movie about two attractive young people in love, in the hope of seeming young and fresh himself, but he is plagued by publicity-seeking actors, demented fellow directors, manic partygoers, and above all by two maddening journalists who follow him about, making his life a misery.

One of these was played by Susan Strasberg, as a bossy character based on Pauline Kael. When Hannaford stops at a red sign, she interprets this absurdly as symbolic of his being branded a Communist. Hanna-ford is haunted also by an obnoxious character named Higgam, an Anglo-Australian busybody who, nosing into matters that should not concern him, gets all the facts wrong. Peter Bogdanovich was said to have essayed the role but was unable to manage the appropriate accent; the biographer and critic Joseph McBride was said to have taken over. Asked by many if I was annoyed, I replied that I couldn't have asked for more.

Back in Los Angeles, Richard and I decided we wanted to see the big Christmas tree at Rockefeller Center and so we took off to New York on the Monaco project without unpacking. Barbara arranged for me to go to the offices of the prominent attorney Alan Arrow, who represented Baron Christian de Massy, Rainier's nephew, whose story this would be.

After my experience with Hal Wallis, pleasant though it was, and aware of what the role of ghostwriter could do to a reputation and a career, I was less than enthusiastic as I sat with the sulky, handsome Baron, the smooth and charming Arrow, the skillful Barbara, and others in the office high up in a grimly impersonal building. But when the six-figure advance and a royalty split were mentioned, I gave in. Lunch with Christian at the Peacock Room of the Waldorf worked out well and I rather liked this moody, unhappy, handsome young man.

But I was unsuited to the project from the beginning. Christian's life was racing cars, and I didn't know Formula One from the formula for dynamite. Second, I was gay, happily settled with one partner now in the dreaded age of AIDS, and quite unable to share Christian's enthusiasm for the women he picked up. I no longer smoked or drank, even wine, and certainly didn't want to accompany him to bars and nightclubs.

He should have had a rough, outgoing, young, womanizing, hard-drinking and hard-smoking, macho, bilingual automobile correspondent with a profound knowledge of racing from the Grand Prix down. It was a very serious case of authorial miscasting.

Christian's life was disappointing to him: he was inflamed by a hatred of Prince Rainier, who had deprived him of a car racing career, all he wanted in life. His fondness for Princess Grace was a redeeming feature, and his accounts of her support of him were the only passages in the chronicle that I could deal with easily. I would turn up morning after morning at his father's home in the San Fernando Valley. That genial old man, the former husband of Rainier's sister, Antoinette, was on his uppers and working of all things as a professional tennis coach; Christian's American stepmother clearly was unimpressed by this change of fortune. The setting of our daily meetings was a gloomy, mirror-flanked dining room furnished in the heavy, oppressive mahoganies of the Monaco house the couple had left under a shadow following the disapproval of Rainier and his circle at court.

The publisher and Barbara Lowenstein naturally wanted blood for their money; I was realistic enough not to resent this—the "blood," of course, being a solution of Grace's death. But as Christian's nervousness increased about writing the book at all, and of causing possible legal repercussions from Monaco, so did his willingness to discuss her ending disappear.

I came to the conclusion, which I hold today, that Grace had a stroke at the wheel of her 1952 British Rover automobile; that her foot moved in a convulsion from the brake to the accelerator as she came down a deep curve of the Grande Corniche, the perilous high road that runs along the Maritime Alps of the French Riviera; and that the car therefore ran at immense speed to her destruction. It is possible that her daughter Stephanie, frantic as the car plunged, turned the wheel so that instead of crashing over a cliff the car careened through a wall, thus saving Stephanie's life. But I found no response from Christian to this reasonable theory, and he gave no satisfactory explanation in the final text.

The work with him was marked by frequent quarrels that left me drained. In one of these, Christian became hysterical as he questioned my use of the word *cleavage,* of which he had never heard, to describe the area between a woman's breasts, as revealed by a low-cut blouse. What followed was worse. Susan Leon, daughter of a William Morris agent, was the editor and disliked me as much as I disliked her. Unhappy with the book, she wanted it called *Fall from Grace,* and I pointed out to her that three other books of that title were already on the market. She hated my title, *Palace,* saying it was cold and distant; luckily, Christian approved it.

She expressed dissatisfaction with the manuscript on grounds I found unsatisfactory and held up my much-needed completion payment for months while she and Christian locked themselves up in her father's Beverly Hills house, puffing away at cigarettes until the room was virtually invisible. Forced to wait for the money, I let them stew in their own juices, disgusted by the whole matter (though Christian did have the decency, after a party I gave for him at my house, to apologize for his behavior toward me). *Palace: My Life in the Royal Family of Monaco* turned out to be bland

and innocuous, rather better written than I thought while doing it, and deservedly unsuccessful. The last I heard of Christian he was selling luxury cars in Miami.

If I was miscast as ghostwriter for Baron Christian de Massy, then I was doubly so as the unauthorized biographer of Marlon Brando. I cannot recall why I undertook this assignment, but I suspect it was because Susan Leon had held up the final payment of the advance on Christian's book, and even Barbara Lowenstein had failed to move her or the publisher. Whatever the reason, I should never have taken on the job.

I admired Brando's best performances, most notably in *The Men,* in which as a paraplegic war veteran he gave a straightforward, moving, and unmannered interpretation of a very masculine man's fear of impotence, and in *On the Waterfront.* Still, I couldn't forget his sneaky attempt to seduce Richard and the self-contempt that accompanied that attempt as he, unsure of his own legendary sex appeal, offered him a Mercedes and life in Tahiti as inducements. Of course, I would make no mention of this in the book; it would have been an invasion of privacy.

I realized I couldn't interview *The Godfather's* Francis Ford Coppola. My friend Michael Powell, the great director of *The Red Shoes* and *Black Narcissus,* had years before wanted him to back a film in which I would be the central figure, either playing myself or with an actor impersonating me, about the pursuit of Errol Flynn as a Nazi agent; Powell, as part of the British spy network in Hollywood in 1940, when he was working on Korda's *Thief of Bagdad,* knew the truth of my findings on Flynn and wanted to immortalize them. Coppola turned him down on the ground that he disliked Errol Flynn, whereas in fact I was certain the real reason was that he didn't like me.

He lived in a Beaux Arts mansion on Pacific Heights in San Francisco, furnished, as Michael Bennett's was, in abattoir modern, that is to say, with cloth lips for a couch, a table like a human kidney, a lampshade like a heart. Skilled and exciting as *The Godfather* was, I found I disliked it for glorifying the Mafia, and I challenged Coppola directly on this, and the fact that the Mob itself hadn't disapproved of it. I said that in their 1930s gangster films, Warner Bros. had never tried to glamourize Cagney or Bogart; *The Godfather* was unreal. He had the grace to admit what it was: a fairy story, a legendary take on a royal family. I wasn't mollified; I thought and still think that the film and its success were morally inexcusable. The film was outrageous in its glorification of evil, a picture of a fine family that had deep loyalties and love of parents and just happened to kill when they felt like it. Coppola's protest that *The Godfather* was a picture of American big business made sense, but it left big business, and that included Paramount and its owner Charles Bluhdorn, off the meat packer's hook.

Several years elapsed. I saw Coppola once, at a party in San Francisco, and he was understandably distant. In 1976, I decided to do a piece on Brando and *Apocalypse Now*. Almost nothing had been in print about the film, and since Coppola had gambled at least $8 million of his own money on it, I felt it might make a fascinating subject for a *New York Times* article.

I called the press agent for the film, who coolly informed me that I must interview nobody, that I would not be given any information or photographs, and that Coppola would not be available for comment. My back was up. The red flag, as they say, had been shown to the bull.

I had no idea what the picture was actually about, beyond a rumor that it was based on Joseph Conrad's novel *Heart of Darkness,* which had fascinated, among others, Orson Welles and the Polish director Andrzej Wajda. I knew that Coppola, like Hitchcock, couldn't work without illustrative sketches covering virtually all the master shots of his pictures. A visual continuity had to be worked out for him. I knew that only six men in the business were capable of doing this, and that the best of them was Hitchcock's man Tom Wright. Knowing that Hitchcock was between movies, I guessed that Wright would have worked for Coppola. I called him at Universal. Sure enough, he had done a complete visual breakdown for *Apocalypse Now*. Would I, he asked, like to see what the picture looked like?

I drove to the studio immediately. Tom Wright showed me his inventive and detailed sketches, which told me all I needed to know about the look of the film, its story, and most of its characters. Then I heard that John Milius, who had written the script, was dissatisfied with Coppola and would grant me an interview. Through the army, I found Vietnam veterans who told me more still. I reached the art director, Angelo Graham, by phone in the Middle West, figuring that in a motel on a long, dreary night after a day's work he would want to do nothing except talk to someone in Hollywood. I was right. We talked for two hours.

The *Times* rightly felt that we needed an actor in the picture to comment on its making. Marlon Brando turned out to be as elusive as ever. He no longer had an agent. His lawyer was uncommunicative, and Brando seemed permanently en route to Tahiti. Dennis Hopper had been asked to say nothing. He had been effectively silenced by Coppola. Martin Sheen, also, would say nothing, and Harvey Keitel flatly refused to give an interview. That left only Robert Duvall among the principal players. The play in which he was appearing on Broadway, *American Buffalo,* was in difficulties and needed publicity. The press agent for the show agreed to let me talk to Duvall in his dressing room on the telephone for half an hour before he went onstage for an evening performance, provided I mentioned that he was the star of the play. This seemed only the mildest of bribes, and I couldn't seriously object to it.

It took several days for the press agent to reach Duvall. The actor seemed not to be answering his telephone. Just as I was leaving to do the interview with Milius, set for 3 p.m. one afternoon, the press agent called from New York to say that Duvall would speak to me at 4 p.m. our time, 7 p.m. his, at the theater.

It was an impossible situation. I needed at least two hours for the Milius interview. I also needed the Duvall interview. How could I possibly squeeze in both? And then, the press agent said, Mr. Duvall would grant the interview only if I tape-recorded it through a rubber plug attached to the telephone.

I didn't own a plug of that kind. Somehow, I had to conduct the interview with Milius, buy a plug, find a telephone, and make the call. I rushed over to Milius's office only to find myself confronted with a twenty-minute delay, while he was in conference with his associates on his first film as a director, *Big Wednesday*.

Figuring that I had about twenty minutes to buy a plug and reach a telephone, I realized I would only have ten minutes for the Milius interview. There was no time for preliminaries. I zeroed in on every main point, obtained some sharp quotes, and fled, no doubt to Milius's amazement, from his office.

Disliking freeways, I was forced to take one. When I reached a well-known recording equipment shop, I found they were out of plugs. I made my way down LaBrea Avenue in dense traffic and found another store. They had one plug left, the cheapest kind available. I looked at my watch. There was no time to get home. I couldn't record the interview standing in a booth because there would have been nowhere to balance the recorder. I had to get to a hotel. Fast.

The nearest hotel was my old haunt the Hollywood Roosevelt. As I drove into the parking lot there was a scene only Hitchcock could have shot. Hundreds of pigeons completely covered the parking lot from one end to the other. The asphalt, the cars, even the shoulders of the people.

I had no alternative. Despite screams of fury from the bird-fancying parking attendant, I let off a blast from the horn that sounded rather like the last trumpet, and the birds flew up into the sky. I parked the car and found I had only a twenty-dollar bill in my pocket. I thrust it into the attendant's hand and broke an Olympic record running into the hotel.

I called the theater. The line was busy.

It was busy for the next ten minutes. At last the line was clear. Duvall gave me a very entertaining interview, with little or nothing good to say for Coppola.

The article was enthusiastically approved by Seymour Peck. In the meantime, Coppola and his lawyers were on the phone to my bosses at the paper, doing their utmost to quash the story. They failed, but Duvall suddenly decided to withdraw the interview, presumably under Coppola's influence.

For a week, the piece was delayed, and I suspect even trembled in the balance. But at last it was run with a much-cleaned-up version of Duvall's remarks run minus his name.

I still couldn't understand what Coppola was beefing about. He had no reason to believe I would write damagingly about his film. Yet he had even had his press agent threaten the paper with legal action if they printed any stills from the film.

A few nights after the story appeared, my editor, Guy Flatley, was at a party when he met Mary Anita Loos. She said, casually, "Did you know that my friend Maureen Orth of *Newsweek* has just been in the Philippines writing a story on Francis Ford Coppola's new picture?"

Guy called me to tell me this. Now I understood everything. Coppola wasn't annoyed because I had broken through the smoke screen on the picture. He was annoyed because I had scooped *Newsweek,* with which he and his company had clearly made a deal; no interviews and no information to the other media, in return for a *Newsweek* cover story.

But the joke, finally, was on them. First of all, my story beat Maureen Orth's so that hers had to be held over a week. It would have seemed too much like a rip-off of mine. By delaying the story two weeks, it ran slap into the jubilee of Queen Elizabeth of England, which supplanted it as a front-page story. It was pushed into the back and was barely noticed. Poetic justice.

It can easily be seen that after these episodes any chance of talking to the principal figures of Brando's recent career was lost. Instead, I concentrated on his personal life, but there again I was confronted by serious obstacles.

The danger of litigation hung over every day of work. I felt like a ship's captain in World War II, zigzagging with a freight of high explosives through the world's oceans, with enemy submarines in pursuit. I hated writing a whitewash, but that is close to what the book finally became. When Christian de Massy's panic removed much that was damaging to Prince Rainier and the Monaco principality, I had known what it was to write less than a frank account. Now I had to eliminate fact after fact to render the book publishable, preempting no-doubt serious eliminations that would be called for by the publisher's legal department.

In a desperate effort to extract something positive from the star's private life, I found athletes who had seen him run like a deer in college. Elaine Stritch, not then the grand doyenne of the stage she is today, remembered that she dated him, and he charmingly left her untouched at the bedroom door; my friend Stella Adler was full of praise for his careful, modest (!) attending of her acting classes in New York; Jean Simmons found him surprisingly gentle on *Guys and Dolls* (Frank Sinatra told me he was appalled by Brando's lateness and brooding over meaningless lines, while Sinatra wanted to finish the work in one take and go home). I couldn't face talking again to the loathsome Elia Kazan, my meeting with him my worst memory of writing the Hepburn book; but I did find Hubert Cornfield, who had directed Brando in *The Night of the Following Day*, intriguing, and Hubert's uncle, Bernard Cornfeld, the infamous swindler of tens of thousands, truly fascinating.

Completely without conscience or regret, Bernie Cornfeld, powerfully built, round and bearded, lived in a fake British mansion in Beverly Hills once owned by George Hamilton. A grand hallway and living room were lined with paintings of handsome men and women from the Tudor period on; Cornfeld told me that some of the earlier ones were Holbeins, but a quick inspection when he wasn't looking showed me that they were not.

He said that these were his ancestors, that he came from a long line of British bluebloods. I was certain he came from no more distinguished an origin than a long line of carpet merchants, but I said nothing.

He bragged that he had spent two years in a Geneva prison, with caviar, Dom Perignon, and pâté de fois gras served to him regularly by besotted wardens. In return, he gave his captors tips on hot stocks, which after he was released proved to be worthless. His cellmate, he said, was a thief who specialized in stealing grand pianos; the man would arrive with his gang in a furniture van when the house owners were away, and no neighbor looked surprised when the pianos were carried out and driven away. I asked Cornfeld, why only pianos? He said that his cellmate was "very musical" and laughed.

I had to admit, disgracefully overlooking the countless families he had wrecked with his Ponzi-like schemes, that Bernard Cornfeld was an engaging rogue and monster, and I am ashamed to say that we actually became friends.

His nephew Hubert had his own fantastic story to tell. He said that he was having an affair with a well-known actress who was suffering from depression from lack of work. One night, as he entered her on the floor by his fireplace, she was groaning with apparent pleasure when he realized she was actually in pain. He withdrew and she whispered in his ear that she had taken poison. She said she wanted to die at the moment of being taken by an attractive male and within seconds she was dead. He had a lot of explaining to do to the police.

The writing of *Brando: The Unauthorized Biography* carried its share of sinister side benefits, but I was glad when the job was done. To this day, I wish it had not been published, but it was unchanged by the editor and was not too badly received.

With two dud books in a row, I seemed to be at a very low ebb, though surprisingly my calls were still returned by agents and publishers and even film people. It was then that, out of the blue, the greatest opportunity of my life arose, and would result in my going back to the very top of the heap.

17

$\mathcal{T}$he mid-1980s were very good years. Of many spectacular parties at the time, perhaps the most spectacular was held to celebrate the covering over of the Universal Amphitheater, which had previously been open to the sun and stars, a major handicap in winter, when rain was frequent. Doris and Jules Stein invited me to sit next to them in the privileged front seats of the rented bus that took an incredible collection of celebrities across Coldwater Canyon from Angelo Drive to the San Fernando Valley and thence to the amphitheater, where Frank Sinatra would perform. The James Stewarts, the Cary Grants, the Robert Mitchums, the Minnellis—these were only a few of the illustrious couples who were with us in Hollywood's most expensive and exclusive caravan.

I was seated at a table with the Steins, the Wassermans, the Minnellis, and the Sinatras after the show, in which Sinatra had given one of the greatest performances of his life. I decided that it was time to take a high dive, to test the waters on how these illustrious figures felt about my book on Errol Flynn, so criminally treated by numerous lesser industry lights.

I asked Jules what his chief memory was of Flynn; the others leaned forward, expressing approval of what I had written. Stein and Lew Wasserman had been Flynn's agents in his heyday. "Keeping him out of jail," was the answer, and the group dissolved in laughter.

In contrast to this joyous event, there was the painful news in 1988 of the death of my beloved friend Colin Higgins, the brilliant American Australian writer and director of *Nine to Five* and *Harold and Maude*. Handsome, muscular, athletic, extremely witty and charming, he was to me not only a fine and inspiring companion but I was, I am certain, despite my deep commitment to Richard, in love with him. There could be no chance of a responding interest; he would never find me attractive. His sexual interest was in Mexican boys, like another close friend, Mark Nixon, who was murdered in Cuernavaca by hustlers of less than sixteen years of age.

Colin was stricken with AIDS. I had never been fond of Shirley Mac-Laine, recalling what I felt was unwarranted temperamental behavior on a talk-show tour in which we were simultaneously promoting books. But her speech at Colin's memorial tribute at the Directors Guild was beautiful and poetic and reduced me to helpless tears.

A tribute of similar character to Orson Welles in the mid-1980s was not as impressive. The most eloquent and thoughtful of those who spoke of him was Geraldine Fitzgerald, who had once been his mistress and whose personality in films I had always admired, despite Pauline Kael. The occasion was memorable for the striking beauty and star presence of Welles's companion, the Yugoslavian sculptress Oya Kodar.

Richard's sumptuous decoration of the house and our parties, though small, were much discussed. Jules and Doris Stein; Lee and Vincente Minnelli; Jean Howard, legendary mistress of Louis B. Mayer ("best food I ever ate at a party"); June (widow of Oscar) Levant and her husband, Henry Ephron, father of Nora; the Minnellis—these were frequent and valued guests along with Anna Sten, Miliza Korjus, and most memorably the great comedian Fritz Feld and his wife, Virginia Christine, famous for the Folgers coffee commercials as "Swedish" Mrs. Olsen.

It was Virginia who figured in that period's most memorable episode. I had picked up in an obscure junk shop on Santa Monica Boulevard a superkitsch papier-mâché artifact: a prop from an old Universal mummy movie, a sarcophagus so blatantly fake that instead of having Egyptian hieroglyphics on the outside, it had the name of the dead—PRINCESS ANANKA—in English lettering.

As soon as she saw it, Virginia's eyes lit up. To everyone's astonishment, she opened it and stood inside with her arms crossed. She asked me to close the door. I warned her there were no air holes; she insisted. Everyone told me I should pull her out at once; she might faint. I called out to her; she did not respond. Then we heard a frantic knocking and shouting. I opened the mummy case and Virginia, very pale, tottered out.

A chorus of voices asked her what she thought she was doing. She replied with the statement that she had played Ananka in the film in which the sarcophagus was used, and by going into it had returned to her natural habitat. A quick scotch and soda fixed her up, and to general laughter and applause, the party went on.

I forget who gave me the idea of writing what would turn out to be my biggest success to date, *The Duchess of Windsor: The Secret Life.* It may have been Jules and Doris Stein. Or perhaps, as with so many of my books, the idea came to me in the dark of the night and I sat up thinking: This is my next work.

My agent Mitch Douglas of ICM suggested we approach the sophisticated and charming young editor Thomas Ward Miller at McGraw-Hill, a distinguished house chiefly known as a publisher of college textbooks but with a very strong trade list. On the briefest of outlines, Miller snapped at the idea.

The story of the plain and flat-chested woman from Baltimore who cost the king of England his throne had been told frequently over the previous fifty years, but with my customary cheek I was sure I would find much that was new, and I did.

I was convinced that the duchess was far more than simply a skilled seducer, that she was in fact, as had been hinted, a direct collaborator with Hitler. I was sure also that she had hidden behind a bland narrative in her memoirs, *The Heart Has Its Reasons,* the truth of her life in China in the 1920s, and that her lawyer Maître Suzanne Blum in Paris and her memorialist Michael Bloch knew far more than they had agreed should be in print.

In December 1986 I flew to London and Paris with Richard to interview people who were close to the Windsors. Lord Ironside, son of a former commander in chief of British forces, confirmed unhesitatingly that his late father knew the duchess had leaked official secrets to Nazi Germany. In Paris I spent an hour with the imposing Comte René de Chambrun at his offices on the Champs Elysées, pretentiously known as Le Cabinet Chambrun. The son-in-law of the French collaborationist Pierre Laval, who had been executed by the Free French, he told me all I needed to know by his protective stance on the Windsors.

I proceeded to the outskirts of Paris, to meet Lady Diana Mosley, widow of the British fascist leader Sir Oswald, who had both been arrested at Dolphin Square while I was living there; she now lived in the Château de la Gloire, a crumbling early-nineteenth-century minicastle once owned by one of Napoleon's generals.

Over *oeuf diable* and *veal milanese* she issued a warning. "You mustn't say," she cautioned, "that Hitler was the best man at my wedding to Sir Oswald. He was the guest of honor." A nice distinction, I thought, and then she began to rant. She said that Hitler would have won the war if he hadn't wasted his time murdering six million Jews, which drained his manpower; they should have been sent to Northern Australia to hunt crocodiles or Madagascar to find badgers. She said that Hitler was a wonderful man and a dear friend and that he would have been the savior of the world if only the wretched Churchill, who admired him so sensibly early on, hadn't changed his mind to obtain personal power in England and had forced his country into war. As for her sister Unity, who fell in love with the führer, she said that a marriage of the pair would have been superb and would have produced fine children to keep the peace of the world.

This delicate shadow of her former self seemed to me mad, bad, and dangerous to know, and I wondered what she would have said if she had found out I had some Jewish blood on my father's side. At all events, I made no adverse response and left her in a good temper; what she must have felt when my book came out I dare not hazard.

Further research in London resulted in friendships with such figures as Hugo Vickers, diligent recorder of Windsoriana, and the royal historian Kenneth Rose. Back in Paris, I gave a speech at the gathering of world historians at the American University and formed a warm acquaintance with the historian M. R. D. Foot. A party following at the Russian embassy was wonderfully charged with menace; despite the fact that several of the historians who joined me in addressing the assembly were Russians themselves, I thought I might be kidnapped and whisked off to Moscow at any minute. Instead, I merely got frowns as I declined offers of vodka. Back in Los Angeles, I decided I must find a man named Count Alfred de Marigny. While the duke and duchess were governor and his lady in the Bahamas during World War II, banished there because they were rightly considered dangerous to British national security, one of the great unsolved murders of all time had taken place.

Their closest friend on the island, Sir Harry Oakes, was found murdered in his bed, the room partly on fire, on the night of July 7, 1943. His son-in-law, the contentious de Marigny, was accused of the crime on the slender basis of singed wrist hairs caused when he lighted a hurricane lamp at a party several miles away. Despite an airtight alibi, the Duke of Windsor made sure de Marigny was arrested at once and stood trial; he was acquitted chiefly because the black members of the jury, who owed him much for his support of African-British water rights in Nassau, overrode the whites. Where, I asked myself, could he possibly be now?

Before I saw him I had to determine the facts for myself. Richard and I were by coincidence already booked on a Caribbean cruise, our fifth, and I made arrangements in the Bahamas to visit the Nassau courthouse where the de Marigny trial had taken place. The archive was in a cellar, and the charmingly ebullient and buxom custodian, an African British lady in a flowing pink muumuu, led me down some rickety steps to a room haunted by white ants and roaches in the sticky heat. To my amazement, she found the trial transcript in minutes and handed it to me; with some persuasion, I managed to have her let me copy it on an insecure Xerox machine and made off with the bulky document, and accompanying photographs and charts, to my ship.

The transcript proved to be amazing. Every report I had dredged up from old newspaper files said that Sir Harry Oakes had been shot and burned to conceal the bullet wounds; not a word of this was true. In fact, he had been stabbed by his killer with a triangular sharp instrument around the left ear's mastoid bone; the wounds were between two and two-and-a-half inches deep, enough to penetrate the brain. He had been set on fire in gunpowder patches, lighted but left smoldering, when the windows blew open in a storm and rain poured in.

It was easy to see the trial was a farce. Windsor had deliberately had two shady detectives from Miami come in, get de Marigny's fingerprints transferred from the drink they offered him to a Chinese screen in Sir Harry's room, and obtain other fake evidence to convict him. When I published my findings in the subsequent book, I wrote, charitably, that I wasn't certain the duke was an accessory to Sir Harry's murder. Today, I take a different view.

After a prolonged search in New York, I found the instrument that had caused Sir Harry's death, the only one that fit the size and shape of the wounds. It was a lanza, or shallow-water fishing spear, and Harold Christie, whom I suspected of murdering Sir Harry or rather engaging a man to do the job, ran the shallow-water spear-fishing concession in the islands.

In Los Angeles I contacted Sergeant Louis Danoff of Hollywood Homicide, and Dr. Joseph Choi, assistant county coroner, and showed them pictures of the deceased. They confirmed that the murder had all the signs of a ritual killing; whoever ordered the crime had engaged the services of a Palo Mayombe black magician, part of the diabolical cult known as Brujeria that practiced in the islands and in South Florida. They showed me similar photographs of recent killings in downtown Los Angeles.

I gradually assembled a case: Sir Harry had been about to ruin Christie, by pulling in his IOUs; Christie hired a dwarfish Palo Mayombe murderer to destroy his friend; on the night of the tropical storm the killer stabbed the sleeping man with the fishing spear; he lost his way going out and left bloody handprints on walls and mirrors at a height of no more than five feet; Christie got away with it due to influence with the Windsors; and the duke, after de Marigny was acquitted, three times tried to have de Marigny killed to suppress the truth.

Luck came to my rescue again. I picked up a copy of *Variety*, the show business daily I almost never read, and found, as if guided to it, a tiny, obscure item at the bottom of a back page that said that Alfred de Marigny, the accused killer in the famous unsolved Oakes case, was planning to cooperate in a film version of his life. It added that he now lived in Houston, Texas.

Incredibly, he was listed in the Houston telephone book, in the wealthy suburb of River Oaks. He agreed to see me and I flew though a violent storm to a very bumpy landing. I expected to go to my hotel and telephone the house for an appointment when to my astonishment a voice on the public address system told me to come to the airline counter. When I arrived, a woman, worn but still attractive in late middle age, greeted me with the statement that she was Mrs. Alfred de Marigny.

I wondered what had driven her to come to the airport in person, and I soon found out. She said, looking me very sharply in the eye, "Do you think my husband did it?" I didn't know how to respond, so merely said, "After thirty years of marriage, Mrs. de Marigny, you mean you don't know?" And my tone of voice told her what she wanted to hear, that I was certain of his innocence.

De Marigny turned up and took care of my luggage; we drove to the house in River Oaks, that elegantly sinister enclave of the very rich, and home of the recently ruined silver kings. De Marigny told me that he was certain Oakes was shot; I said that I was equally certain that was wrong, and I produced the photographic charts and trial transcripts from Nassau.

He was fascinated, but, stubborn character that he was, he ignored the documentation when he later came to write a most inaccurate memoir and account of the case. I realized that this charming Mauritian was his own worst enemy: mischievous, ill advised, opinionated, and undiplomatic. But completely innocent of murder.

Back in England again, I had two memorable encounters. I took to lunch at the Dorchester Grill Leslie Field, royal jewelry historian and for mer editor of the society magazine the *Tatler*, my mother's favorite reading as a child. I wanted to interview Field because she was said to be one of the few people who had seen the elusive, notorious document known as the China Dossier.

This lengthy report had been prepared in 1934 by King George V, grandfather of the present queen, with the purpose of destroying Wallis Simpson's reputation in the eyes of her lover, the Prince of Wales. It had disappeared into the recesses of the Round Tower of Windsor Castle, because of royal spin doctoring, and it had been kept secret and (as it is to this day) declared nonexistent by many close to the queen.

Mrs. Field told me that the dossier showed Wallis drug peddling and gambling for high stakes in China in the 1920s, backed by wealthy lovers, including a Chinese general. Later, I found that the file had been taken by the impeccably respectable courtier the Honorable John Coke to his employer Queen Mary, who was appalled by its contents. Others who were shown the dossier included the duchesses of York and Kent, and Winston Churchill, in 1951, while on a painting holiday in Marrakech. The dossier revealed also that Wallis had been a society prostitute, the mistress of Mussolini's future son-in-law Count Galeazzo Ciano (a fact later confirmed to me by his widow) and of an Italian admiral. It was clear that the Prince of Wales, later the Duke of Windsor, refused to accept the reports on her and that his supporters have denied their existence ever since.

One who did not deny was the duke's equerry, Sir Dudley Forwood. I went by train to see him at his house in the New Forest. He greeted me at the railway station not in a Rolls-Royce or a Daimler as I had expected but in a beaten-up prewar Hillman Minx, the British equivalent of a Volkswagen. It was full of scraps of paper, chicken feathers, and the smell of turpentine.

The elderly, charming gentleman, survivor of years with the Windsors, told me as an opening statement that his present wife was one of the few (he had married several) who wasn't a lesbian. With that, he placed a gnarled hand on my knee and, at imminent risk of being driven back to the station, I removed it gently, saying that I was spoken for; I showed him the wedding ring I still wore for Norine and now for Richard.

He sighed resignedly and drove on. As soon as we arrived at the airy, sprawling house, Lady Forwood greeted me warmly and, after asking me to tea and whether I liked crumpets (I lied that I did), without further ado asked me if I would be writing about the duchess's Casanova Clip.

I assumed she was referring to a valuable item of jewelry and was amazed when this seemingly respectable lady, exuding good breeding, told me (and I had only been in the house for five minutes) that it was a technique of tightening the vaginal orifice that could improve a semiflaccid male's strength on entry by gripping the base of the penis. She went on to ask me if I had come across the duchess's use of fang chung. Used as I was to the oddities of the British upper class, I was amazed by the frankness of the question. Fang chung was, according to my research, the art of sexual stimulation in which the duchess specialized and which to his lasting gratitude had rescued the duke from impotence. It involved the relaxing of the insecure male through a long and carefully modulated hot oil massage of the nipples, stomach, thighs, and, after a deliberately postponed delay, the genitals. The exponent of fang chung knew where the nerve endings and centers so often neglected were to be found in the male body; the technique could also be used to prevent premature ejaculation by applying pressure of the fingers in the area between the urethra and the anus, thus stopping a quick climax.

Sir Dudley said that when he was the duke's equerry he had seen the duchess, dressed in white as a hospital nurse, thrashing the former king as he wore only a diaper, whimpering for more. "That's why my husband's knees are so bad," Lady Dudley said. "He spent his life kneeling at keyholes."

Sir Dudley addressed a more serious matter. He gave me the first account he had given anyone of his and the duke's meeting with Hitler at

Berchstesgaden. He said that after a few seconds in which he addressed the führer in Hitler's native tongue, Hitler stood up annoyed and told a translator to render the duke's words in English. When later the duke asked the translator the reason for the führer's action, he was told that Hitler felt humiliated because the duke was addressing him in High German, the language of the upper class, and Hitler spoke the low class German learned in humbler circumstances.

Luckily, my Rome correspondent Donatella Ortona's father had been chargé d'affaires at the Italian embassy in London when the duchess was leaking secrets to Mussolini. Even more fortunate, his best friend was Mussolini's ambassador to the Court of St. James, Count Dino Grandi, during that period, and the two men (Grandi was blind, living in a castle near Bologna) were mines of information.

Two years in preparation, research, and writing, *The Duchess of Windsor: The Secret Life* involved hundreds of interviews and thousands of pages of documents. At last the job was done and I handed Tom Miller at McGraw-Hill the bulky manuscript. Enthused, he accepted it at once.

To my combined disappointment and relief, McGraw-Hill planned no major talk-show tour, just appearances on *Good Morning America* and a few other major shows. I decided on a tactic: although the duchess was still known to many, and the auction of her jewels in Geneva had made headlines, I felt that she wasn't an automatic draw as a book subject unless I could come up with a strong selling gimmick.

Before the *GMA* interview with the coolly detached Jane Pauley began, I took the unusual step of suggesting a question to her; startled, since this had probably never happened with any other guest, she wrote it down. The question was: how could a not beautiful, obscure, and certainly not wealthy Baltimore girl bring down the British throne by seducing a king?

In answering the question, I thought of Shelley Winters, who had appeared recently to promote her book of memoirs. Zaftig, no longer attractive, and all too volatile in her behavior, she had, she told her talk-show hosts, enjoyed passionate affairs with some of the best-looking men of her era, including the gorgeous Italian star Vittorio Gassman and the American beauty Anthony Franciosa. Many of the millions of zaftig female viewers must have asked themselves, how had this overweight woman done it? They had forgotten that when she was young, Shelley Winters was pretty, sexy, and voluptuous.

I answered that the duchess had overcome the duke's lack of sexual confidence; she had applied certain techniques, both physical and psychological, that assured her an absolute but loving power over him; and what was the throne of England to compare with discovering he was after all not a wimp and weakling, but a man?

The approach worked; the book was twenty-three weeks in the top half of the *New York Times* best-seller lists, was high in *Publishers Weekly* and in England, and number one in France. Who could resist finding out about fang chung? I was set for life.

I began to think about a life of Cary Grant. I had first met with the star after visiting Alfred Hitchcock at his cottage at Universal Studios; I had dropped in, at Grant's invitation, to see him at his own little house nearby.

I was told, then or later, that there was a trompe l'oeil painting he had ordered from the studio's art director Alexander Golitzen; annoyed by a view of nothing but oleander bushes and a brick wall, he had ordered a replica of a country scene to replace the window so that one would seem to be looking out at a garden with a gravel path, a wicker gate, a fence, and beyond them a hill with sheep gamboling on it and beyond that again a gray English sky. He wanted to feel he was back in the West Country of his birth.

When the painting was completed, he sent it back, annoyed; he said the art department had made a very serious mistake. They denied it, and he pointed out that the knotty pine door's one open knot failed to show the sky. The painting had to be done again before he would accept it. I found Grant as fussy as the story would indicate; as we talked, he stared for a long time at two books that were not in perfect alignment on a shelf and then, unable to stand the sight any longer, set them exactly side by side. He flicked a tiny fragment of dust off a table with a Kleenex and then deposited the Kleenex, with a flourish, neatly folded, in the wastebasket.

His hair was too perfect: razor cut, it had obviously been checked and rechecked in a mirror. His eyes were strange: they had the peculiar blankness of a ventriloquist's dummy. The enormous horn-rimmed glasses seemed to be lensless; he was, I could tell, and others later confirmed it, wearing contact lenses.

He walked me into his inner sanctum, a pretty office with, at its center, a circular flowered table he told me he had painted himself. "Kind of gays things up a little," he said. The term had only just come into use, and his wink told me a very great deal.

I had a sense of a man who carried with him countless secrets, and it wasn't surprising to find that he had been involved with Secret Intelligence in World War II, or that, of all things, he had been an under-the-table Hollywood movie agent at the height of his screen career, representing, with his partner Harry Edington, Garbo, Dietrich, Leopold Stokowski, Rita Hayworth, Joel McCrea, Edward G. Robinson, and Rosalind Russell. Few secrets in Hollywood were better kept than that one.

It was clear to me soon after laying the groundwork for a new biography of Grant that his bisexuality was known to everyone in Hollywood. Edith Gwyn was the author of a racy daily column in the *Hollywood Reporter* from the early thirties on, and a diligent search of her contributions over many years showed she was privy to her industry's secret facts and slipped them to readers. She hid barbs in a continuing gag involving movie titles that advertised the wrong stars: Dietrich was in *Male and Female,* Garbo in *The Son-Daughter,* and Grant in *One Way Passage.*

Roy Moseley, with whom I had worked on the Merle Oberon biography, again came in as my fellow author and was indispensable as a finder of rare facts and an interviewer of people who had never talked about Grant.

Most notably, he had friends in Grant's former assistant and chauffeur Ray Austin, who witnessed Grant's love affair with Howard Hughes, and in Grant's first wife, Virginia Cherrill, costar of Charlie Chaplin's *City Lights,* who spoke of Grant's cruelty.

More than one man I interviewed said he had idolized Grant until Cary came to his house wearing a dress. Grant's gay relationship with Randolph Scott was astonishingly open; they would go to premieres and parties as a pair, without female stars, and no studio chief could change this. When they made the movie *My Favorite Wife,* and checked into a hotel in Pasadena, everyone expected them to occupy separate suites; to the shock and astonishment of their fellow actors and crew, they moved into the same room and shared a double bed.

A fan magazine correspondent from Spain took photographs of Grant and Scott in 1941, at their home in the Los Feliz district of Los Angeles, which told all too clear a story. Perhaps the couple thought the pictures wouldn't be seen in America after the war, but they were, by collectors; they went unpublished in the United States until our book appeared.

Joseph Longstreth, agent for Caryl Chessman, also knew Grant, who told him that he knew of Errol Flynn's Nazi activities at a party at the Beverly Hills home of Gilbert Roland and Constance Bennett on May 20, 1941. Grant told Longstreth he had reported the matter to the authorities and, to his distress, nothing was done.

I found fascinating real-life parallels with Grant's famous film *Notorious,* directed by Alfred Hitchcock. The heroine, played by Ingrid Bergman, has a Nazi sympathizer father, who commits suicide in a Miami jail. This was a direct parallel with Charles Bedaux, host to the Duke and Duchess of Windsor, and Nazi contact, who killed himself in prison in identical circumstances in that city. One of the Bergman circle in the film was played by Sir Charles Mendl, another British agent. Bergman herself had been under suspicion as she had made a film in Berlin and then had joined the allied cause. Leopoldine Konstantin, playing the mother of Claude Rains's Nazi villain, was under suspicion also, as he had been a frequent guest of George Gyssling, the Nazi consul general in Los Angeles, with her husband, the writer Géza Herczeg.

As for the group of spies surrounding Rains in the film, Reinhold Schünzel, once a director, had been falsely accused of refusing to make the anti-Nazi movie *Escape* because he was a Nazi sympathizer; Frederick Ledebur was an Allied agent. But the strongest parallel of all was in the central scene in which Grant, though in love with Bergman, lets the FBI send her into bed with Rains and even into marriage, to determine the secrets that will clear up her record as a suspect once and for all.

As for the aforementioned matter of the uranium deposits found in the film in the mountains near Rio, the parallel was again exact, and based on Grant's findings. Hedy Lamarr, whom he knew very well, had married the Nazi industrialist Fritz Mandl and fled his house when she overheard him talking to Hitler in her living room. Mandl had gone to Buenos Aires where he began developing nuclear weaponry, storing samples of dust in fireproof steel boxes in his house. The use of wine bottles as places for the dust in *Notorious* was a sly reference to Mandl's interest in fine vintages.

There was yet another parallel between Cary Grant's role in *Notorious* and real life, also reported in no other book. In late 1940 a Spanish spy, Count Carlos Vejarano y Cassina, arrived in New York, and Sir Charles Mendl, who should have known better, introduced him to Grant and Barbara Hutton, who in turn gave Vejarano financial support in finding accommodation in Hollywood. Vejarano's purpose was to determine Grant's activities, now extensive, in investigating such Nazis as Errol Flynn, Hilde Kruger, and George Gyssling.

Grant arranged a screen test for Vejarano and took Spanish lessons from him for a fee; he obtained work for Vejarano as a translator into Spanish of screenplays at Columbia. On November 26, 1943, J. Edgar Hoover had Vejarano arrested in New York. I found the attorney Milton S. Gould, who handled the case. Gould confirmed that Grant and Hutton were devastated by the arrest, not just because they had been duped by an enemy agent but because they would have been ruined if their relationship with Vejarano had been revealed. The trial and Vejarano's deportation to Spain went unmentioned in all published sources; the FBI files were very clear.

Roy Moseley's researches in England uncovered much new information on Grant's family origins, and many new details of his marriages not only to Virginia Cherrill but to Barbara Hutton, to the mysterious Betsy Drake, and to the charming Dyan Cannon, survivor of a newspaper headline that read, "DYAN CANNON DISCHARGED."

The book appeared to great success and went on many best-seller lists; the reviews were on the whole good and I began a talk-show tour.

The tour turned out to be grueling. Many hosts attacked me for writing that Grant was bisexual; on a shock-radio show, a woman called in saying she knew why I said Grant was gay, because he had thrown me out when I tried to climb into bed and make love to him. I said that she was the one he rejected; I had already satisfied the star when she turned up, angry and frustrated. This fiction, rendered in terms of unbridled vulgarity, pleased the host enormously.

The new decade of the 1990s began with an ambitious project: a dual biography of Queen Elizabeth and Prince Philip, with Roy Moseley listed as coauthor. Although indispensable in his help on Merle Oberon and Cary Grant, in this case he had little to do with the finished work, but he deserved the shared credit, and the money, for his devoted and exemplary work in the past.

There were of course scores of books on the royal couple, but much of their story had been tactfully omitted, as the chief authors were British, and some clearly had possible knighthoods in mind. Both of these principals had seemingly been above reproach, except for Philip's oft-quoted and ill-advised gaffes in public places. But certain matters concerning them had never surfaced and seemed to me of vital interest to a public readership that had grown more sophisticated and demanding of inside information than any before it.

The chief interest for me in the queen was the never-discussed matter of her personal investments. This subject opened by me was overlooked again when *Elizabeth and Philip: The Untold Story of the Queen of England and Her Prince* appeared in 1991; hence the fact that I relate it here, in a period in which money and business affairs are far more prominent in people's minds than they were seventeen years ago.

I found that the queen was a master of stock manipulations; she inherited her skills from the Queen Mother, a canny Scotswoman with a finger in many pies. In 1968 the monarch had bought, through Courtaulds, the vast international textile corporation, in which she had a majority shareholding, a 38,000-acre cotton plantation, one of the largest in the American South, at Scott, Mississippi. It was worth $4.5 million at the time (at least ten times as much today) and employed hundreds of black laborers; with great skill, the queen's advisers had engineered it so that as well as reaping profits on a colossal scale, the so-called Queen's Farm was granted $1.5 million a year from the U.S. Department of Agriculture as a subsidy it emphatically did not need.

In a long-forgotten entry, I found in the *Congressional Record* for January 28, 1971, that Senator Thomas McIntyre of New Hampshire had brought up this inconvenient matter at an introduction of a bill on farm subsidies. He charged that the queen had been the beneficiary of $120,000 for one fallow year following the four-year cycle of crop growing, a perfectly normal procedure, which she could and should have paid for herself.

I talked to Congressman Silvio O. Conte of Massachusetts, a specialist in matters of foreign investment, and he stated that the Queen's Farm was anonymously part of her Crown Lands, quite inappropriate in America. Under congressional pressure, Courtaulds sold the farm very profitably for

$44.5 million. The queen also owned, with her mother, substantial properties in New York, rivaling those owned today by such billionaires as Donald Trump and Steven Roth. They included the Jack Dempsey building on Broadway and much of the grind movie district west of Broadway as well as stretches of Eighth and Ninth avenues and West Forty-first to Forty-eighth streets.

Digging through records established these ownerships. Until it collapsed in the famous Nick Leeson scandal, Barings, then the royal bankers and investors, played a role in these acquisitions.

Other shrewd royal investments paid off handsomely. The queen had a heavy holding in General Electric, which came up year after year as the most successful company of its type in the world.

She also had a substantial (perhaps a majority) shareholding in the colossus known as Rio Tinto Zinc, with her principal private secretary, Sir Martin (later Lord) Charteris, elected to the board. RTZ specialized in lead, copper, iron ore, bauxite, aluminum, coal, and graphite glass as well as nuclear energy.

Her greatest profit came from her conviction that the North Sea off British shores contained vast resources of oil, an idea few had cottoned to before. She had a holding in British Petroleum that, with RTZ, played a major role in exploiting the vast petroleum North Sea resource known as Argyle Field that would make her and England even richer than before. The prime minister, Harold Wilson; Harold Lever, chancellor of the Queen's Duchy of Lancaster; and postmaster general Edmund Dell assisted the queen in the matter.

During a U.S. Senate Foreign Relations Committee hearing, U.S. attorney general Edward U. Levi and Senator Frank Church charged that an international cartel, including RTZ, was fixing uranium prices worldwide. Evidence was obtained in minutes of a 1974 meeting of RTZ in Johannesburg, in which cornering the dangerous element was discussed. Nothing came of this.

The queen's interest in General Electric was remarkable. She owned two million pounds of GE shares, at a time when she was more or less openly in support of Margaret Thatcher's Conservative government. GE was perhaps the most consistent and substantial financial supporter of Thatcher's electoral campaign. Lord Weinstock, head of GE, put every effort behind Thatcher; his running of GE resulted in demands by the Labor

Party that he allow the company to be nationalized in view of its meddling in politics and downsizing and dismissal of thousands of employees.

The queen entered numerous investments on both sides of the Atlantic under the name of Houblon Nominees. Doreen Houblon, granddaughter of the sixth Earl of Carrick, had strong racing and personal connections to the queen and received both the MCO and DVO from the monarch. Her book on riding, *Side Saddle,* was among the queen's favorite works.

Houblon Nominees was part of the Bank of England, which meant that the queen benefited directly from the largest national financial institution. The directors of the B of E were also the directors of Houblon; one was a Bowes-Lyon, related directly to the Queen Mother.

In addition to these revelations, all ignored when the book came out, because at that time finance was not big news, I found that the four sisters of Prince Philip were married to prominent Nazis; Sophie was the wife of the SS Death's Head leader Prince Christoph of Hesse. They were excluded from the royal wedding in 1947, as too many questions would be asked so soon after the war; but at the coronation in 1953 they had to be let in. All in black, in Westminster Abbey, they seemed to be dressed for a funeral rather than for the greatest of royal occasions; by now, the fever-pitch atmosphere of anti-Germanism had died down and their presence created very little stir. There were ripples when Prince Philip fought too strenuously for a united Germany and when Prince Michael of Kent married a woman whose father had served Hitler as a soldier in World War II, but these were far too little and much too late.

The picture that emerged of the queen was clearly removed from that drawn by Helen Mirren in the famous film of 2007. Her iron will, financial shrewdness, wheeling and dealing in cotton and New York real estate; her peremptory attitude to those who crossed her; and her implacable hatred of Princess Diana were all glossed over. But it is true to say of the movie that if it had portrayed the real woman, it would not have been a smash hit. Nor would it have succeeded if it had been a hagiography.

19

ouis B. Mayer seemed an ideal subject for me: the greatest of the motion picture industry's leaders, he was apparently unblemished by personal scandal, except for the false charge that he had dandled the child Judy Garland on his knee and filled her up with drugs, and that he had dumped his first wife when she was charged with being a kleptomaniac.

I felt I could write a sober, unsensational, and respectable account of the scrap merchant's son in a Boston ghetto who later dominated the movie industry as nobody did before or after him. And I had no difficulty, with *Cary Grant* turning up on best-seller lists, in obtaining a contract from Putnam. In this case, I decided to write the book alone.

I was lucky again. The details of Mayer's birth in Russia and immigration to the United States were loosely reported in the existing records and most inaccurately in his late daughter Irene's memoirs; his grandsons Danny and Jeffrey could cast no light on the facts. So I was fortunate that glasnost, the newly opened peaceful connections to the Soviet Union, also included the availability of documents in Moscow that had been hidden for some seventy years, since the revolution.

From these, obtained by a Russian contact, and from obscure records of the family's early arrival in New York and Halifax, Nova Scotia, I was able to unravel Mayer's fascinating early years. Most of all, I was able to see that he wasn't raised in America but in Canada, which explained to me for the first time why he was addicted to British writers, directors, and stars; worshipped the British royal family and Winston Churchill; and spearheaded pro-British propaganda in the period between the outbreak of war in Europe and Pearl Harbor, when so many Americans were isolationist.

I found that he had supported Allied Artists, the aforementioned British Intelligence group in Hollywood. I found the records of a congressional hearing in November and December 1941 in which the isolationist Senators Gerald Nye and Arthur Vandenberg condemned MGM and other studios for ignoring the Neutrality Act, which forbade Americans to enter into propagandist activities condemning Nazi Germany, with which the United States was still not in a state of war.

Mayer thought such attacks egregious; Pearl Harbor brought the committee's hearings to an end. He had made the anti-Nazi *Escape* and *The Mortal Storm,* and now he made *Mrs. Miniver,* an outright attack on Germany, in which Greer Garson as an English housewife took in a German soldier who had parachuted onto her property.

Mayer, I found, had, with Ad Schulberg, his mistress and agent and mother of Budd Schulberg (*What Made Sammy Run?*), for years rescued countless Jewish writers from all over Europe and the Balkans, putting them under contract to rewrite scripts or work in various other capacities at the studio.

His biggest challenge came from Leni Riefenstahl; my old friend Bob Vogel of MGM foreign publicity told me the story. Riefenstahl had visited Hollywood in 1938 in the wake of Kristalnacht, the horrifying pogrom against Jews initiated by Hitler when a Jew was accused of killing a Nazi diplomat agent in Paris. Top of her list of people to see was Gary Cooper, a frequent guest of Nazi consul general in Los Angeles George Gyssling and a former guest of the Albert (brother of Hermann) Goerings in Berlin. But wisely, Paramount spirited him off to Mexico.

Next on her list was Winfield Sheehan, former head of Fox Pictures, later joined with 20th Century, and a Nazi sympathizer whose wife, the famous Viennese opera star Maria Jaritza, was also an admirer of Hitler. They had Riefenstahl stay at their Hidden Valley ranch, where they, on instructions from Dr. Joseph Goebbels, raised the famous Lipizzaner horses of the Spanish Riding School in Vienna to protect them against Allied air raids for the duration of the war.

Mayer asked Vogel if he should receive Riefenstahl. Walt Disney was giving her a tour of his studio and a dinner party in her honor. Vogel said that if she came to the studio a Jewish grip might drop an arc light on her head and kill her; if he refused, Hitler could close up MGM in Berlin. Mayer decided he would not have Riefenstahl at the studio. She declared herself unwilling to settle for a private visit to his house, and he was relieved.

He still managed to keep open the Berlin branch. Thus, he was upset when Luise Rainer, who had twice consecutively won Academy Awards for performances in pictures he made, protested with a placard outside the Beverly Hills Hotel calling for Leni to go home. He terminated Rainer's contract.

This darkened my picture of Mayer, and I soon found other unflattering aspects of his life. Despite his horror of Nazism, he allowed Winfield Sheehan to make a Hitlerian movie right under his nose: *Florian,* about the Lipizzaners, and an excuse to bring them to California. The movie was outright fascist in its reference to racial strains. In one scene, a Lipizzaner mare gives birth to a black foal; when someone expresses horror, he is reassured that the animal will turn white in the third year. The movie was suffused in such sentiments and early scenes of violence in Germany were put down not, accurately, to Nazi storm trooper activism but to Communists. That Mayer allowed such a picture to be made and released is a lasting blemish on his name.

Nor was his behavior much better in the matter of John Gilbert, the great silent star ruined by sound. I was able to establish that when Gilbert arranged to marry Greta Garbo at a Santa Monica beach house, Garbo failed to turn up, and Mayer, seeing Gilbert's hysterical state, screamed at him to fuck the dame and forget about marrying her. Gilbert carried Mayer into the bathroom and began to strangle him to death until Eddie Mannix, studio chief and former bouncer at New Jersey's Palisades Amusement Park, dragged Gilbert loose and saved Mayer's life. Gilbert was doomed.

The matter of the death of Mayer's cultivated producer Paul Bern was a much-discussed mystery, as closed off as the Sir Harry Oakes affair in the Bahamas, and an equal challenge to me as a literary detective.

For many years, it hadn't been a mystery at all, but a seemingly straightforward case of suicide, the motive his sexual impotence with Jean Harlow, his wife, who would also die young. But for years, the picture had been changed: the story around Hollywood was that he had been murdered by Dorothy Millette, his former, common-law wife, who had arrived at his house at night, shot him in a jealous rage, and then flung herself off a boat to her death into the Sacramento River.

250

The latest exponent of this account seemed to be incontrovertible. The producer-writer Sam Marx, a friend of mine for many years, was in a position to know: he had been an executive at MGM in 1932, when Bern died; he was part of the inner circle that ran the studio; he helped handle the police at the time of the criminal investigation; and now he had produced a book, *Deadly Illusions,* which purported to support the murder theory with evidence, including a highly questionable document he claimed to have been given by a retired official attached to the grand jury records room, always considered inviolate and for the indefinite future.

No such document was shown me, and I decided that the case was unproved. Satisfied that Bern's death was in fact a suicide, I began exploring files that had been ignored by previous writers.

The autopsy report, based on carefully recorded forensic findings, left no doubt that Bern, naked in front of a three-paneled mirror, had pressed a revolver to his temple and shot himself. The suicide note was not, as every source said, placed on a mantelpiece and then secretly removed by Louis B. Mayer, but written in a green morocco visitor's book police found on arrival at the house, with a rubber band placed around the appropriate page to make sure it wasn't missed. Mayer wasn't at the house.

I found probate files, unopened since 1932, that showed that Bern had bought numerous books on the worship of the penis in ancient cultures, a study of female sexuality alleging women's total dependence on men, and a volume on male hormonal disturbances that could lead to sexual failure. No further evidence was needed to show what was troubling this unhappy man.

But when everything seemed to be sewn up, I found a further clue. In an obscure and forgotten entry in the *Los Angeles Times,* I found a reference to Bern's hysterical attack of grief at Santa Monica Beach when a man with whom he was intimate was drowned in a freak wave. I then heard from various women who said he had been capable of intercourse with them. I found that his insecurity and sexual ambiguity had increased drastically with Harlow, who was at the time the precursor of Marilyn Monroe as the most desired woman in America. Given her challenging and raucous nature, displayed harshly in her screen performances, she must have temporarily rendered him neuter.

The finished work had been signed up by Phyllis Grann, the formidable editor in chief of Putnam's publishers, as part of a two-book deal, the second to be decided. No sooner had she received *Merchant of Dreams:*

Louis B. Mayer, M.G.M., and the Secret Hollywood than she and her editor George Coleman turned it down.

They said it was too specialized, too serious and imposing, for the mass audience for which they intended it. But unable to find fault with it, and with the contract specifying lack of quality as the only reason for declining it, they had to pay the substantial second payment of the advance. Dan Strone of William Morris offered the book to numerous editors, all of whom stated that the book either didn't work or couldn't be marketed or both. The well-known editor Betty Prashker kept the typescript at her bedside for weeks and finally said she couldn't take it on. It looked as if it would be my first book not to find a publisher when Donald I. Fine, the famously irascible independent, took it on, to his ultimate high profit, with an advance of five thousand dollars, the smallest I had received.

I was in very good hands; Sarah Gallick, the editor, was one of the best I had ever had, and I followed her suggestions for cuts without a murmur. Beautifully produced, expertly promoted, the book put me back on top with an appearance on *Good Morning America* and I was even sent to London for the British publication and interviewed by the BBC's Sheridan Morley and many others. Reviews were favorable in both countries; the book sold well. It was time to fulfill my contract with Putnam for a second work, and this time it had to be bedrock commercial.

Louis B. Mayer as a name spelled prestige, importance, even greatness; the next name I came up with spelled scandal, squalor, and foulness.

Howard Hughes had been on my mind for years, but I had shied from writing about him because I found so many aspects of his character repulsive. When I mentioned him to my editor George Coleman, a desirable, handsome gay and gifted young man, at dinner at the Edwardian Room of the Plaza Hotel in New York, he instantly became excited. Had Hughes been the lover of Cary Grant, he asked. I wasn't rude enough to remind him of my Grant biography.

I embarked on a dark journey, which was rather like exploring the Mato Grosso of the Amazon basin in 1895, with headhunters and dangerous animals, reptiles, and poisonous insects at every turn. As always, fact after fact contradicted everything that had been written before; I realized, not with a sense of one-upmanship but sadly, that many writers simply copied each others' books.

As with Merle Oberon and many others, the subject's birthplace was completely wrong. The account of Hughes's father, a wildcatter who shot men's hats off if they stood in the way of an oil claim, had been grossly misreported. Nobody had obtained his mother's letters to him or records of his schooling; I did, and there was an enormous amount to fill in.

There was the marvelous story, not told properly before, of his flight around the world in 1938 when Katharine Hepburn packed the sandwiches and he put Ping-Pong balls in the fuselage as flotation devices should the plane crash into the stormy Bering Straits.

Disliking flying, I did so much research with veteran pilots, mechanics, and the staff of museums of aeronautics that I could almost have flown a 1930s biplane myself. It became clear that Hughes had no idea he was controlled, like other humans, by the force of gravity; time and time again, he made the mistake of overloading his craft, with the result that he had a series of horrific crashes, most notably in Beverly Hills in 1946. I talked to the actress Rosemary DeCamp, who had been in her bedroom when she heard a roar, looked up, and found herself looking into the sky. Hughes had ripped off her roof.

If there was any persistent myth, it was that Hughes became mentally incompetent in later life; ill he was, incompetent never. His masses of memoranda, never previously obtained, showed a an antic dedication to wheeling and dealing until the day of his death, his notes to his aides written in a perfect, round, schoolroom script.

The unexplained reason for his terror of germs had to be understood, and research in Houston, Texas, where he was raised, provided the answer. As a child he had lived in the yellow fever zone; the word QUARANTINE was almost certainly the first word he saw. Hence his mother's overprotectiveness and his own lifelong panic at the possibility of contagion.

My good luck returned. It was essential I unravel Hughes's mysterious and unexplained connections in Nicaragua that led to his financing of a Nicaraguan force at the Bay of Pigs and earned him the concessions of Nicaraguan railroad and roadway ownerships. But what could have become of the late Nicaraguan president Somoza's men with whom he dealt in the capital city of Managua?

Astonishingly, François du Sardou, a Puerto Rican friend who was expert in Latin American affairs, revealed that every surviving member of

Somoza's cabinet, and his girlfriend, lived together in a mansion in the Rossmore district of Los Angeles, a stone's throw from the home of Mae West, Patricia Barham, and Hughes himself at one time.

This was as incredible a find as *It's All True,* Dr. Erben, or Merle Oberon's birthplace, and I was able to conduct interviews with everyone in that house, filling in a chapter of Hughes's life that had remained unknown. Even more extraordinary, my researcher had as first cousin no less than Bernard Barker, the chief burglar of Watergate, who granted me many hours on tape, the first he had given anyone.

I hadn't associated Hughes with Watergate, placing all the blame, as the world did, on Richard Nixon. But Barker, and later Professor Stephen Ambrose and William Colby, former head of the CIA, confirmed that indeed Hughes not Nixon was the real figure behind the burglary. Even Woodward and Bernstein had been silent on the matter, and when, later, I met Carl Bernstein on a talk show, he was notably cold and dismissive: another Dwight Macdonald in my life.

There was no doubt in my mind, after weeks of delving into the facts, that Hughes had financed the famous caper, that his purpose was to remove from Democratic files the evidence of his illegal wheelings and dealings, and that the mission failed. I found that the meeting of the conspirators in New York was bugged by a British agent hired by the Democrats, and the agent confirmed that.

The Democrats knew the burglars were coming and arranged a plant among the raiders to make sure that Band-Aids were placed on the doors horizontally, as indicators.

Meanwhile, all the significant documents had been removed to the Democratic headquarters in Miami. Nixon of course took the heat afterward for a rogue operation he hadn't authorized; Hughes did not. But when Nixon was asked by Charles Colson (the evidence is on tape) to sum up Watergate in two words the answer was HOWARD HUGHES.

Yet another sensational incident had gone unreported. In June 1974 Hughes organized a fake burglary of his Hollywood offices, so that hundreds of pages of incriminating documents could be brought to him in the Bahamas. Although staff members of the time remained anonymous, the evidence was complete. Another matter was Hughes's immunity from various prosecutions that year and after. It emerged from Colby and others that he had supplied the government with spy satellites, UFO-like camera-equipped craft that surveyed Soviet installations, free of charge. In return, Hughes was excused from paying income tax, the official reason being that he ran the tax-free Hughes Medical Institute, which in fact was nonexistent, occupying a hut on the University of Miami campus.

Although Hughes's involvement in Watergate achieved mysteriously little press attention, the emphasis being on his affairs with the male and female stars, one matter I uncovered did achieve international notice. This was the matter of *The Conqueror.*

This very bad film about the life of Genghis Khan, bizarrely starring John Wayne in the title role, was shot, despite warnings to Hughes, in a nuclear test fall-out area; the director Dick Powell had even made a previous film, *Split Second,* about a group of people in a similar location threatened with nuclear poisoning and death. Hughes had failed to inform Powell or his stars that the danger existed, so bent was he on using that particular location, and he even imported nuclear-affected sand to the studio to continue with the shots.

As a result, he can be named as a mass murderer, since John Wayne, Susan Hayward, Pedro Armendariz, Agnes Moorehead, and Dick Powell all died of cancer, along with most of the crew. His self-centeredness had never been more cruelly displayed, and writing this part of the book was very painful indeed.

A best seller, *Howard Hughes: A Secret Life* was very well reviewed and was optioned very quickly by John Malkovich as a vehicle for himself.

That seemed to me good casting; Malkovich had the correct gauntness, a tortured, haunted element in performance that would work well in the portrayal. The problem was that he would not have been convincing as the dashing young airman who made the 1938 world flight and bedded so many men and women, his physical attraction overwhelming to all who met him. And I felt that to portray only the older, bizarre Hughes would not be successful commercially; the picture would undoubtedly cost in the hundreds of millions.

I had several pleasant lunches, spreading over most of a year, with Malkovich's partner Russ Smith, always at the Polo Lounge of the Beverly Hills Hotel. Charming and well informed, Russ made an ideal companion; my chief disappointment was that I never met Malkovich. Soured by American politics, he was among those expatriate Americans who railed against his native country and lived in Provence, scene of my honeymoon, of Dirk Bogarde's house, and of Peter Mayle's famous escapist books later on.

The question of a screenwriter came up; I almost suggested myself, but then I remembered that contracts for Hollywood writers called for eight drafts and that everything was rewritten, often on a day-to-day basis on the set, and tailored to the demands of producers, stars, and directors. I had seen all my books appear virtually as I had written them, with the exception of valid editorial changes in *Kate* and acceptable cuts on *Merchant of Dreams*; otherwise, for better or worse, my published work was my own. Now if I were taken on as adapter, I would be subject to the demands of my colleagues; and such an idea was (and is) unacceptable. As I had no track record on screen or stage, it was unlikely I would be taken on anyway.

Malkovich and Smith settled on the British playwright Terry Johnson. Much as I liked Johnson when I met him for lunch at the Bel Air Hotel, I thought this was a very serious mistake. An English intellectual, whose plays were highly wrought exercises in style, he was the last person to write a mainstream commercial script, and far too young to have any grasp of the life of Hughes's times. With no background in Hollywood, Texas, or New York, he would, for all his imaginative skills, be unable, I was certain, to carry off this most difficult of assignments, even working in tandem with Malkovich.

It turned out I was right, and at a stormy meeting at the Hassler Hotel in Rome, Johnson broke with his colleagues. The project finally lapsed, only to be taken up after a few weeks when Michael Mann and his Forward Pass Productions optioned the property. But more of this later.

With *Howard Hughes* still doing well, I suggested to Dan Strone and Tom Miller that I write a biography of Rose Kennedy, the matriarch, whose life had been overlooked in favor of her illustrious sons. The idea was accepted at once, without an outline, and I embarked on new research that yet again resulted in surprising major discoveries, all of them ignored up to then and calling for discussion here.

If there were two things for which Joseph Kennedy, Rose's husband, was famous, they were his affair with Gloria Swanson in the late 1920s and his collaborations with Hitler. Although I had been deceived in previous books into writing on the basis of insufficiently explored matters, I found both beliefs to be untrue, and was able to correct them; just as my revisionist histories that showed heroes like Errol Flynn to be villains provoked annoyance worldwide, so did my cleaning up of the record of an antihero, Joseph P. Kennedy, upset many historians.

I was fortunate in finding, at the University of Texas in Austin, where the Howard Hughes files had proved indispensable, a great cache of Kennedyana, including letters to and from Kennedy and Gloria Swanson that showed their relationship to be strictly business; they showed not a single indication of desire, much less its consummation. Swanson perpetrated the myth in her memoirs: she had Kennedy staying with her at the Poinciana Hotel in Palm Beach when he made love to her; he wasn't at that hotel at the time, but in New York.

She claimed that he left Rose's stateroom on the ship *Ile de France* and commuted to her cabin night after night on a transatlantic crossing, and Rose was too dumb to notice. But they were not (the passenger lists confirmed) on the same ship at the same time. Swanson was deeply in love with her husband, the Marquis de la Falaise, who exchanged passionate love letters with her at the time; Falaise was a close friend of Rose and Joe and surely would have, as a cuckolded French nobleman, acted very differently.

Certain that the story was a fabrication, I wondered why Swanson had invented it or, rather, confirmed the oft-told account of it in book after book. I contacted her two daughters, both of whom said that she had been forced by her publishers to include the fake story, because without it she would not receive a million-dollar advance, which she needed to prop up her husband's failing health food business. One daughter said that her mother sobbed to her, admitting everything and expressing sorrow and guilt that she would hurt Rose, Eunice, and other family members, none of whom as it turned out condemned the fictitious memoir when it appeared. Subsequent lives of Jack Kennedy have failed to take note of the evidence, including a skillful biography written by a good friend of mine, the excellent Robert Dallek.

I determined that Kennedy, so far from being anti-Semitic, had embarked, at the onset of World War II, on a mass immigration plan for Jewish children to America, which President Roosevelt implacably prevented. I found records, not previously accessed, showing that on November 15, 1938, Kennedy had a meeting with British prime minister Neville Chamberlain at 10 Downing Street to arrange for the migration.

Kennedy had 600 children housed in Scotland, 2,000 in Africa, 800 in France, 200 in Liberia, and more in England itself, under the shelter of

Boy Scout camps. He also arranged for the Teamsters in New York to place Jewish children with families in New York City. Roosevelt blocked the deal.

Still described then (and now) as a Nazi sympathizer, Kennedy gave a press conference on December 17, 1938, in Washington denouncing Hitler and later made a coast-to-coast broadcast on the Jewish William Paley's CBS network still further providing bitter criticism of the Nazi regime. Cole Porter even provided a musical, *Leave It to Me,* in which Kennedy (disguised as a Mr. Godhaus of Kansas) was shown kicking a German in the stomach and proving supportive of the Jews. But the bitter liberal assaults went on and on.

Rose's intense Catholicism, so often the butt of liberal jokes, led her to a close relationship with Pope Pius XII, who on August 24, 1939, made an anti-Nazi speech on the radio, of which she approved, and on August 31 summoned a meeting in Rome of foreign ambassadors calling for an end to German conquest of Europe and a permanent peace. Later she was very much with her husband when he broke the anti-Semitic laws against club memberships, stating he would resign from several as member and sponsor unless they admitted Jews.

The most important question was Rose's attitude toward John F. Kennedy's assassination. From interviews and letters, it became clear to me that Rose and her family, led by Bobby as attorney general, were certain that Oswald acted alone.

Otherwise, why would she agree to stay with Joe at Hyannisport after Thanksgiving with no bodyguard, only an old night watchman, and why did Bobby have the *New York Times* announce on its front page that he would vacation with his wife and children in North Florida, and give the exact location? Surely conspirators would seek to eliminate him, since he would know too much; the attorney general would unravel the secrets of such a conspiracy, if he didn't know them already. Yet there are many to this day who still believe Castro, or the Soviet Union, or both, or perhaps the Mafia, were bent on killing Kennedy.

My most fascinating interview was with William Colby, former CIA chief, at his home in Georgetown, Washington, D.C. He said unequivocally that John Kennedy was a victim of Adlai Stevenson; that Stevenson had urged him to have President Diem of South Vietnam ambushed and murdered, a foolish act since Diem, though corrupt, was a bulwark against

Communism; that Stevenson had also told Kennedy to remove the air cover at the Bay of Pigs, as otherwise, Stevenson as ambassador couldn't face the United Nations Council. By now, it was clear that the book was no longer a biography of Rose alone, but of her whole family, and of an era. It would become a major hit in France.

20

A decision to take leave from writing books was precipitated by a personal crisis. Richard, who all his life had enjoyed seemingly excellent health, working long hours at double shifts in hospitals, including his own Kaiser Permanente, because he had no interest in sharing my active social life or sitting alone at home at night waiting for me to return, had gradually, and with the characteristic self-neglect of people in the medical profession, unwittingly become ill. He was diagnosed with diabetes and now, untreated for years, was faced with end-stage kidney failure.

He had to retire and spend days in the gray limbo of a dialysis room, a tiny television set suspended from the corner of the ceiling, surrounded by unhappy patients, his blood slowly and uncomfortably exchanged. It was painful to visit him there, to take him there each day and pick him up, to anticipate waiting years for a kidney transplant. One night I returned from the San Fernando Valley to find him lying on his bedroom floor, his face the color of wax, his breath almost imperceptible. It was clear that he was dying.

I called the local fire station to send the paramedics. They should have taken only five minutes to arrive; they took twenty. By a shocking coincidence, another man had collapsed similarly, just down the street, and with fire victims in our tinderbox city, only one ambulance was available.

It would be melodramatic to say those were the longest twenty minutes of my life. It would also be accurate. By the time the paramedics walked into Richard's room, he was in what doctors call Code Blue. He was, in a technical sense, dead. His heart had stopped beating; he wasn't breathing.

By thumping his chest and applying a resuscitator, the team brought him back to life; I was too grateful even to speak.

They took him to Kaiser, where he had a slow but sure recovery, marooned in an emergency room where I found him surrounded by bleeding accident victims, men and women in bandages after household abuse, and a black actor with a gunshot wound. The noise all night was almost unendurable; then at last Richard was able to come home.

I asked him if he remembered anything from Code Blue. He replied that he had felt himself leaving his body and standing near it, where a tall man in a black suit was waiting for him. Behind the man there was a large door; it was partly ajar and through it streamed a brilliant light. The man told him it wasn't his time yet and pushed him back into his body.

Years before, in the pragmatic pages of *New York* magazine, I had read a similar story, of a youth in New York, seemingly killed by a motorcycle gang, whose brother had also been knifed to death; in Code Blue, the younger brother saw his sibling floating above his head telling him to return to the world of the living; rough, strong hands pushed him back into his body.

I remembered, too, how an actress friend of mine had fallen on Ventura Boulevard in the San Fernando Valley, her glasses driven into her head as her face hit the sidewalk; she had been rushed to Tarzana Hospital, where an operation saved her; she had experienced Code Blue in the private ward. And in that state, she had felt herself rise floor after floor through ceilings to the roof, where she saw pigeons and scraps of what seemed to be iron; she descended to a room next to the operating theater, where she saw a mess of dirty paper plates and Styrofoam cups strewn about after a party. When she described all this to her doctors afterward, they told her it was a fantasy, but she could see from the way they looked at each other that she had described everything she couldn't possibly have seen with mortal eyes.

I had heard of dialysis at sea, a treatment that was available on certain cruise ships. Voyages in the Caribbean were Richard's greatest pleasure, especially because of his shopping sprees in Charlotte Amalie, St. Thomas. I took him aboard the *Veendam,* of the Holland American Line, sailing from Fort Lauderdale, and at first he seemed to be doing well.

But the dialysis room was cramped and uncomfortable and the treatment suddenly stopped being effective; he collapsed late one night after a cabaret show, and began sweating and shivering. He told me in answer to my question that he was certain he was very ill. I got hold of a wheelchair and pushed him the full length of the ship to the ship's hospital. They said he was beyond their help so I wheeled him back to the stateroom; the phone rang and the captain was on the line. He said that Richard and I were to be evacuated at once; he wouldn't be responsible for a death at sea.

I exclaimed that we were in the middle of the ocean; where could we possibly go? He told me we were about twenty nautical miles off San Juan, Puerto Rico, and would be sent there. It was wet and windy outside; a terrible night. A stewardess arrived to help me pack.

Richard was placed on a gurney. We went up to the boat deck by elevator, late-night passengers parting to admit us, staring at us with a very human mixture of sympathy and brutal curiosity. A lifeboat had been lowered from its davits, and with some difficulty Richard was winched into it, still on his gurney and mercifully asleep under heavy sedation. I wished I had been, as we were lowered twelve decks into the choppy, rain-swept sea; the ship was lighted from stem to stern, every porthole blazing as the entire vessel turned out to see us go.

I sat in the prow with a junior officer, staring out into the storm. When first we arrived at the port of Old San Juan, customs, military, and immigration officials were there to greet us. An argument broke out when, partly in Spanish and partly in English, the local authorities said we would not be admitted, as Richard might have a communicable disease. Luckily, the *Veendam* assistant cruise director talked them into letting us stay on land, explaining that Richard had kidney failure, not any threatening illness.

The ambulance bumped alarmingly over the ill-laid cobbles and asphalt of Old San Juan until we reached an emergency facility at 2 a.m. At this late hour, the squalid hospital was crowded with screaming children, sobbing parents, and rows of gray-faced, helpless citizens; there was a flu epidemic and the emergency hospital staff was stretched to the limit. But the *Veendam* men were superb: they made sure Richard went to the front of the line and was wheeled into the only large, clean room.

A doctor emerged and told me in broken English with moments of Spanish that Richard would not last the night and I might as well leave. When I refused he had me taken out by armed orderlies as the *Veendam* officers left with my warmest thanks. I found a motel nearby. I walked into the depressing room to find all the lights on; when I tried to turn them off, the switches didn't work, nor did the central switch at the door. Wrapping my hand in a towel, I managed to unscrew all except one and fell on the bed fully clothed, unable to sleep, feel, or even think.

In the early morning I called the hospital medical facility to find that Richard had been transferred to another in New San Juan. When I arrived there, climbing up steps coated in decades of bird dung, I found that he had had a very narrow escape: a pacemaker he had been given for temporary use the previous night later malfunctioned on another patient, and the man died.

I moved to another hotel to be close to him; when I arrived there I ran into a nightmare scene. I was greeted by an enormous pack of Doberman pinschers, snarling and prowling on insecure long leashes; they were, the clerk at the reception desk told me, there because they were drug sniffers and there was a congress going on of the Drug Enforcement Administration. All my life I have had an unreasoning fear of that breed of large dog, perhaps triggered by some forgotten childhood incident, while loving most pooches and wishing often that I owned one. The sight of these slavering monsters prowling about was bad enough, but one slipped its leash and came charging at me; its controller barely stopped it in its tracks. The reason for its aggression I couldn't determine; certainly, I didn't use or carry or smell of drugs.

I went to the hospital twice that day, the cab driver fighting through a violent mob that was demonstrating for Puerto Rican independence; by nightfall, there was a minor riot, but nothing, not even gunshots around the taxi, could hold me back. In between these trips to see Richard tortured in his bed, and trying to persuade nurses and doctors to take better care of him, I wandered the tropical grounds of the hotel, seeing the green and creamy waves beating on the wind-riddled rocks, hearing the mournful cries of seabirds.

At last Richard turned a corner and should theoretically have been brought on orders from Los Angeles Kaiser Permanente Hospital, which he had served so faithfully for forty years, to its central facility in Atlanta by private plane, a mandatory requirement in cases of life or death. But Kaiser refused to fulfill that arrangement and I had no alternative but to return to Los Angeles and insist that they proceed. They didn't, and Richard arrived home in terrible shape. But eventually, after a five-year wait, he had a transplant, from a young male skier who had died in an accident at Aspen, Colorado, and it worked.

There followed weeks of a daily ordeal; I had to rise at 4 a.m. each morning to drive him through darkened, empty streets in rainy winter weather to UCLA for essential blood monitoring. Our first trip almost malfunctioned.

We arrived in good time for a dawn registration with the specialist kidney team; if we were late, we would not be able to have another appointment for a week, and that might be too late. When we reached UCLA, the map I had been sent proved useless; it was between Christmas and New Year, when Los Angeles effectively closes down, and there wasn't even a security guard to guide us. I drove past empty booth after booth; not a soul to be seen.

Then out of nowhere an African American appeared, with an angelic smile, and without being asked, told us exactly where to go. I thanked him and drove off; when I looked back, there was nobody to be seen. Had he perhaps visited the facility and guessed what we were looking for? Or was it a visitation, sent to assist us? I'd like to think that.

It was clear that even with Richard in his recovered condition, I still couldn't risk taking trips away from home, to New York, Paris, and London, or even to the Los Angeles outer areas, when he might have a relapse and reject his new kidney. Therefore, I decided, after the long interval when I had taken care of him and had written nothing, that I must suspend, at least for the time being, my life as an investigative biographer.

Instead, I would have to find a new form of work that would keep me at home. I thought of fiction, but it was very hard to place. Then I thought of playwriting; it never occurred to me that I mightn't have a talent for it. I was quite certain I could write anything, in any medium, if I chose, and I was still a published poet, and could go on writing poetry.

If you're going into the theater world, there is nothing I can do for you. I took you on because you are a big, best-selling author. Not a Clancy or a Grisham, of course, but big enough. There's no money in theater and I'm not even in touch with our theater people at William Morris. It's a closed shop; if you're not part of a charmed circle in New York there's no hope for you. Sorry."

These words of my agent Dan Strone, with no words of sympathy for Richard, concluded our professional relationship; although, as I shall relate, he did try to restore it years later. His discouragement when I announced my intention of entering an entirely new field, of which I had no knowledge, by embarking on playwriting, which I had never even considered (apart from the play at St. Peter's about a spy in an RAF camp), spurred me on. And now quite suddenly, at sixty-five, I discovered an entirely new talent I had no idea I had.

I knew I could write plays and see them produced, and one night the entire plot of a comedy came to me. *Murder by Moonlight,* originally called *Murder at the Double,* was a satire of the Agatha Christie mysteries of the 1930s, set in an English country home where a young man, bent upon seducing the mistress of a rich household, disguises himself as her Australian cousin, sweeping her off her feet right under her husband's nose. Murder in the potting shed and games of false identity followed, there was an obligatory séance scene, and the comic detective provided, at great speed, a mad solution involving twins.

Without seeking a production, I followed the play, which wrote itself in two weeks, by writing another: *His Majesty Mr. Kean.* I took the basic structure of a work by Alexandre Dumas, about the early-nineteenth-century actor Edmund Kean and his romantic conquest by a young woman he had sponsored; I replaced the antiquated dialogue and approach with another, more geared to contemporary audiences in its cynicism, irony, and amorality.

Murder by Moonlight was first tried out at First Stage, an excellent small Hollywood theater company devoted to workshopping. Plays were shown with the actors reading from texts, not a process I liked, but I wanted to hear the words spoken. I also disliked the idea of audience comments afterward, knowing that I wouldn't alter a word. Indeed, Edward Albee, whom I met often at the bookstore of a mutual friend in Los Angeles, told me he never would approve any workshop, or interference with his writing, and advised me to follow his example. I have.

Moonlight was beautifully acted by the First Stagers under the benign guidance of the group's creator, Dennis Safren. The cast's British accents and stylized playing were perfect, led by the wonderful Susan Ziegler. By chance a local promoter, Ed Gaines, was present; he had called my phone number by mistake, and when I heard his name I asked him and his wife to attend. They did, and he signed me to a contract on the back of the program.

With its plethora of speaking parts, *His Majesty Mr. Kean* was beyond the resources of First Stage, so I researched California theaters to see where best to send it. The Music Center's Ahmanson Theater and Mark Taper Forum were the ultimate; but Gordon Davidson, the amiable man in charge, would take on only surefire successes from New York, and rightly so; it would be hard to fill his theaters with the work of a first-time playwright, notwithstanding my track record in publishing.

Instead, I found that California State University at Long Beach had, astonishingly, the best-endowed theater in the state. The energetic board had managed to talk the Sacramento authorities into providing a million dollars to support the most handsome of venues, and a trip there to see a performance convinced me that the producers could put on a show as lavish as any to be found on Broadway.

I telephoned Ron Lindblom, the brilliant young director whose productions had earned rapturous reviews from local critics, and was delighted he had heard of me. "What've you got?" he asked me, and when I mentioned *Kean* he told me to send it to him at once.

I forwarded it by Federal Express, firmly expecting to wait for months or even years, for a reply. I had been warned by writers I knew that even when a play was requested it could lay gathering dust on a shelf until the writer was plunged in despair, and finally not used at all. Not so in this case. Within twenty-four hours, Lindblom called and said that *Kean* would be put on at his next season, as the fourth and final work, always a great honor. I drove to Long Beach to see him.

Bearded and benign, flashing electric energy and enthusiasm, Ron became an instant friend and supporter. Within a few days, he had made plans for an elaborate production with no expense spared, in the smaller of the theaters he helped to run: he would, through the inspired use of platforms and mirrors, achieve a multipurpose stage that could evoke nineteenth-century London. Later, when he showed me the costume books, obtained with great difficulty from libraries all over the world, he explained how the pastel colors and silks of the Regency would be reproduced on the stage.

There was a minor stumble. Ron had recommended as *Kean*'s director Charles Marowitz, whose major reputation in England as a pioneer of avant-garde theater at the Open Space in the 1960s had preceded him when he removed to Malibu a decade or so later; he was now attached to the Cal State–Long Beach team. I was excited by the idea of having a British legend as mentor and executant, but disillusionment soon set in.

I met with Marowitz, Ron, and various colleagues in a boardroom at the school; Marowitz seemed interested but oddly unenthused and I began to feel uneasy. Then he made a Dwight Macdonald-ish mistake that put me off him completely, making me feel he was not by any means the theater authority he seemed to be.

One of the most famous phrases applied to Edmund Kean was the poet Samuel Taylor Coleridge's "To see him act is like reading Shakespeare by flashes of lightning." When Marowitz attributed the quotation to his idol William Hazlitt, I hadn't the nerve to correct him but made a mental note to be careful of him in the future.

I was wise because soon afterward I received from him a copy of my play covered in notes on both text and margins that proved to be totally useless. He even had had the nerve to cross out my best scene, borrowed from *Jane Eyre,* in which Kean, disguised as a gypsy, tells the actress who wants to know her fortune that she will soon succumb to the embraces of a powerful and handsome young actor: himself, of course. When the restored scene was played before an audience, it invariably brought the house down and it remains the best I have ever written.

I told Ron Lindblom I rejected Marowitz out of hand and he kindly agreed to take over as director. I could have asked for no better choice.

Ron made no changes and asked for only minor cuts in the text, respected my approach and language, and cast the play brilliantly with a mixed student, professional Equity, and non-Equity cast, which mastered swordplay, knockabout comedy, orgiastic scenes, passionate trysts at night, and above all the accents, from Cockney to upper class, that are often so difficult for Americans. A dazzling Kean and a no less dazzling Prince Regent, the future George IV, electrified me; I could scarcely have asked for more from the National Theater of Great Britain, and in Ron Lindblom I had found an undoubted genius.

The opening night was unforgettable, the highlight of my life to date. In his wilderness of mirrors and ramps, Ron created a London world I would have thought impossible to capture without a million-dollar production. The audience of students and faculty laughed continuously for over two hours. Even the youngest, to whom the Regency must have seemed utterly distant and foreign, responded to the bawdy, uncompromised sexuality, the romping humor, and the violent scenes of action. Matt Southwell as *Kean* was given a deserved standing ovation.

The play's success was repeated in a brilliant performance with scripts at the Williamstown Theater Festival in New York. There, the director Maria Mileaf elicited fine acting from a cast led by the admirable Robert Joy, of *Atlantic City* and *Ragtime,* today a leading figure of *CSI New York,* and one of my closest friends.

With both Broadway and the Los Angeles Music Center out of bounds for so elaborate a work, I could have asked for no more. Then *Murder by Moonlight* found an equally excellent home.

When Edmund Gaines dropped the option, I sent the play to Jeremiah Morris. This immensely talented director, with long theater experience in New York and Los Angeles, had, with his business partner Robert Kane, fought for ten years against very heavy odds to create El Portal, the most beautiful and opulent theater built since the Music Center. Building ordinances, stubborn Sacramento officials, and North Hollywood obstructionists had all stood in their way but at last they succeeded in battering everyone in their path and were ready to announce a first season.

I sent *Murder by Moonlight* to Morris with a statement that I had to have a commitment to the opening season by Saturday at 2 p.m. or I would have to give it to another producer. He responded at five minutes to the hour to say he had great fun reading it and would have even more fun in putting it on. He scheduled it at once as the second play in the season; hired Peggy Shannon, head of the popular Sacramento Theater Company, to direct; whipped up an excellent cast; and didn't change a word: A playwright's dream.

Once again, the British atmosphere was caught with loving care. The sets, of a London flat and a country home, the one converted into the other by the use of moving walls, were so accurate I could find no fault in them; I felt I was back in Dolphin Square and our country home the Mount. A voice coach worked with me and with the cast to ensure a range of accents from broad fake Australian to Mayfair. The play ran to packed houses and earned very good money for me and for the theater, and I was spurred on to write other plays.

My *Fighting the Gorilla* was a contrast: a deliberately vulgar satire of Hollywood in its story of the rise from an ad agency mailroom to running a studio by two attractive young men, the origins carefully hidden for legal reasons.

I sent the play to the African American Riant Theater in Tribeca, New York, and they accepted it at once; they made a significant and brilliant casting decision. In the story, a studio chief dies at the end of the first act from an overdose of drugs; in the second, he's replaced by a twin and nobody knows the difference, an echo of l'affaire Corinne Griffith.

Cyndy Marion, the inspired young director at the Riant, chose a superb black actor to play both parts, a savage comment on the fact that no African American, despite the industry's lip service, had ever run a Hollywood studio. This proved a triumphant decision and the play was a hit. Not a word was changed.

The *Village Voice* insisted on calling the play *Fucking the Gorilla,* which amused me a great deal; the prissy *New York Times* would use only the original title. The show opened with the star as a mailroom boy walking front stage and telling the audience that it was a gorilla; that if a movie flops, the gorilla sucks; if it is a hit, the studio fucked the gorilla. The New York audience broke up at the line every time (it got no laugh in Los Angeles).

Richard Johnson, of the all important Page Six of the *New York Post,* and the boxer Evander Holyfield, guest columnist that week for the *New York Daily News,* mentioned the play's production, and Holyfield stated that if his fans and readers wanted one kind of gorilla they should go to the new Gorilla Park at the Bronx Zoo; another kind was to be found at the Riant Theater in Tribeca, in a play by Charles Higham. Both columnists added that my *Howard Hughes* would soon be a major motion picture.

I was reading these indispensable columns when the telephone rang; Michael Mann's assistant was on the line. How dared I, she said, mention that the film of Howard Hughes was to be made; Mr. Mann detested advance publicity. I said that he must be the only human being in Hollywood who took that point of view and that nothing in my contract forbade me to talk about it to the press. When someone else on his staff called me to say that I would never work in Hollywood again, the ultimate cliché, I said that I had never worked in it in a professional sense, only written books and articles about it, and that I never would work *for* it. I heard that Mann became hysterical at my response; I trust he didn't break his head against a wall.

My next theater experience was less colorful, but unsettling. The multimillionairess Justine Compton, a remarkable patroness of the arts, was an old friend; in view of her small stature and unqualified chutzpah, I dubbed her Mighty Mouse.

She was a fascinating, mysterious figure behind the scenes of show business. She was said to have been the sponsor of some of the new figures of the British and French movie *New Wave* who emerged in the 1960s; certainly she was a woman of great cultivation. I had attended many of her Los Angeles parties in the 1980s, cantinas on Sunday afternoons where one would meet Kirk Douglas, Burt Lancaster, François Truffaut, and French stage stars like Jean-Louis Barrault and Madeleine Renaud, and the great cinematographer Nestor Almendros, whom I counted as a friend.

Despite an outward appearance of good cheer, Justine was restless and dissatisfied, longing to be a success as a writer; but her ambition went unfulfilled. She had married and split from the brilliant theatrical director Harold Clurman and then from a notable Beverly Hills tennis pro. For no discernible reason, after decorating her grand Mario Lanza Bel Air mansion with taste and skill, she moved next door, where she created another brilliant environment and then quite suddenly left for New York and a perfectly ordinary if expensive apartment.

Then she at last achieved the success she longed for; she bought the old Century Club, which dated back to the Civil War, and converted it into the Century Theater. She fought the New York civic authorities to a standstill and managed to overcome the threat of a handicap elevator that could have ruined the structure, declaring it a historical building and supplying instead an ingeniously constructed wheelchair ramp.

I sent her a play about Edith Wharton and at first she seemed excited and at various parties told her friends we would be working together, an exciting prospect indeed. She tried to lure the legendary Tammy Grimes out of early retirement to play the Wharton part and arranged a luncheon for us to meet at the Players Club in Gramercy Park, with its morbidly reconstructed death chamber of Edwin Booth.

Tammy and I hit it off at once, but I soon realized that she wasn't going to return to the stage; she was too happily settled in the country with a very attractive man. Then Justine summoned me to a meeting, announced she was dyslexic and couldn't read my play, but had had it read to her and that it needed work; she wanted a new opening scene in which Wharton, at her house near Paris, took her own books down from shelves and began reminiscing about the ill-fated love affairs that formed the basis of my plot.

I disliked the approach and when I tried to manage it, which I shouldn't have, Justine withdrew and instead embarked on a season of Ibsen, which she directed very capably herself. We parted company for good.

Then came an equally unsettling experience with the veteran Broadway producer Arthur Cantor. He fell in love with my version of Booth Tarkington's novel *Alice Adams,* filmed once with Katharine Hepburn, and called it lovely; but it soon emerged that he had no money to produce it. When he opened a play out of town by a South African writer about a mysterious portrait with Julie Harris, he failed to post bonds for the cast, had no cash to supply, and his career was over. Equity was furious with him and he died not long after.

I don't regret one hour of my seven years in the American theater. The fact that I didn't have to rewrite a line was amazing and gratifying. There can be no thrill equal to sitting in a darkened auditorium seeing and hearing actors bring to life characters that didn't exist until I created them. But there was no money to speak of in the medium. I was forced to return to the world of profit-making books.

I tasted sour apples in dealing with Michael Mann on *The Aviator,* the film version of *Howard Hughes*; my agent Dorris Halsey had to fight hard and bitterly to get me the option renewals called for by the contract, and matters didn't improve when Martin Scorsese took over as director. Finally, it came to the point that the picture would be made, and a deal was concluded. Which, alas, though financially rewarding, denied me screen credit.

The deal had, if truth be told, been threatened from the beginning. The reason lay in the original negotiations. Fired years before because of personal differences, Dan Strone had wanted, he told me by telephone from New York, to come back on board for the one deal because Creative Artists Agency, representing the principals on the Hughes project, had approached him by mistake, thinking he still represented me. I had no agent at the time.

I agreed that in view of the situation I would concede on this specific basis but warned him that I wanted this one to be wrapped up at once, with no nonsense at all.

A week went by with no word from him. I had become restive when an old acquaintance from my *New York Times* days, Bob Bookman, the veteran, highly skilled CAA agent, who now lived in Hughes's Hollywood house, called me to say that the deal was in imminent danger of collapse.

He said that Dan Strone wanted the name of the star CAA wanted to perform as Hughes, and CAA was not prepared to release the name. Strone, he said, would not proceed unless he knew.

I called Strone at William Morris and dismissed him again. Then I called Bookman to say I was prepared to sign the option agreement. It arrived within three hours, brought by motorcycle from Beverly Hills by an antic, humorous Cockney. The movie entitled *The Aviator* concentrated on Hughes's positive side: his early heroism, his charm, his relationship with Katharine Hepburn, his mental disturbances that were no fault of his, his defeat of a Senate committee after World War II. Many people called me, saying they thought the film betrayed the book, but I pointed out that to show the real-life monster he was, sitting for hours in hotel rooms naked except for a diaper made of toilet paper, swatting flies and farting, would scarcely make for box office cinema.

I was invited to the preview screening in Hollywood, at the imposing Kodak Theater. It exhibited all the fine craftsmanship of Martin Scorsese, and the period costumes, hair, and sets were as perfect as anyone could wish. Leonardo DiCaprio's performance was remarkable considering his youth, rising to a fine pitch of intensity in his confrontations with the senator, played by Alan Alda in the final scenes. The book went back onto some best-seller lists, and my agent Dorris Halsey's associate, the outgoing and enthusiastic young Whitney Lee, sold it in foreign languages for a treasure. I was on the map again.

$\mathcal{I}$ began work on *Murdering Mr. Lincoln* in 2003. In this new detection, I found that the president was the victim of a conspiracy led by the Kentuckian anarchist George Nicholas Sanders, head of a belligerent group that met in Canada and of which John Wilkes Booth was merely an instrument. Sanders's voluminous papers at the National Archives in Washington, where John Taylor, peerless head of the Modern Military Branch, again proved after many years an invariable help and supporter, proved to be a diamond mine; they had scarcely been examined by historians.

I ploughed through scores of volumes of Civil War reports from the front lines, maintained at the Los Angeles Central Library, a formidable structure with its steep banks of plunging escalators that brought back an earlier fear of heights, descending floor after floor to the History Room at the bottom. In that room, inhabitants of Skid Row had found a home and not only on rainy days; surrounded by snores, gripes, and threatening glances, especially in the washroom, I began examining the library's peerless collection of materials. Microfilm and Xerox machines, long showing signs of wear and tear, were dilapidated and plagued by countless technical problems; with rare exceptions, the staff were notably unhelpful in aiding me, klutz that I am with anything mechanical, to handle the microfilm.

My breakthrough was in establishing the guilt of John Surratt (whose mother, Mary, was hanged), who was acquitted at his trial, a year after the other conspirators. This amazing story had gone untold, and if I am proud of one single thing in my career as a historian it is in solving the mystery of how Surratt got across the Susquehanna River to arrive in Washington, D.C., in time to confer with John Wilkes Booth, when every historian had written that it was impossible.

The book was commissioned by the ill-fated and notorious Judith Regan of ReganBooks. Her editor Cal Morgan, whom I met at the offices in New York, was quiet, subdued, and seemingly enthused at the idea of the book and signed it on a short outline. But then, after it was delivered, there were weeks, then months, of unacceptable silence.

The final payment on a book that had cost me dearly in time, money, and travel was grossly overdue and there was no indication that he or Regan had actually read it; certainly it was among my best and most sparely written works. Finally, Cal Morgan sent me numerous tightly packed, single-spaced pages of comments (presumably backed by Regan's own) that showed a complete lack of understanding of my style, my approach, even my language, and called for a potentially disastrous rewrite.

Typical of Morgan was his complaining that I had used the world "comely" for a man and "stopped" instead of "stayed" at a hotel. I withdrew from my tax shelter IRA the first half of the advance Morgan had paid and returned it to him. My contract stipulated that I had the right to do this if we couldn't agree on final form and content. This left me severely out of pocket.

Dorris Halsey sent the book to Michael Viner, publisher at Millennium and creator of a popular line of cassette books; he was the husband then of one of my favorite actresses, the beautiful Deborah Raffin. He accepted it; it was handsomely published by him; then he went bankrupt.

Viner gave a celebratory party for me, also for Sidney Sheldon's birthday, at his house; the street in Beverly Hills was not numbered and I had to park my car at the top of a hill and walk down, counting the houses until I found the correct one. I heard heavy footsteps behind me and turned around, thinking it might be a mugger. I saw a man as tall as I am and much broader; he looked baffled. "I can't figure this but," he said, "I can't find the place." I suggested with a laugh he follow me up the driveway and added, "You could find the moon, but couldn't find this *house*." The man was Buzz Aldrin.

21

For eighty years, historians and criminologists were puzzled by four great unsolved mysteries: the deaths of the prominent gay Hollywood director William Desmond Taylor in 1922 and of the even more prominent Thomas H. Ince two years later; the Sir Harry Oakes case of 1943; and the Black Dahlia affair. By this time I had, of course, solved the third of these, while doing research for *The Duchess of Windsor*; the Black Dahlia was solved by the murderer's son.

The Ince affair I had not written about, but I researched it in detail in the year 2002 and made notes of records in the county court archives; I wasn't allowed to Xerox them and they have since disappeared.

The circumstances were clear: on the night of November 24, 1924, Ince was aboard William Randolph Hearst's yacht off the California coast when he was found doubled up in agony and taken ashore. In over eighty years of books and articles, no writer had obtained the autopsy report, which disclosed clearly that, far from being shot by an angry Hearst, who mistook him for Charlie Chaplin and, firing through the bulkhead, killed him because he thought Chaplin was making love to Hearst's mistress Marion Davies, Ince died of gastritis, a looped bowel, and peritonitis, and his body was embalmed to prove there was no bullet wound. The probate files, also missing today, showed that his relatives, many of them alive in Thousand Palms, California, had for decades fought over his will, but none in the countless depositions claimed he was a victim of foul play.

As I described earlier, I had taped Mary Miles Minter's account of the killing of William Desmond Taylor and dismissed it, based on the available evidence; her panic in retrieving my cassette interview with her was to me a clear indication of her guilt. Until she died, I couldn't write the truth; project after project intervened, and my book on the case, *Murder in Hollywood,* planned as early as 1971, remained an unfulfilled project.

Then, in 2003, I was cleaning out a closet when I came across a large, blue-bound mass of papers I didn't recall I had. It was the police file on the case, or rather a copy thereof, prepared for my late friend King Vidor, who had planned a book of his own.

I had offered to edit that book, in which King, I thought mistakenly, blamed the killing on Minter's mother, Charlotte Shelby. He had failed to make his case, and when I took the manuscript to Robert Giroux of Farrar, Straus and Giroux, Giroux correctly turned it down on that basis.

Sidney Kirkpatrick wrote a best seller, *A Cast of Killers,* on the murder, also pointing to Charlotte Shelby. It seemed time to write an entirely new account, and I at last managed to unravel the facts. I ran them by Marc Wanamaker, a good friend, archivist, and world authority on Hollywood history, who confirmed my findings.

On a certain night in February 1922, Taylor was found shot dead in his apartment; the autopsy report showed that a bullet had entered his back through the ribs, crossed through his body without puncturing a vital organ, and lodged unexited in the right shoulder. A massive cover-up ensued by Paramount, the studio that had as a major star Mary Miles Minter, and by the corrupt district attorney, Thomas A. Woolwine, who was on Paramount pay. Sums of a million dollars and up were handed out in those days to the DA's office to remove criminal dockets; years later, when Clark Gable ran over a woman and child on Sunset Boulevard, and John Huston did the same, a million dollars changed hands and the manslaughters were hushed up.

The evidence I accumulated against Minter was devastating: strands of her hair were found on the dead Taylor's lapel; she owned a .38 Smith and Wesson revolver whose bullets matched those that killed Taylor; she had the opportunity—a fake alibi failed to explain her absence from her house at the exact time Taylor was killed, a time altered by the DA despite the coroner's report. When a housekeeper threatened to reveal her absence, the woman was declared insane by two doctors engaged by Minter's mother, and she was committed to an institution for the rest of her life.

I established the motive: Minter, in love with Taylor, who had directed her in pictures, was furious with him for not making love to her. At a performance of Verdi's *Othello* in Los Angeles, she saw him accompanied by his lover, the set designer George James Hopkins; she turned to them during the opening scene and shouted, "Now I know what's going on!"

But instead of giving up her efforts to seduce a predominantly gay man, she was determined to convert him and visited him at all hours of the day and night, demanding that he satisfy her in bed. His final refusal undoubtedly triggered the fatal embrace in which the gun went off in her hand; if she didn't deliberately fire it—it may have gone off by mistake— she certainly had murder in her heart.

With the aid of a world authority on Los Angeles, my friend Professor Doyce Nunis, I was able to determine the atmosphere of bought DAs, judges, and police in the 1920s; the wholesale distortion of evidence when the facts were clear if the accused murderer had influence; and the unbridled vice of a city that resembled an unlawful frontier town without a sheriff or marshal. California was indeed the Wild West and, in some respects, remains so.

I had a stroke of luck in finding the memoirs of George James Hopkins, Taylor's lover of many years. I recalled that when I had accompanied King Vidor to an interview with Hopkins in 1971, at a typical Hollywood architectural folly, an apartment building in imitation of a nineteenth-century French château but with Norman flanking towers, Hopkins had mentioned that he was at work on a memoir. I remembered also that he had as a companion a young Japanese man; now that Hopkins was dead I wondered if that friend had kept the manuscript, which could perhaps cast light on the case.

In Los Angeles, people move constantly, seldom staying in a house longer than a few years at best, preferring unsentimentally to sell at a profit rather than settle in a permanent home; apartment dwellers are gypsies, often impossible to trace after time has elapsed.

But fortunately one resident in the building had remained since Hopkins lived there. He gave me the name of a man in Idaho who knew Hopkins's Japanese companion, and before a day had gone by I was on my way to an industrial suburb to meet that devoted partner.

I found him lively and charming; with great generosity he gave me the thick, brown bound manuscript of Hopkins's memoirs, "Caught in the Act," which proved to be entertaining, wonderfully detailed, and unhesitating in naming Minter with copious documentation as the culprit. It supplemented the documents I had found at the county courthouse archives.

Murder in Hollywood was published by the University of Wisconsin Press to excellent reviews on both sides of the Atlantic, and even Bruce Long, the world authority on the case, gave me his approval, with some minor demurs.

*I*n a conversation with Tom Miller, the original editor of the *Duchess of Windsor,* who had started to work for John Wiley and Sons publishers, we decided I should update that book with new material. Once again, good luck made this possible.

Each Saturday for years I had lunch at the Daily Grill restaurant in Studio City; for a brief time, a remainder bookstore appeared on the floor below it, and while browsing through it I found an excellent book, of which I hadn't heard and might never otherwise have seen, *Shadow Lovers,* by Andrea Lynn of the University of Illinois, about H. G. Wells's affair with, among others, the society beauty Constance Coolidge in the 1930s. Lynn referred at one stage to a secret diary Constance had kept, with details of the Duchess of Windsor, her friend in prewar Paris, and I realized I must obtain this priceless diary at once. Lynn was charmingly cooperative and sent me the many pages in Coolidge's crabbed but readable handwriting; they opened a door to a dark room whose existence I would never otherwise have known.

The diary covered a long period of the late 1930s and proved to be as extraordinary as the lost memoirs of William Desmond Taylor. In March 1938 Coolidge, in Paris, was approached by her friend of the Auteuil horse-racing fraternity, the Comte de Cambaçérès, with word that she was to see a woman named Madame Maroni; oddly, the diary makes no mention of Maroni's Christian name. Coolidge, in response to numerous phone calls, finally yielded to the woman's insistent demands to see her, and made her way to a house in the 17th arrondissement just a short walk from Coolidge's own apartment.

The woman said that, representing a duchess who wished to remain anonymous, she had in her possession letters, documents, and photographs that, if made public, would be extremely damaging to the Duke and Duchess of Windsor; if she could see the duke alone, certain arrangements could be made for his benefit.

With blackmail in the air, Constance said she would look into the matter and left. She at once began to talk to influential figures in the worlds of politics and journalism rather than suggest to Wallis and the duke that they might wish to pay off the informant.

The diary grew more fascinating page by page; it was like a 1930s thriller by E. Phillips Oppenheim or Agatha Christie. Coolidge contacted leading figures of the Sûreté and the Deuxième Bureau and they advised her that "Madame Maroni" was in fact the blackmailer herself; no such duchess existed. The woman was a niece of the Fascist architect Gian Carlo Maroni, a friend and supporter of Mussolini.

She had posed as a maid at the home of the duke's cousin, Prince Philipp of Hesse, Hitler's favorite and a frequent emissary to the Italian dictator, in order to steal photographs and documents showing that the duke had a secret and intimate connection with the bisexual Philipp.

Had the evidence emerged it would have exposed to the world the intricate relationships of the royal families of England, Germany, and Italy that would show collusion in the highest places toward an alliance of supposedly oppositional powers and a restoration of the kaiserdom of Germany and of the heirs to King Victor Emmanuel of Italy, still in the service of Hitler.

If it were found that later the duke had written letters and Philipp had responded, supporting the führer and his scorched earth policies, it could have rocked the British monarchy to its foundations; yet another danger was that the Duke of Kent, brother of Windsor and King George VI, was involved in these correspondences.

There was no alternative: Constance had to advise the Windsors to come from the South of France to Paris at once and take care of the matter. Despite a national transport strike, they managed to reach the city on overcrowded roads and summon the Scotland Yard authorities to the Hôtel Crillon. Faced with threats, the so-called Madame Maroni became frightened and disappeared; her documents were seized by the Sûreté and, I later discovered, sent to Moscow; when they were returned to Paris after World War II, they vanished again.

All of this new information cast a light on a much discussed and mysterious incident in August 1945, when the Communist spy Anthony Blunt and Owen Morshead, a resident architect at Windsor Castle, were sent to Friedrichshof in Germany, home of the Hesse family, supposedly to retrieve certain British royal family letters but in my view to find the Philipp of Hesse/Maroni/Windsor evidence. It wasn't there; hence the fact that for years the royal spin-doctors have said that the mission was innocent. At time of writing, the photographs and papers have not been found; it's a safe bet that if they are, they will wind up at Windsor Castle.

A long trip to Paris in the fall of 2004 proved very productive in supporting much of what Coolidge had written in 1938. There was the delight of finding the building, 36 Boulevard Emile Augère, where the blackmail plot took place.

Long before, some fifty years ago, a railway station named La Muette ("the woman who cannot speak") had existed nearby, and now the deep siding through which the steam trains ran, replaced by the ubiquitous Métro, had become a jungle of uncontrolled weeds, enormous red and yellow flowers, some of them twenty feet high, huge bushes displaying black prickles, and flaking lichen-covered trees. When I walked into the building, a lady concierge who was almost too classic—hair in a bun, clothes gypsyish, manner suspicious—asked me my business. Soon afterward, an elderly male resident appeared and questioned me even more closely. I replied accurately—but made no mention of blackmail. As I left, very fast, the sky, already dark, turned a deep, ominous black. No setting for a blackmail plot could have been more perfect.

Inevitably, the passage of time brought deaths, along with the continuing joy of old friends surviving decade after decade, and the remarkable fact that all of my fellow pupils at St. Peter's in World War II were still living.

David Bradley, belligerent director of the Hollywood Hall of Shame's *They Saved Hitler's Brain* and *Twelve to the Moon,* had shattered our friendship by charging me, in front of the usual collection of the famous of yesteryear, of stealing some of his books. I said to general laughter that I had far too many books already and that if I wanted to I could buy any others I wanted, and even his house. Then I sued him for slander; his insurance people paid me five thousand dollars. We never spoke again.

David was once a generous and decent man who had helped me in the early days of my visits to Hollywood by driving me all over town when I couldn't drive, and he had put me up in his guest cottage on the grounds.

As I have mentioned, his parties were dazzling assemblages of the greatest directors of Hollywood's history. I would stand in a group composed of the great director Henry King, King Vidor, Henry Hathaway, Rouben Mamoulian, and Josef von Sternberg, and sit on the floor watching silent films, impeccably preserved, with the stars who had appeared in them. But Bradley had unfortunate habits; he would make us sit through second-rate musicals because his lover Ken Dumayne appeared in one scene as an extra; he would show previous years' New Year's Day party films, pointing to this or that departed figure with a stubby finger placed directly on the screen, shouting, "He's dead, she's dead" while some of the elderly present shuddered, tough old-timers though they were.

One night, Dumayne, drunk, crashed into several drivers and a motorcyclist, injuring them all; David went to each one and paid them off to the tune of some hundred thousand dollars in total, thus releasing Dumayne from the county jail. Soon after, both men died, miserable and isolated after so many refusals of the famous to attend their increasingly shabby events.

David should have left his fabled collection of New Year's Day films and his old movies, over thirty thousand in all, to the Academy of Motion Picture Arts and Sciences, but instead, in a fit of pique, and later annoyed with his alma mater Northwestern University, which wanted them, he left the lot to Indiana University in Bloomington. The reason was that the library there preserved the largest collection of his idol Orson Welles papers in existence. Working on the Welles biography, I had spent weeks there, with a handicapped student, copying hundreds of memoranda and files, in handwriting—a grueling task. Bradley had been called the 16 mm Orson Welles, for his early efforts *Macbeth* and *Julius Caesar,* made on his late banker father's money and given a warm reception by buffs of the rare and the bizarre. Now he would leave his collection to the same institution that housed his idol and superior.

But Indiana had no facilities, the librarian told me, to store this mass of material; its film courses were limited, and the greatest collection in private hands in America was consigned to a warehouse, instead of being the basis for year-round showings at the Academy or the Museum of Modern Art in New York, its most appropriate venues.

The closest friend of my early Hollywood days was the director Curtis Harrington. He had been generous in giving me time from a busy schedule as director to drive me around Los Angeles; when I developed a painful papilloma on my right foot, and could barely walk, he supplied me with a homeopathic remedy that worked. For years, we would meet every Saturday at the health food restaurant the Source Café on Sunset Boulevard, whose sometime owner, the guru of a sect, after announcing he could fly without wings, plunged embarrassingly and fatally from an airplane in front of his flock.

Of the many parties Curtis gave at his art nouveau house in Hollywood, one stands out in memory: it was for the director and old friend of mine Lindsay Anderson, who was in Hollywood to discuss a film project. During the delicious meal—Curtis was an excellent cook—Susan Strasberg was seen surreptitiously using a toothpick behind a napkin when she thought nobody was looking. Rachel Roberts, the British star recently divorced from Rex Harrison, noticed and said, rudely, in a fake Yorkshire accent, "Having trooble with your teeth, dear?" Susan had her revenge. Rachel announced, "When I was married to Rex we lived in Portofino, Italy. He was so hungry for me that when we were out walking one day he suddenly fooked me against a tree. A man and a woman came by and the woman said to the man in English, 'What's going on there?' 'It's two world-famous people,' the man replied, 'fooking in broad daylight.'" "Well, *one* of you was world famous," Susan replied.

Rachel had a handsome and loving young companion in the Latino decorator Darren Ramirez, and often when we had lunch or dinner she would speak of her fondness for him. But underneath her words I sensed that this talented but plain woman, lacking in obvious sex appeal, never trusted him or believed he could actually be in love with her. Depressive, uneven in temperament, a wonderful friend, Rachel killed herself as horribly as possible, not with sleeping pills or even slit wrists in a bathtub, but by swallowing a bottle of lye.

My friendship with Curtis was threatened early on; I had written the original story for *The Legend of Lizzie Borden,* starring Elizabeth Montgomery, and shown with great success on television. Curtis had approved my theory as expressed in the treatment that Miss Borden had been naked when she committed the murders of her father and stepmother, thus paralyzing them at the sight of her, making it possible to strike the fatal blows, and eliminating any sign of blood on her clothing. One morning I was in Charlie Chan's Printing on Sunset Boulevard when I saw a script of the movie lying there; the production hadn't been announced and I had received no payment. I opened the front page; there was no mention of my name; Curtis was listed as coauthor. I was furious and drove at once to Curtis's house; he told me to fuck off. At a strained meeting between myself and attorneys for the adaptive writers I was allotted a check but only on condition I would not ask for screen credit. Needing the money, unable to afford to pay my attorney any more, I had to concede.

I forgave Curtis and never mentioned the matter to him again. But in the twenty-first century our relationship finally and inexorably cracked apart. His hatred of Jews and blacks was always painful to me, along with his brutal attacks on the decor of my home every time I arranged a screening for him there. When I found out that my father had mixed Jewish origins he told me he would be appalled were it not for the fact that he was sure I had made it up to sustain my career in Hollywood, where the "Yiddim" ruled everything; he blamed them for his not getting work when in fact that is exactly what they had done for many years.

We almost parted for good when he laughed in my face at dinner as I told him the story of Richard's brush with death on board ship and in Puerto Rico, saying it was "extreme." This callousness was unacceptable, and the latest of several examples of his arrogant coldness. At a dinner party at his house when I asked for 7Up, he humiliated me (or tried to) in front of the other guests by saying that he only liked people who drank wine. I never was asked to another.

But the final rift came at a screening of *Forever Hollywood,* my friend Todd McCarthy's documentary of Hollywood history, given its premiere at the Egyptian Theatre in 1999. I ran into Fayard Nicholas, of the dancing team the Nicholas Brothers, whose sibling had died, and I told Fayard that if ever I felt the blues, I would run his dance sequence from *Down Argentine Way,* and feel good again. His eyes teared as he said that was the loveliest compliment he had ever been paid.

Foolishly I turned to Curtis, who was standing some distance away, to tell him of the encounter. He looked at me with contempt and hatred, and at last I knew that I, who loved African Americans all my life, starting with my beloved Ianthea Matthews in London in the early 1950s, and with whom I had an intense, mysterious rapport (they understood my British intonation with which so many white Americans had difficulties), could no longer count an arrogant racist as a friend. In pain at the loss of a man who had once been my closest companion, I broke off the relationship for good.

Curtis had been a specialist in, and fan of, the macabre, and it isn't surprising to note that when he died, his memorial service was Hollywood Gothic in its bizarrerie. I wasn't there, but friends described the scene: Kenneth Anger, the brilliant creator of the screen's most intense erotic masterworks, including *Fireworks* and *Lucifer Rising,* whom Curtis charged with witchcraft when Curtis found nail parings and hair on his doorstep, appeared and allegedly in a dramatic gesture kissed Curtis's dead face on the lips in the open coffin announcing to all those present that he himself would die on Halloween of 2008 (he didn't), and then he left.

My happiest memory of Curtis I carry from the set of *Dynasty,* the television series in which a powerful family, conveniently located in the same house, quarrel, make love, and make deals under the overall supervision of Ross Hunter's and Jerry Wald's natural successor as kitsch Hollywood producer, Aaron Spelling.

Curtis directed several episodes, all of which starred the very talented and amusing Joan Collins as Mrs. Carrington, Denver millionairess and mistress of men and intrigue. With the vanishing of Joan Crawford from the screen, she provided a welcome shot of sinister glamour and was always, I felt, underrated as an actress.

In one episode, Curtis told me, Mrs. Carrington arrived at the Dorchester Hotel in London to take up residence in the legendary Oliver Messel suite. It was customary for the hotel's manager to greet arrivals of such remarkable wealth that they could afford to pay thousands a night. But on this occasion, everyone overlooked the fact that no manager appeared in the script.

A perfectionist, Joan complained that there was no manager in the cast to greet her and wouldn't continue until the problem was fixed. Unnerved, Curtis called Aaron Spelling, who at once sent for the writers to come in and produce just one line, "Welcome to the Dorchester, Mrs. Carrington."

Their contract allowed for nobody else to write the series dialogue so it was fortunate they were found at once. But who could speak the words?

Handsome actors could be seen wandering about or working as waiters in the studio cafés, looking for a break. Spelling and coproducer Douglas Cramer sent out a search party; a man was found, fitted rapidly with a suit and tie, and sent on set. But when he spoke, Joan still wasn't satisfied. "He's got an American accent," she said. "It won't do."

Curtis had an inspiration. Guessing that Joan seldom read the British newspapers while she lived in Los Angeles, he made up a story, saying that there was an item in the London *Daily Telegraph* that the Dorchester's new manager was American. Joan swallowed the story whole, and played a perfect scene.

$\mathcal{I}$ began work, in 2006, on a biography of Jennie, the Brooklyn-born mother of Winston Churchill, which was successfully published a year later in London and New York. *Dark Lady: Winston Churchill's Mother and Her World* earned me first choice as the *Daily Mail* Book of the Month and much serialization, as well as a smash hit in Rio de Janeiro, where I found I have a strong following. My *Rose: The Life and Times of Rose Fitzgerald Kennedy,* so ill fated when it came out in America, with a particularly ill-advised cover used over my protests of her face sad and wrinkled in old age, was superbly brought out with a glamourous new cover by Cherche-Midi in Paris and became a great commercial and critical success in France with articles in every major magazine and ecstatic reviews.

I began the current book with an account of a time when some inner warning saved my life when I was out running, and I conclude it with other examples. When I was due to fly to Los Angeles on assignment in the 1960s, I had an overwhelming impulse to delay the trip by a day; the plane crashed into Sydney Harbor, killing all aboard. When Richard and I, who went to Las Vegas for Christmas every year, decided on an instinct not to go there one season, the MGM Grand Hotel, where we were booked, burned down.

In my seventies, not yet on the shelf, I also brought out through the Authors Guild a reprint of *Trading with the Enemy,* which is earning new royalties.

It has been said that anyone who can maintain long friendships in Los Angeles is twice blessed. Those who have remained close and loyal to me for over thirty years include Dr. Gerald Turbow, authority on the Europeans in exile in World War II; Jacob Edelman and Robert Kane, fine dramatists, and their wives, Janie and Christine; the actor Robert Joy; John MacDonald, a man of many talents; the gifted ace filmmaker Philippe Mora and his brilliant wife, Pamela; Paul Morrissey, Warholian film director of puritanical movies about sex; James Curtis, author of books on James Whale, Preston Sturges, W. C. Fields, and now Spencer Tracy; Todd McCarthy, leading writer of books (*Howard Hawks*) and chief critic and columnist of *Variety;* Marvin (Eisenman) of the Movies; and Richard Palafox's entire family. Without them, life would indeed have been very difficult.

*T*he last pages of memoir should, I believe, never seek to sum up; as an optimist, I hope for future editions, and additions. But I have a few words to say on the world that has changed so tremendously since my youth.

Those of my generation tend to grumble, as the elderly have always done since time immemorial, about cultural decline, the manners and customs of the young, and the dismal fall of civilization as a whole: Jacques Barzun, a brilliant centenarian, has written best in this vein. But I rejoice. Homosexuality, a crime through much of my life and the exercise of which could many times have landed me in prison, is understood and accepted by more people than at any time in history. The invention of the DVD, the greatest since the wheel, makes home viewing a ravishing pleasure; old, faded, and scratched movies, for years endured on shaky 16 mm projectors, can now be seen in better form than originally, since by some chemical process the contrasts of photography, especially in black and white, are still more powerfully realized. Medicine has improved so much that Richard, who would have died just ten years before his present medication became available, is able to live a full and useful life. And classical music, though recordings are threatened commercially, is superbly presented in a Los Angeles that has grown culturally beyond recognition in the years I have lived here. No less than Placido Domingo runs the local opera, and the great Esa-Pekka Salonen has, until very recently, been music director of the Los Angeles Philharmonic.

The old are upset by rap music, but they don't have to listen to it except when caught in traffic, any more than their grandparents had to listen to swing, bebop, or jazz. True, newspapers are an endangered species, but the big ones aren't extinct yet; and their contents are available, admittedly in condensed form, to everyone on computers. The fact that I am a technical klutz, unable to deal with word processors or even cell phones, not to mention Google, doesn't mean that I don't appreciate the fact that, by picking up a telephone and calling a book finder, I can in minutes have someone order an obscure and hard to find book or movie through various Web sites, when before it would have taken months. Although the Internet is often unreliable as an information source, it is unrivaled as a form of obtaining the forgotten and the obscure.

I believe there will always be books, and, if not newspapers, then even magazines; there is something in many human beings that wants to hold not only a metal iPod but also an actual creation of paper and print. The fact that an African American has become president is a stunning reversal of old shibboleths and prejudices. I look forward to the future, terrorism notwithstanding, and a continuing of the wonderful and terrifying melodrama and comedy of life.

Charles Higham

The biographer, critic, poet, and film historian was born in London, the son of a member of Parliament and advertising pioneer. His five highly acclaimed books of poetry, published in England and Australia, where he immigrated in 1954, and his writings on film earned him the post of Regents Professor at the University of California at Santa Cruz in 1969, an honor accorded annually to only one writer from a foreign country. While there, he made a major find in film scholarship: Orson Welles's unfinished Latin American epic *It's All True,* thought to have been lost in a vault at Paramount. The discovery earned him a spread in *Newsweek* and the posts of Hollywood feature writer for the *New York Times* and official historian of film for Time-Life.

A frequent guest on *Today, Good Morning America,* and *Larry King Live,* and several History channel and A&E biography programs, he was the first authorized biographer of Katharine Hepburn; his *Kate* was a major critical and commercial success and became an international best seller. His next hit was *Errol Flynn,* which led him into the field of politics. His *Trading with the Enemy,* about wartime industrial collusion with Nazi Germany, was critically acclaimed and in turn drew him into a valued association with the late Simon Wiesenthal and with Rabbis Hier and Cooper of the Holocaust Studies Center, where he worked closely with them and gave world press conferences on the matter of Herman Abs, Hitler's banker, and Klaus Barbie of Lyons. His reports were used as major items in the celebrated Bronfman report on Swiss appropriation of Holocaust victims' gold.

His *Duchess of Windsor,* which also dealt with Nazi activities, spent thirty-four weeks at the top of the *New York Times* best-seller lists and was number one in France, where his *Rose* recently enjoyed a major success. His life of Howard Hughes became the chief basis of Martin Scorsese's movie *The Aviator.* He continues to publish poetry in Australia and has been widely anthologized as a leading Australian poet in exile. He is a successful playwright, with productions at the El Portal Theater in Los Angeles, the largest complex built since the Music Center, where he opened the first season; the Cal State Long Beach Theater; and the African American Riant Theater in Tribeca, New York, among others. A recipient of the Academie Française Prize of the Creators, his works have been translated into over a dozen languages. He lives in Los Angeles.

Index

Note: Page numbers in italics indicate photographs.